DECOLONIZING MIDDLE LEVEL LITERACY INSTRUCTION

This text offers pre-service and in-service teachers pragmatic strategies for teaching middle-grades literacy in culturally proactive and sustaining ways. By demystifying big ideas and complex concepts, Domínguez and Seglem provide clear pathways and lessons for illuminating and engaging with race, ethnicity, culture, and identity in the middle-grade English Language Arts classroom. While addressing social justice, equity, diversity, and liberation can seem intimidating or unrelated to classroom practice, the authors demonstrate how weaving such questions into instruction benefits students' development.

The guidance, strategies, and lessons in this book provide an answer to the question: *What does decolonial literacy teaching look like?* Concrete but not prescriptive, the authors encourage us to reconsider accepted logics of schooling, so that we can better support adolescents as they navigate complex identity landscapes. Bringing together disparate conversations around reading, writing, identity, and decolonial thinking, and specifically tailored to the middle grades, this book serves as a comprehensive toolkit for praxis and covers such topics as cultural change, community connections, and racial literacy. Each chapter features tips on reading and writing instruction, Teacher Spotlights, Planning Questions, and Additional Resources to make it easy for educators to apply the strategies to their own contexts.

An accessible entry to addressing challenging questions around identity in the classroom, this book is essential reading in courses and professional development on ELA and literacy methods as well as teaching culturally and linguistically diverse students. For teachers looking to push toward equity and reshape literacy education so that it serves all middle-grade students, Domínguez and Seglem offer plenty of accessible and motivating places to start.

Michael Domínguez is an Associate Professor of Chicana and Chicano Studies at San Diego State University, USA.

Robyn Seglem is a Professor in the School of Teaching and Learning at Illinois State University, USA.

T0388556

DECOLONIZING MIDDLE LEVEL LITERACY INSTRUCTION

A Culturally Proactive Approach to Literacy Methods

Michael Domínguez and Robyn Seglem

Routledge
Taylor & Francis Group

NEW YORK AND LONDON

Designed cover image: © Getty Images

First published 2023
by Routledge
605 Third Avenue, New York, NY 10158

and by Routledge
4 Park Square, Milton Park, Abingdon, Oxon, OX14 4RN

Routledge is an imprint of the Taylor & Francis Group, an informa business

Library of Congress Cataloging-in-Publication Data
Names: Domínguez, Michael, author. | Seglem, Robyn L., author.
Title: Decolonizing middle level literacy instruction : a culturally proactive approach to literacy methods / Michael Domínguez, Robyn Seglem.
Description: New York, NY : Routledge, 2023. | Includes bibliographical references and index. | Identifiers: LCCN 2022061847 | ISBN 9781032251882 (paperback) | ISBN 9781032269634 (hardback) | ISBN 9781003290681 (ebook)
Subjects: LCSH: Language arts (Middle school)--Social aspects. | Children--Books and reading--Social aspects. | Culturally relevant pedagogy.
Classification: LCC LB1631 .D58 2023 | DDC 428.0071/2--dc23/eng/20230223
LC record available at https://lccn.loc.gov/2022061847

ISBN: 978-1-032-26963-4 (hbk)
ISBN: 978-1-032-25188-2 (pbk)
ISBN: 978-1-003-29068-1 (ebk)

DOI: 10.4324/9781003290681

Typeset in Perpetua
by SPi Technologies India Pvt Ltd (Straive)

CONTENTS

CONTENTS

PREFACE

Why This Book?

There is a Mexican proverb, popularized by Gloria Anzaldúa (2015), that goes like this:

> Caminante no hay puentes, se hace puentes al andar (Traveler, there are no bridges, we make them as we walk.)

As we travel through the complexity of our own educational landscapes—the ones we grow from, and the ones we teach in—we often come across places that feel impassable and treacherous, where no help exists to keep moving forward. While neither we, nor anyone, can do the work for you, this book is meant to help you keep moving, by providing you with guidance, tools, and ideas that can be used to build bridges over and through those daunting challenges we inevitably face if we are committed to equity and justice in education. It is a book about some big ideas for *thinking* the world differently, specifically, for thinking the world differently in a *decolonial* way. They are ideas—like the concepts of social justice, equity, and diversity—that might feel very familiar. They are also ideas—like coloniality or decoloniality—that may feel unfamiliar and complex. And they are ideas—like race and racialization—that might seem scary and intimidating. And it's possible that as you are reading this, you are wondering what all these ideas have to do with middle-school literacy. As we hope you'll see by the end of this text, they have everything to do with it. The big ideas and concepts that we are about to introduce, explain, and weave through an array of chapters and lessons on how to organize learning in your classroom may be the most significant things shaping the lives of your students, whether you, or they, know it or not.

Whatever context brought you to this text, we are glad that you picked it up and that you are reading it now. Whether you are in a position to completely reinvent your classroom exactly as you see fit, or in a school where things are tight, difficult, and feel a bit like you can't breathe, this book is for you. Because we cannot think of anything more important to do in this era of standards, censorship, pressure, and panic than taking the time to imagine alternative ways to be together in the classroom, supporting students' learning.

How to Approach This Book

One of, perhaps the most, frequently asked questions we are asked when we are working and talking with teachers about the idea of decoloniality is: Well, what does that look like? Sometimes this question is earnest and hopeful; sometimes it's defensive and accusatory; and sometimes it's incredulous. All of that is understandable, because for teachers, old and new, it is difficult to imagine things working differently than the ways that they have worked for so long, for these ways are the same patterns, logics, pressures, ideologies, and practices that shaped us. The grammar of schooling as we have long understood it feels comfortable and normal because it is comfortable and normal. Even for those of us that grammar and logic of schooling hurt.

We know how ELA classes, curriculum, and pedagogy are *supposed* to work, because we experienced years of it working that way. We know how teachers and students are *supposed* to interact and relate to one another because we have experienced countless interactions with teachers that set our expectations. We know what ELA activities and tasks are *supposed* to involve because we did those activities ourselves. We know what the goals of literacy learning and schooling are *supposed* to be, because we managed, whether easily or with some trouble, to meet those expectations, and wind up as teachers. We know how things are *supposed* to work, because our schools, districts, communities, and other institutions reinforce these all the time. That is part of the coloniality we discussed earlier.

Schools and classrooms are supposed to work in certain ways because we are socially and culturally conditioned to be epistemically obedient to them. This is a process called *cultural normativity*—the cultural pressure which leads us to feel comfortable, safe, and attached to the ways things *are*, even if those things obviously do not work very well for many people, and maybe even us. That cultural normativity, those 'supposed tos,' reflect echoes of colonial marginalization, and just do not work for many students, especially historically marginalized and BIPOC students. But because we are so immersed in it—so used to it, comfortable with it, and obedient to it—that vision of what schooling is supposed to be like can feel inevitable. The challenges we face are so big, the institutions so embedded, that the prospect of doing things differently—substantially differently, as in the case of a decolonial approach—can feel disorienting, scary, impossible....and that is where that question comes from: What does it LOOK like?

Here is the thing though: there is not a singular answer to that question, and so, though we hear it all the time, it is never easy to answer. In fact, prescribing a singular answer, and a singular, alternative, way for schooling to look, would be—even if humanizing—at least a tad colonial. That is not to say there are not some answers to these questions, but it is important to note, right from the outset here, that decolonizing, culturally sustaining, and culturally proactive approaches to teaching are always going to be local—grounded in and growing from your knowledge of your students and your community.

In this text, our goal is not to give you an exact road map of what to do to decolonize your classroom. Not because we are withholding information, but because it cannot be done. There is not a map out there for *your* classroom, in *your* context, to do that. But that does not mean decolonizing your classroom cannot be done. The pressure to teach the way you are 'supposed to' can be strong, but it is not inevitable. As the feminist science fiction writer Ursula LeGuin (2014) reminds us, the power of the institutions around us may feel inescapable, yet "so did the divine right of kings. Any human power can be resisted and changed by human beings. Resistance and change often begin in art. Very often in our art, the art of words." Those words are a good reminder that though challenging, a decolonial vision of the future is possible, and what better place to start that process of imagination than in the literacy classroom?

What to Expect from This Text

Now, with that said, as you read, you'll likely see things that a) involve strategies you have seen before, and b) are ideas, concepts, and suggestions from white authors or scholars you might not associate with decolonization. This is not accidental. Rather, it is a reflection of our conscious attempt to undertake what Stevens et al. (2017) call an "academic raid"—drawing from the ideas and concepts that are familiar and present in Western thinking and repurposing them towards decolonial ends. As we have and will discuss, decolonization is not a quest to exclusively rely on a single tradition or source of knowledge, nor is it an impossible task to re-construct some imagined pre-colonial positionality, ignoring the realities and impacts of modernity and everyday life in and beyond schools.

In fact, the very idea and process of operating in either exclusionary, or appropriative, ways reflect the way coloniality has and continues to socialize us to think that something might only have value if it comes from a particular person or perspective. That attitude, no matter how it is directed, is dehumanizing and limiting. We should absolutely be attentive and reflective around the ways power has operated in our perceptions of ideas, resources, and pedagogical strategies, and we should take active and attentive steps to increase the diversity of the resources in our classrooms. But simply swapping out one cultural referent for another and then continuing to treat knowledge the same way does little in the way of decolonizing and humanizing culture, one another, or our classrooms. Basically, it is not just about swapping out the texts, but about changing up the questions we ask ourselves and our students, around ideas altogether.

So what does all of this mean? It means that yes, you will see some things that look familiar. It wouldn't make much pragmatic sense for us to come up with new names for variations of practices that you have seen in classrooms before. Rather, that would be a foolhardy, and, we think, egotistical attempt to 'Columbus' (appropriate or steal) the broad contours of things we know excellent teachers already do and have names for. Instead, what we will ask you to do is not just assume we are endorsing them as you understand them now—in fact in most cases, that is very much NOT the case—and instead pay attention to the differences and new questions we encourage you to leverage as you apply them.

We should also note, as we talk about what to expect, that we see this text as fitting into an array of other resources that support the skills needed to be a great literacy educator. Essentially, don't expect this book to do all things. We don't go deeply into reading development or language acquisition theory because that's not what we're here to do. We don't detail every step and variation of developing writing process messaging, nor do we spell out how you should lesson plan. You can find those resources elsewhere, and we encourage you to do so, and put them into conversation with the ideas and lessons we spell out here. You see, we've found doing those sorts of things to be less than generative, because prescribing them, as we noted above, is never going to really align to your local context. They feel like the stuff we want, but they are not really the things we need. Like someone else's shoes, they never quite fit or feel right, but too often, because they are there and seem easy, we keep on using them rather than imagining our own versions of praxis, driven by conceptual understanding of where we want to go. So with this text, our goal is to lay the groundwork for you to understand the big ideas associated with decoloniality and how they link up with, in, and through the literacy classroom, so that you have the vision and guidance to organize your instruction in new, humanizing, decolonial ways.

Visionary Pragmatism

As we will discuss further once you get into this text, pursuing decolonial thinking in your praxis and classroom is not (necessarily) about engaging in some kind of jarring, radical, bombastic practices that clash with the daily demands of being a teacher. Sure, we hope you will push the envelope in lots of ways, but we also recognize the importance of making it work within your constraints—things like school policies, administrative asks, and the sheer time it takes to create lessons. Considering that, we ascribe to Patricia Hill-Collins' (2009) advocacy for visionary pragmatism. In this way of approaching social change and progress, the key is to strike a balance between the big ideas and principles that guide our vision and the reality of how we might have to make compromises as we gradually work towards change in the mundane minutiae of everyday life. Essentially, we want to be anchored in a clear, compelling, and ambitious vision of the future shaped by values and principles that speak aspirationally to who we could be, but not so caught up in the abstract and ideal that we cease to be able to function when things don't go according to plan. We need to be intentional with every choice we make in the classroom, but also flexible and kind with ourselves to recognize that sometimes, we just have to make the best choice possible, even if it strays from our vision a bit.

Our hope is that this text will set you up to be able to act with visionary pragmatism in your school and classroom, guided by decolonial and humanizing principles. That is going to look very different based on who you are, your context, your school, your students and all sorts of other factors. But if we are engaged in intentional, pragmatic action, guided by aspirations of a world where coloniality (more on that word later) and marginalization are being disrupted, that's how change happens. Those small, intentional, principled steps—doing what you can, in the space you can, with the tools you have—are what move us towards a new way of thinking about the world.

Moving forward, you'll find this text broken into a few sections:

Part I: In Dialogue / Desconocimientos

In Part I, we begin with Paulo Freire's concept of dialogue. We recognize that to fully engage in dialogue around any change, we must clearly communicate how we see and define ideas. We also use Gloria Anzaldúa's work to expand upon this concept, recognizing that through *desconocimientos* we must undo old knowledge in order to create new knowledge together. As such, we begin by examining what coloniality means and how it appears in schools, using this information to help illuminate the need to give up our current understandings of school. Then, we turn to the significance and importance of racial identity and racial literacies to middle school. Here, wwe point to the developmental readiness of middle schoolers to critically examine racial experiences, recognizing that this is a critical time in our students' lives to undo the harmful messaging they have received around the construct of race.

Part II: In Praxis / Travesias

In Part II, we shift to praxis or action. We look at the *travesias*, or voyages, we must undertake in order to critically reflect upon and transform our worlds through action. Within these chapters, we identify specific points along our *travesias* that lead us toward decolonization. We suggest specific actions and ways of being that can be used for each new terrain.

Part III: Pragmatic Vision / Conocimientos

In Part III, we come full circle and return to reflection to develop a critical awareness of who we are as decolonizing educators in order to act and change the realities of our educational contexts. We examine how to navigate restrictive landscapes, as well as how to sustain our commitments to decolonizing middle level instruction.

As we try to imagine a decolonial classroom (and world), with our visionary-pragmatist mindset, we are all setting off anew to create our own maps: maps that have not ever existed before. With that in mind, in this text, what we do hope to accomplish, and how we hope you will see this text, is as a guide to cartography (map-making), complete with descriptions of big ideas to consider, discussions to help us see clearly the challenges we will face, suggestions for ways to be disobedient to the logic of schooling, and examples of ways in which folks have brought a decolonial sensibility to classrooms. We hope you will take this text up not to replicate things that you read exactly as we describe them, but use everything we share here to spark your imagination, and, as decolonial thinker Augusto Boal notes, see the world as it is, and consider the world as it *could* be. So when folks ask us, as you might be doing, *What does it look like, this decolonial literacy teaching?*, let us consider some possibilities, so that you can imagine, and enact, that reality as you and your students need it to be, and find out together what a decolonial future will look like.

References

Anzaldúa, G. (2015). "Now let us shift… conocimiento… inner work, public acts". In A. Keating (Ed.) *Light in the Dark/Luz en lo Oscuro* (pp. 117–160). Duke University Press.

Collins, P. H. (2009). *Another kind of public education: Race, schools, the media, and democratic possibilities*. Beacon Press.

LeGuin, U. (2014, Nov. 19). *Acceptance speech – Medal for distinguished contribution to American letters*. National Book Awards.

Stevens, V.A., Stevens, P., & Nicholas, S. (2017). Raiding and alliances: Indigenous educational sovereignty as social justice. *Journal of Critical Thought and Praxis, 6*(1), 18–37.

Part I

IN DIALOGUE / DESCONOCIMIENTOS

Paulo Freire has impacted the world of education through his work in critical pedagogy. Dialogue has long been a cornerstone of his work because, through conversation that is based in love and mutual respect, humans can come together to question the world as we currently know it and create new knowledge together. Gloria Anzaldúa helps us expand upon this concept, prompting us to notice that as we confront new ideas, we are also in the process of undoing old knowledge. Desconocimientos captures this idea, that we are unlearning and disrupting old patterns, challenging ways of thinking, and abandoning thoughts and beliefs that no longer serve us for who we want and need to be.

This part of the book engages us in *desconocimientos*, pushing us to undo what we know about school. It prompts us to engage in dialogue around *why* we conceive of and perpetuate school practices that marginalize, dehumanize, and harm students who do not fit into colonial ways of being and learning. Chapter 1 provides a historical overview of coloniality, illuminates the subtle and not-so-subtle practices that schools regularly engage in that perpetuate coloniality, and shares why decolonizing education is necessary to rectify the damages done to students who are a part of marginalized populations. Chapter 2 tackles the concepts of race and racial literacy and connects these constructs to decolonization. It introduces you to the Coloniality of Being, of Power, and of Knowledge, and it challenges the notion that middle schoolers are too young to engage in real conversations around race. Our hope is that through dialogue around these big ideas—these big social and cultural problems— we can disrupt colonial schooling practices and engage in desconocimientos.

DOI: 10.4324/9781003290681-1

1

1

WHY DECOLONIZE OUR CLASSROOMS?

Coloniality and Decoloniality: A Primer

We recently came across a line by Isabel Cañas (2022) that struck us as particularly evocative of the way colonialism remains pertinent in our lives:

> Colonialism carved the landscapes of our homes with ghosts. It left gaping wounds that still weep.
>
> (p. 342)

We suspect that for many of our readers, the terms that sit at the center of our text are perhaps both familiar and unknown. That is an obvious contradiction, so let us explain. Essentially, we suspect you may be familiar with and have likely heard of or seen the terms decolonial or decolonize, in part because their use has proliferated in educational activist circles, social media, and around everything from diets to media to relationships. And if you haven't heard these terms, that's OK too! But we also suspect that even if you have come across these concepts before, it was not in a context in which their rich conceptual history or the critical way they connect to the idea of coloniality (which is a much less popularized term) was fully explained. These terms evoke both ghosts of the pasts and wounds of the present, but the connections between the two are rarely explored, explained, or clarified. With that in mind, we want to kick things off by offering some context and a primer on these terms, some related ideas, and their connection to our everyday lives and work in the classroom. Let's begin with a foundational question: *Why do we need to decolonize if colonization ended decades ago?*

Colonization v. Coloniality

We suspect it is safe to assume that all of our readers are, at least on a very cursory level, familiar with the idea of colonization as a geopolitical process, and with the generalities of European colonization (or modern colonization) that began in earnest in the late 1400s and early 1500s, and extended at least through the world wars in the 20th century. This isn't a history book, so we won't try to dive too deeply into the specifics of this period, including things like its fuzzy start and end dates or effective duration, pivotal moments that shaped it, or the wide variations of the characteristics of colonization

DOI: 10.4324/9781003290681-2

across this period as perspectives and political and social realities shifted. Yet it is worth-while—and indeed essential—to carve out some clear, obvious understandings of what the effects of 500 years of European colonization were. While this is certainly not a comprehensive list, modern European/Western colonization:

- Devastated indigenous populations in Africa, the Americas, Asia, and Oceania, with millions and millions of lives lost through active conquest, disease, starvation, or other forms of subjugation
- Upended existing stable social, political, and cultural systems that were replaced with European control or proxy control through local collaborators
- Devised previously unimagined systems of human and cultural classification that facilitated and reinforced European, and local proxy, control and domination of social and economic resources
- Disrupted existing, stable economies and labor markets in favor of extractive economies that exploited and depleted local natural resources, while also leaving these new economies under the control of European entities or their proxies
- Created the fluid, complicated category of social organization that we understand today as race and racial identity
- Created nation-state borders that both divided cultural, kinship, and ethnic groups and forced groups of divergent cultural and ethnic traditions together
- Disrupted long-standing patterns of cultural knowledge, belief, relationality, kinship, community, literacy, language, and art, in some cases almost destroying these traditions and knowledges almost completely
- Imposed European social, political, and cultural systems, values, and structures as a new, hegemonic way of life

We could go on (and on) but suffice it to say that the impacts of European/Western colonization and colonialism were stark. They were violent. They were far-reaching, and, without making any sort of idealized, romantic claims about the perfection, innocence, or accomplishments of pre-colonial indigenous societies, we can note that they were universally detrimental to the indigenous peoples of Africa, the Americas, Asia, and Oceania.

Over the course of the West's era of colonization, nearly the entire globe, in one way or another, fell under the direct control or indirect economic and political dominance of some Western power. This expansive impact that created the idea of 'the West' to describe Europe/modernity (inclusive, eventually of the U.S.), continues to shapes the way we see, understand, and divide the world ourselves today (Said, 1978). Consider that it is commonplace to think of our global community in terms of the 'First World'/Global North (i.e., the U.S., Canada, Europe, particularly Western Europe, and the Anglo-Oceanic nations) and the 'Third World'/Global South (i.e., nations of Africa, the Americas, Asia, and Oceania). Yet while the terms persist, the political arrangements—colonialism—that created them have, as we learned in history class, ended—most in the wake of the Second World War, though several not for quite some time thereafter—and colonialism as a political system is broadly seen as a thing of the past.

But here's the thing: while these *de jure* (i.e., by law; official, stated, policies and political arrangements) relationships of colonial control, whereby a Western power actively maintained political, economic, and socio-cultural dominion over a non-Western, Global South nation and its people, are largely no more, the *de facto* (i.e., in practice, unofficial, practical arrangements) systems and structures of that era remain in place. As Maldonado-Torres explains, colonialism has given way to *coloniality*; or in other words, the official systems of governance are gone, but their shadow (and impact) linger on, continuing the patterns of domination that centuries of political and economic control had left in place. Coloniality then:

> ...refers to long-standing patterns of power that emerged as a result of colonialism, but that define culture, labor, intersubjective relations, and knowledge production well beyond the strict limits of colonial administrations.... It is maintained alive in books, in the criteria for academic performance, in cultural patterns, in common sense, in the self-image of peoples, in aspirations of self, and so many other aspects of our modern experience.
>
> (Maldonado-Torres, 2007, p. 243)

To unpack that a bit, consider some of the realities of colonialism we noted above. They live on in the U.S. and elsewhere, as coloniality, in the way our world works today. They are alive and well in the fact that our maps and system of time are centered on Great Britain (e.g., Kaul, 2021), in our statistical lack of meaningful political representation for BIPOC individuals (e.g., Segura & Bowler, 2006), in Western private ownership of natural resources, and/or control of industries central to economic development (e.g., Galeano, 1997; Gonzalez, 2011), in the ways that Global South nations have had to grapple, for decades, with internal tensions created by colonial borders (e.g., Hernández, 2018, Lefebvre, 2011; Pasternak, 2020), in the dismissal and appropriation of BIPOC culture and knowledge (e.g., Mignolo, 2011; Tuhiwai Smith, 2021), in the imposition and proliferation of toxic gender roles and relationships (e.g., Aldama, 2001; Collins, 2004), in the clear-cut, structural stratification of wealth, community, and economic control along racial lines (e.g., Roediger, 1991; Rothstein, 2017), in the hegemony of English and other European language and literacy practices (e.g., Alim et al., 2016; Rosa, 2019), in practices and patterns of BIPOC disposability, including the school-to-prison pipeline (e.g., Alexander, 2011; Dutil, 2020), and of course, in our present understandings of race and racial identity, and the far-reaching, ongoing impact of this (e.g., Bonilla-Silva, 2006; Gómez, 2022; Omi & Winant, 2014). In short, colonialism may be over, but the *patterns of control* that it left in place remain firmly entrenched to this day, echoing both on the political stage and also in the classroom.

Day-to-Day Coloniality

Now, one of the complaints that is often leveled when we start discussing terms like *coloniality* is that they are 'too theoretical,' and that reflecting on a concept like this, as well as all these legacies and impacts we have just mentioned, has little to do with teaching (generally) or applicability to teaching literacy (specifically). To be sure, some of the authors we have cited could reasonably be called decolonial theorists, whose work is, well, dense, and not obviously productive in helping us figure out what to do in the classroom with our kids tomorrow. We get that. But we also want to invite you to question that logic and argument, because it is a suggestion that would have us, essentially, ignore the past and its legacies in order to only focus, mechanistically, on instruction as some form of triage wherein we treat the symptom, but forever ignore the cause. There are root causes and historical legacies and conceptual narratives that produce the challenges we see each day. They can be addressed, but through different forms of thought and action than transactionally dealing with issues as if they appeared from nowhere. If we boil things down to just the pragmatic, just the transactional, what do we lose?

Theory exists for a reason; it gives us ways to speak concisely and precisely about complicated things, to understand how things that occur in our real world are connected, and to carry both real and symbolic meaning. In short, we see these ideas not as too abstract to have relevance to our teaching lives, but as incredibly salient to understanding how schools work, how we must understand the literacies we and our students arrive in our classrooms with, and how we might imagine schooling and literacy instruction to work differently. In that spirit, let us try to ground the idea of coloniality through three examples that each introduce a fundamental aspect of coloniality, and show how very alive they are in our daily lives: one about Harry Potter, another about psychological research, and a final one about school discipline and pedagogical approaches.

Harry Potter and the Colonial Zero-Point

As we have stated, coloniality represents the way that ideologies and relationships from the era of colonialism are perpetuated into and through the present, post-colonial era. One of the starkest ways in which that happens is through youth literature, and one of the most striking ways we have observed that occurring in our era is through the global phenomenon of Harry Potter.

Even if you haven't read the books or seen the movies, we're guessing that you're familiar with the Harry Potter series and franchise. Since its release, it has become among the most popular young-reader and middle-grades texts ever, stretched into spin-off series and an expanded universe, and translated into countless languages. It was, and remains, a sensation, and given that the creator is English, it's no surprise that Harry Potter is English himself, or that his story and the world he inhabits are Anglo-centric. Ms Rowling was writing a world that felt familiar, and while critique of those stories might certainly be warranted, we are not overly bothered by the nature of the original seven books.

Rather, we actually want to pick up with what happened after the series ended, and the demand for more about the world of Harry Potter beyond Hogwarts that followed. Specifically, in the wake of the series' conclusion, Ms Rowling (and, by that point, her creative team) launched *Pottermore* and the 'Wizarding World,' (2022) an online space that effectively expanded the Harry Potter universe and canon beyond what we saw in the books. Interestingly, one aspect of this was a map that identified where the other wizarding schools in the world were. In this cartographic exercise, each continent of the world was assigned a single school—Uagadou in Africa, Castlebuxo in South America,

Ilvermorny in North America, and Mahakatouro in Asia—with the exception of Europe, which had three (those portrayed in the original texts, Hogwarts, Durmstrang, and Beauxbatons). The astute observer will note that the demographics of this distribution are imbalanced at best. Europe, with roughly 9% of the world's population, has three schools to serve it, while Africa with 17.5% and Asia with 59% of the world's population (not to mention the immense, vastly divergent cultural traditions and worlds these percentages represent) have only one each. Subsequent Harry Potter universe expansion has added one in Russia, and hinted at the existence of three more (Harry Potter Wiki, 2022). Even so, the math still skews heavily towards Europe.

Beyond this basic demographic issue, one can also notice that in at least two cases—North and South America—the names of the wizarding schools are in the language of colonizers, assuming, implicitly, that organized schooling was non-existent until after colonization in the 1500s, while in the case of Africa and Asia, continents with, literally thousands of distinct indigenous languages, one school, with a pseudo-indigenous/local language name is sufficient to capture the 'cultural flavor' of these entire, massive continents. All of these assumptions created by the map and subsequent Pottermore canon are, intentionally or not, a reflection of myopic, colonial imagination of what the Global South world must be—small, parochial, culturally homogeneous, and dependent on the West for the structures of civilization and social organization.

And to be clear that this is not just us overanalyzing, as we can see, for instance, in the work of Mills (2016). These same concerns and questions were raised with Pottermore and Ms Rowling, who offered the rather unsatisfactory and ahistorical answer that wizards elsewhere in the world simply homeschooled their children (the ahistoricity arises because a strong argument can be made that broad, collective public schooling actually first emerged in the Mexica Empire, which would arguably indicate that if anything, we would expect Europe to be engaged in homeschooling while cultures in the Global South created schools). The conclusion that one arrives at, following the development of this broader world, is that this isn't just an imaginary magical world, but an imaginary magical world that is inextricably linked to, and imagined through, a colonial lens, or a *colonial zero-point* (Castro-Gómez, 2005). That is, a world and imagination fixed with the West at its center, assuming that structure, order, development, knowledge, and civilization itself must emerge from and begin with contact with the histories and traditions of the West, ignoring that complex, well-developed civilizations and cultures existed, and in many cases had practices, that pre-dated similar developments in the West.

Ms Rowling has every right to compose the story she wants to, and to imagine a world of her own creation as she wants to. As we said, it's her story, her world. Yet throughout the series and the storytelling that has emerged since its conclusion, Harry's existence in a global, post-colonial world has been firmly established. That was Ms Rowling's choice, as was her approach to imagining and portraying relationships, equity, and power (socio-political, not magical) in and across that more broadly imagined world in deeply colonial terms.

The issue we are trying to raise here is that when—even in this context of Ms Rowling's intellectual property—stories by creators from the West imagine and portray the Global South and non-Western worlds in colonial ways, reflective of the ideologies and attitudes towards the Global South that were present during the colonial era, they are both perpetuating and reinforcing the notion that the only valid cultural referent to begin with, the zero-point, begins with the colonial West. This is a notion that is profoundly limiting and profoundly harmful to non-Western (i.e., BIPOC and other marginalized youth) folks, perpetuating a lack of not just phenotypic representation (of folks who look like BIPOC folks), but ontological marginalization as well—of how folks think and feel and relate to the world. It isn't just that historically marginalized, racialized individuals aren't the protagonists in stories, it's that BIPOC stories are strange, foreign outliers. It's that BIPOC ways of being and understanding the world are not worth considering.

Pottermore didn't need to become explicit about wizarding schools elsewhere in the world; it could have deferred to local cultural diversity or sought out indigenous creators who could have expanded it in culturally coherent ways (Mills, 2016). And it didn't need to become defensive and ahistorical in defending the colonial way in which it had composed that perception of a broader wizarding world when it failed to do that. And beyond all that, the *Magical Beasts* franchise didn't need to expand its scope of characters in such a way as to make the marginality and peripheral role of Global South peoples and nations so glaring. But it did. And through that active choice, it has continued to double-down on a colonial perception of the world as its mythology and storytelling has expanded across subsequent media. *Harry Potter* surely isn't alone in doing this, but it is among the most popular properties in world media, and one in which its imagination seems steadfastly committed to holding on to that colonial zero-point. And that's why we share this analogy; it is a stark example of the ways in which colonial attitudes, ideologies, and zero-point are being kept alive long after the end of colonialism, perpetuated in ways that are subtle and seemingly benign, but no less significant.

The Müller-Lyer Illusion and the Western Cultural Archive

If coloniality has shaped our way of seeing and thinking about the world, it has also impacted the way we value and defer to particular forms of knowledge. Tuhiwai Smith (2021) calls this accumulation of Western knowledge, and the appropriation and consumption of non-Western knowledge, accrued across the 500-year history of colonization and reinforced through academic practices and social and cultural messaging in colonial schools, the *Western Cultural Archive*. Essentially, what she means is that just as coloniality insists on a particular point of view and reference, that colonial zero-point, it also puts brackets around what knowledge counts, what knowledge and questions are valuable to ask and explore, and what ideological possibilities exist to draw on when solving problems—this is the Western Cultural Archive, an accumulation of things that the West has either produced itself, or claimed and placed under its control.

To consider the relevance of this to ourselves, let's consider the following psychological illusion test, the Müller-Lyer illusion, which asks us to consider which of the two lines is longer.

Have a guess? In the test, developed way back in the 1800s, the idea is that this is a gut reaction: a first impression, not a studied decision. Careful observers (or folks who have seen this before) will note that the lines are the same length. But a quick, perceptual guess tends to lead to different conclusions, because of the optical illusion of the

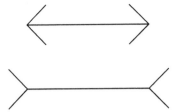

Figure 1.1 The Müller-Lyer illusion demonstrates how people can perceive the world differently based upon their experiences.

opposing ways the arrows at the ends are depicted. Specifically, when we review the meta-results of this test, it turns out that the majority of people who are administered the test in the U.S., Canada, and Western Europe assume the bottom line is longer, often by a substantial amount. The illusion of the arrows, informed by our regular existence within a built world of boxes (i.e., buildings and rooms) with straight edges and straight-line perspective, colors our perception. But the normalcy of this data is called into question when the same test is administered elsewhere, say, with rural communities in Western Africa (McCauley & Henrich, 2006). In these communities, where straight-edged buildings and 90-degree corners are largely absent, the illusion of lines and straight-line perspective do not interfere with assessing the length of the lines, and the lack of difference is clear, even on a cursory examination. But this discussion is less about the mechanics of this particular psychological test, and more about the knowledge that has been produced about it.

In a post-colonial world, it is simply the case that most research—as knowledge production—has been conducted in the U.S., Canada, and Western Europe ('the West') (Henrich, Heine, & Norenzayan, 2010; Román Quirós, 2021). What this means is that when we try to create a picture of useable knowledge based on this test and its results—i.e., what is normal and abnormal in terms of human psychological perception or human behavior—our understanding of 'normal' is necessarily a reflection of what is normal to the West, not necessarily what is actually normal to global humanity. And so when communities in the Global South, like those folks in West Africa (and elsewhere), perform very differently on this psychological battery, or say, in their literacy practices and skills (see Heath 1983; Scribner & Cole, 1981), their performance is demarcated as strange, different, peculiar, Other. They performed differently than *normal* because their way of life, and the ways of knowing and being that produced their results—essentially their community's valued practices and knowledge—are not *colonially* normal. Rather than understand them as culturally contextual normative practices that disprove the assumed wisdom of the existing 'normal' range of outcomes, these folks' results become objects of study for the Western Archive to examine and classify (Grosfoguel, 2013). They exist, but they still don't 'count.'

To turn back to this as an analogy, we can think of how the Müller-Lyer illusion works in the same way as so many of our schooling and literacy practices operate. BIPOC students arrive in our classrooms with a huge array of ways of thinking, learning, being, speaking, writing, telling stories, listening and engaging in community dialogue, and sharing their knowledge. Their practices are countless and diverse, and as intellectually complicated, if not more so, than the practices that normative schooling values (e.g., Heath, 1983). Yet ultimately, even when we are outwardly and explicitly concerned with equity, we often default to the norms and practices of schooling—to the Western Cultural Archive—and our classrooms become spaces where, as Paris (2012) notes, institutions "are implicitly or explicitly trying to get working class kids of color to write and speak like middle class White ones." Students arrive as complex multilingual, mult-iliterate, communal learners, and find themselves labeled as failures, outliers, and Others because their competencies and skills fail to align with the normative ways we want to see language spoken, stories told, writing composed, and tasks individually performed. This insistence on particular forms of knowledge, and ways of being, is an echo of colonial education systems that worked to 'civilize' indigenous peoples, and it continues on as a central element of coloniality, a *de facto* assumption, built into our schools, that the ultimate goal for our students is not to master complex literacies and develop *their* skills, but to approximate those forms of knowledge and literacy that the Western Cultural Archive deems valued and important, even if these norms and competencies aren't that globally normal at all.

Broken Windows, Teaching Like a Champion, and Colonial Power

Our third analogy is less an analogy, and more a conceptual map of a very popular, yet deeply colonial, racially charged, and particularly insidious family of patronizing, colonial ideas that have come to live in our schools. Specifically, the notion of 'broken windows,' and its connections to modern 'no excuses' approaches to classroom management and pedagogy. The idea and phrase "broken windows" emerged in a 1982 essay by James Q. Wilson and George Kelling. In this essay, Wilson and Kelling suggested, essentially, that the socio-economic struggles of marginalized, BIPOC communities were down to their cultural pathology; that the presence and tolerance of a broken window in their home or community was not reflective of folks stretched to their limits, with neither the time, nor resources to address small, superficial, non-pressing concerns, but emblematic of a people who, without a firm, guiding hand, would allow their communities to descend into chaos and disorder and become a blight on their cities. Their solution: intensive policing, for if you stop the broken window, or other minor infraction from occurring, you stop the endemic pathology of these communities from spiraling into more serious crime, like robbery, murder, drug use, etc. It's critical to note here that Wilson and Kelling didn't have data to back up this conclusion. Their essay was not based on evidence and research, but rather it ignored and rejected the substantial evidence and documentation by sociologists at the time that explained how persistent racism, bias, and structural segregation of economic opportunity were negatively impacting communities of color (e.g., Coleman et al., 1966). Wilson and Kelling were driven by an ideological assumption—a colonial one—that it couldn't be the structures of White society that were at fault for BIPOC communities' continued struggles and marginalization, but rather must be a pathology in the communities themselves. To be very clear: their suggestions were borne not of a desire to help, but of resentment of the Other.

Over the next few decades, this ideology gave direct birth to, among many other laws and policies, New York City's infamous 'Stop and Frisk' law, which was widely understood to criminalize and target people of color, and Arizona's SB 1070 anti-immigrant law, which essentially legalized racial profiling in the state. Both laws were eventually ruled to be (at least in part) unconstitutional by the U.S. Supreme Court for the racial profiling and animus they codified. Yet policing wasn't the only place this idea of 'broken windows' took hold. Indeed, well after it had emerged as an element of these draconian laws and clearly earned reproaches for its racial implications and assumptions, Abigail Thernstrom and Stephan Thernstrom (2004) *directly cited* Wilson and Kelling as the ideological roots of their text *No Excuses: Closing the Racial Learning Gap in Schools*. Fueled by this repackaging as 'no excuses,' the racist, colonial broken windows ideology would continue to pop up in school, school district, and especially charter school policies, and as a driving theory in the work of Doug Lemov, who encourages those who want to *Teach Like a Champion* (2010) to "sweat the small stuff," again directly citing Wilson and Kelling and an idea that was long established as being inextricably linked to racial profiling and perceptions of BIPOC communities as culturally pathological. Essentially what we are getting at is this: these ubiquitous, popular approaches to schooling and teaching *necessarily* reflect, replicate, and reinforce colonial ideas—specifically, the notion that doing or valuing anything other than what an authority directs you to is a form of cultural pathology. Like Wilson and Kelling, *No Excuses* assumes that the structures of schooling or the nature of pedagogy can't be the issue, so it must be the students who are wrong.

Chances are you either already have, or at some point will, encounter one of these texts, or educators, administrators, or school policies inspired by them, by the popular notion of 'no excuses,' or even directly by the idea of 'broken windows.' And these are not the only examples of ubiquitous policies, ideas, and pedagogies—often cloaked in a language of equity and high expectations—that are rooted in the deficit-based ideologies of coloniality. Think Ruby Payne's (2005) ongoing and self-enriching lament about BIPOC youth and their "culture of poverty," or E.D. Hirsch's (1988) equally lucrative concern that multicultural education is undermining (Eurocentric) cultural literacy, or the way notions like 'grit' and 'growth mindset' have been weaponized as ways to dismiss students with complicated affective lives, and provide intellectual alibis to teachers unwilling to continue working with them (e.g., Leonardo & Zembylas, 2013; Ris, 2016; Rose, 2015). The ideologies behind these and other ideas speculating on why BIPOC and other marginalized children struggle may not seem that big a concern, especially if they can help you organize your lessons and classroom management more effectively, or provide a handy motivational tool. Yet ideas, and our expression of them in practice, have symbolic meaning that, try as we might, cannot be ignored in practice. Despite their glossy sheen, there is malice and resentment behind ideas like these that never goes away. The water, so to speak, is poisoned from the source, and so long as we cling to it, that racist, colonial well continues to shape our relationships to youth and historically and culturally marginalized communities in subtle and not so subtle ways.

In short, we can't salvage colonial ideologies, or the practical applications that flow from them; they are rooted in a *coloniality of power* (Quijano, 2000) that will always work to reproduce inequitable, dehumanizing power relations, regardless of our best intentions. Whether we intend it or not, the moment we begin replicating 'no excuses' discipline policies or pedagogies (or anything else borne from the ideologies of coloniality), we are replicating a system of power and a pedagogy that is fundamentally rooted in the resentment of the Global South and the post-colonial, racialized Other. No Excuses isn't about high standards—not really—but about control, and upholding the idea that doing anything besides what we are told, or allowing any affective or lived experience to draw our focus away from what we are instructed to do by our colonial overseers, is wrong, Other, pathological. In schools across the country, BIPOC and marginalized kids are being inundated with a message: whatever your practices, literacies, and ways of being are, they don't particularly matter. Do as those in (colonial) power say, or else face consequence and ostracization—there are *no excuses* but to comply, there are *no excuses* but to consent. It may be couched in all sorts of smiley-face stickers, growth mindset or social justice language, and 'positive behavior plan' worksheets, but the point is this: ideologically, there's very little difference between a 'no excuses' approach to classroom pedagogy, management, and discipline, and the draconian, 'Stop and Frisk' laws the courts have shown us time and again are racially biased, unconstitutional, and rooted in beliefs about the cultural pathology of BIPOC communities. They see BIPOC culture as the problem, and want those students to be someone else. As educators, we can be better than that, and find solutions to challenges of management and learning that aren't based on pedagogies of resentment and an obedience to the colonial logics of schooling.

Thinking Differently as Decoloniality

It is our hope that each of these examples has helped to spotlight how different aspects of coloniality live and work in our daily lives. In our post-colonial world, in which our present lives, society, economies, and relationships are shaped by the legacies and echoes of our own past history, coloniality is, "the air we breathe every day" (Maldonado-Torres, 2007, p. 243). It is, and has been, there, even if we were not aware of it. We could go on and on with further examples and analogies of the ways different dynamics of schooling, society, culture, politics, economics, etc. are shaped by and reflect the legacies and dynamics and relationalities of colonialism, but that would be a different text. And, more to the point, it is our hope that you will begin to do some of that critical analysis work yourself. Our focus for this book is on classroom literacy praxis, and specifically, what can be done in classroom literacy praxis to resist and disrupt coloniality on a day-to-day basis. These examples are not meant to be comprehensive, but to be emblematic of the type of critical thinking and examination that a decolonial educator needs to be doing all the time.

For, you see, coloniality may be ubiquitous, it may be structural, and it may be daunting, but it is not invulnerable, and it is not inevitable. In each of the analogies above, choices were made—choices to adhere to the logics and legacies of the ideologies and stories and assumptions of coloniality. Continuing to operate from a colonial zero-point, ignoring the vast and spectacular contributions of Global South cultures is a choice. Continuing to perpetuate the norms and expectations of the colonial West, and the Western Cultural Archive, and how it lives in and defines what are expected and acceptable ways of being in literacy classrooms is a choice. And relying on coloniality to shape how we see and relate to the ways of being and affective lives of BIPOC youth is also a choice. In each of these cases, as the pressures of coloniality confront us in different ways in classrooms, we face a choice: will we accept the colonial way of seeing the world, and be obedient to how it expects us to act, or will we choose something different, choose to be subversive, disruptive, resistant, and—as Mignolo (2009) says—"epistemically disobedient," rejecting the ideologies of coloniality altogether?

In our estimation, this is what the work of decoloniality—or the undoing and disruption of coloniality—involves. *Epistemic disobedience* is not just learning a new set of tools or picking up showy, performative lesson and curriculum activities that are more 'humanizing' or responsive. Epistemic disobedience requires that we are critical in our analysis of praxis, finding ways to see where coloniality emerges in our daily lives, particularly in our teaching and interactions with students and curriculum, because only once we see and name coloniality, can we recognize the ways in which we are being asked to obey it. And only once we are conscious of the ways that we are being asked to be obedient to coloniality can we become strategic, targeted, subversive, and intentional in our disobedience.

That is our goal with this text: to not give you guidance on reflexive, transactional skills to enact—that's not good teaching—but guidance on how to think about your classroom, your curriculum, and your relationships that will place you in a position to be making thoughtful, conscious choices about how to resist and disobey coloniality, whether that be in grand, spectacular fashion, or, more likely, in subtle, subversive ways at the margins, and ultimately, ensure that you are leading your students' literacy development in the most humanizing, liberatory way that you possibly can.

Being Clear about Decolonization

As we mentioned earlier, the term decolonization, and the idea of decolonizing things has become a bit of a ubiquitous phrase in certain circles, on the internet, and on various tracks of social media. While we are glad that more people are beginning to question colonial legacies, it is also the case that sometimes when a thing becomes trendy, it can easily lose its richness and substance. We only need to look at common ideas and terms across education to see how that plays out. James Banks' (1993) revolutionary call for multiculturalism in pedagogy and curriculum in the early 1980s became, over time, so misunderstood and watered down that today, multiculturalism is seen dismissively, and often understood in superficial terms—having diverse texts in the classroom library, or celebrating whatever cultural month it is. That could not be further from what Banks had in mind.

Gloria Ladson-Billings' (1995) vision of a culturally responsive pedagogy faced a similar challenge, and now, the phrases 'culturally responsive' and 'culturally relevant' are everywhere in our schools and district policies, even as the practices we put in place for BIPOC students continue to be dismissive of their cultural practices and perspectives. The concept of culturally responsive, in the popular education imagination, barely scratches the surface of the rich, complex engagement with communities and reciprocal learning between educators and families that Ladson-Billings laid out. And the entire idea of social justice has become something of a nebulous, ameobic specter that individuals from across the ideological spectrum can twist into a justification for their particular approach to problems impacting marginalized communities, even if those approaches' origins, roots, and evidentiary outcomes replicate new or different forms of social marginalization or injustice (Domínguez, 2017). We are thinking here of how certain perspectives in education (referenced above in regard to 'broken windows' thinking) suggest that in the name of social justice, marginalized youth need rigorously disciplined and reductive educational experiences to close achievement gaps, without ever questioning the deficit, cultural pathology, resentment-based thinking that framed the problem of achievement gaps that way in the first place (Ladson-Billings, 2006). Essentially, it is a worrying trend that sometimes our best, most important and critical ideas will so easily become watered down. If we only take the time to understand things on a surface level, our implementation and enactment of those ideas—how we live something out—will be, well, superficial.

As we begin this book on decolonizing middle-grades literacy, we are deeply conscious of that potential and tendency for superficiality. Indeed, we are conscious of conversations and challenging questions that have been raised of whether authentic decolonization within institutions is even possible, given their colonial origins and echoes (Hernández, 2018). That is a heavy thought for us educators to sit with, given that we are in many ways necessarily bound to the dictates of institutions. But though this thought is challenging, our attachment to the hope and possibility inherent in embracing a decolonial way of being is not diminished; yes, we want to steer purposefully away from superficiality, but we also know there are ways to live out these commitments pragmatically within the day-to-day, mundane grind of teaching.

So with all this in mind, we want to be deeply attentive to, and guided by, Tuck and Yang's (2012) reminder to us all that decolonization is *not* just another metaphor for social justice. Decolonization is not just language to use to keep up with trends on social media, or a phrase to toss out to bolster our credentials of support for BIPOC students. It is not an identity to take on about being the most 'woke,' or a skill picked up in a two-day professional development workshop. Decolonization involves making real, tangible, active, and continuous changes to what we do each day, to how we live our lives, and to how we think about the world and our relationality to others, actively aware of how colonization has, and continues to, shape our lives and the ways we see one another. Decolonization requires us to consider how racialization and ethnic and cultural identity necessarily impact our experiences and social power and what we can do to help our students understand and disrupt unequal power structures, including giving up some of our own social power along the way. It requires us to think about big questions around the value and position of knowledge, about sovereignty and agency, and to question assumptions and structures that we may be comfortable, and even pleased with. In short, decolonization is going to involve some real work, and some real change, both in our day-to-day actions, and in how we see ourselves, others, and possibilities for how the world can work.

Even as we say this, we recognize the constraints we all exist within in schools and classrooms. It is unlikely that you will be able to throw out the bell schedule, reimagine and enact a wholly different way to approach subject-area learning, or toss out state- and district-mandated standardized assessments (if you are in that position, well, do so!). We are in the same positions in our universities and in the classrooms and middle schools we work with. The structures of society and education are enormous, locked in place both by the legacies of coloniality that created them, but also by their sheer size and normality in the 21st-century world. Change is difficult, and big change, decolonial change that requires serious, uncomfortable self-reflection, is even more difficult, because it would involve rethinking the entire thing (institutions, structures, and all) and starting from scratch. With that in mind, we believe it is incredibly important to be very careful about the claims that we might make around the verb 'to decolonize,' and would even say that reaching a point where our classrooms are 'decolonized' in the past tense, is impossible because there are both so many aspects of society (and our schools) on which to work, and because decolonization is an ongoing and continuous process even after taking steps forward. So where does that leave us?

Well, it is here that we think about some of our most interesting, and delightfully mischievous, middle-grades students. The ones who, even when the rules were supposed to be incredibly strict, and the environment impossible to disrupt, still find a way to thumb their nose at the system, often in ways that are sneaky and hardly perceptible. Following from our earlier discussion of being *epistemically disobedient*, it is our hope that you will emulate those students, and, even in very constraining circumstances, even if it is just in the margins, find ways to be *disobedient* to coloniality in your pedagogy. That sense of disobedience is our goal—not for us to walk around making claims that decolonization in your classroom is 'done,' or that you are now a 'decolonial teacher' for having read this text, both of which are attitudes that risk watering down the decolonial to superficial status, like so many other good ideas before it. Even when we are committed to this work, it is important to recognize that not everything we do reflects (or qualifies as) decolonial action. That is OK, because it is realistic.

Rather, to ensure we are not taking decolonial work for granted, or reducing it to a metaphor, we hope you will seek to be constantly engaged in the action of decolonization, and reflective of the depth of coloniality all around us, in our lives, and our institutions. Appreciating where we are able to decolonize, and where we might just be doing our best to be humanizing in colonial circumstances, is a critical and continual process. We must constantly look for new spaces, places, and opportunities to disrupt and decolonize, disobey colonial logics, and imagine new possibilities for how we might be together in learning spaces. And in our estimation, it is okay to start small, surreptitiously, and look for cracks at the margins in which to engage in decolonial work. Don't get us wrong, that is still going to be difficult, and it needs to be accompanied by a sense of urgency for being as broadly transformative and disobedient as we can be, but it helps us recognize that humility and an appreciation for constant growth are decolonial values we want to be striving for too.

Questions to Consider in Reflecting on Coloniality

1   What is my level of historical knowledge around the impacts of colonization on people, cultures, and societies in the Global South?
2   How do I see elements of coloniality in my life and world? Where do I see the patterns of power, or social and cultural expectations of the colonial zero-point, present in my day-to-day life?
3   How much are my own expectations about schools and schooling, and the things I am comfortable with in education, a reflection of the Western Cultural Archive?
4   What are ways I can think of right now to be epistemically disobedient to the ways coloniality wants my students and I to behave and perform?

Resources to Explore

Growing Our Knowledge of a Neo-Colonial World

To really explore and unpack coloniality is going to take some time, and some reading and exploration. While we have mentioned and recapped some of the big, central theoretical ideas that drive this field as a whole, they don't make for scintillating or accessible reading—but that doesn't mean there aren't great resources to explore. Here's where we suggest diving in to start exploring perspectives and analyses of coloniality:

- A good place to begin is with Juan Gonzalez' *Harvest of Empire: A History of Latinos in America*, Roxanne Dunbar Ortiz' *An Indigenous Peoples' History of the United States*, Paul Ortiz' *An African American and Latinx History of the United States*, and Ronald Takaki's *A Different Mirror*. Each of these texts traces out what we know as counter-narrative histories—history told from the perspectives of those whose experiences were marginalized, and upon whose losses dominant narratives of history were built. Each of these texts is essential reading for everyone—adult and student—and most have young people's versions available, which make them student accessible.
- Straddling the line between theoretical and relatable, Roberto Hernández's *Coloniality of the US//Mexico Border: Power, Violence, and the Decolonial Imperative* lays out in detail the ways coloniality still pervades our lives, with a particular focus on how we have long viewed the southern U.S. border, or the dividing line between the U.S. and the Global South.
- Finally, we can't speak highly enough of *Teen Vogue*'s (De)Colonized Series (https://www.teenvogue.com/tag/decolonized). From straightforward articles defining terms and concepts like the article "Colonialism Explained" (https://www.teenvogue.com/story/colonialism-explained), to narratives, reflections, and analyses of social movements and current events, the editors at *Teen Vogue* have done all of us educators a great service here.

References

Aldama, A. J. (2001). *Disrupting savagism: Intersecting Chicana/o, Mexican immigrant, and Native American struggles for self-representation.* Duke University Press.

Alexander, M. (2011). *The new Jim Crow: Mass incarceration in an age of colorblindness.* The New Press.

Alim, H. S., Rickford, J. R., & Ball, A. F. (2016). Introducing raciolinguistics. In H. Samy Alim, John R. Rickford, & Arnetha F. Ball (eds.), *Raciolinguistics: How language shapes our ideas about race,* 1–30. Oxford University Press.

Banks, J. A. (1993). Multicultural education: Development, dimensions, and challenges. *The Phi Delta Kappan,* 75(1), 22–28.

Bonilla-Silva, E. (2006). *Racism without racists: Color-blind racism and the persistence of racial inequality in the United States.* Rowman & Littlefield Publishers.

Cañas, I. (2022). *The Hacienda.* Berkley Books.

Castro-Gómez, S. (2005). *La Hybris Del Punto Cero: Ciencia, Raza E Ilustración En La Nueva Granada (1750–1816)* [*The Hubris of the zero point: Science, race, and illustration in New Granada (1750–1816)*]. Pontificia Universidad Javeriana.

Coleman, J. S., Campbell, E., Hobson, C., McPartland, J., Mood, A., Weinfeld, F., & York, R. (1966). The Coleman report. *Equality of Educational Opportunity,* 1–32.

Collins, P. H. (2004). *Black sexual politics: African Americans, gender, and the new racism.* Routledge.

Domínguez, M. 2017. "Se Hace Puentes Al Andar": Decolonial teacher education as a needed bridge to culturally sustaining and revitalizing pedagogies. In D. Paris and H. S. Alim (Eds.), *Culturally sustaining pedagogy: Teaching and learning for justice in a changing world* (pp. 225–245). Teachers College Press.

Dunbar-Ortiz, R. (2014). *An indigenous peoples' history of the United States* (Vol. 3). Beacon Press.

Dutil, S. (2020). Dismantling the school-to-prison pipeline: A trauma-informed, critical race perspective on school discipline. *Children & Schools,* 42(3), 171–178.

Galeano, E. (1997). *Open veins of Latin America: Five centuries of the pillage of a continent.* NYU Press.

Gómez, L. E. (2022). *Inventing Latinos: A new story of American racism.* The New Press.

Gonzalez, J. (2011). *Harvest of empire: A history of Latinos in America.* Penguin.

Grosfoguel, R. (2013). The epistemic decolonial turn: Beyond political-economy paradigms. In W. Mignolo & A. Escobar (Eds.), *Globalization and the decolonial option* (pp. 65–77). Routledge.

Harry Potter Wiki (2022, November 1). *Wizarding Schools Map.* Harry Potter Wiki. https://harrypotter.fandom.com/wiki/Map:Wizarding_schools

Heath, S. B. (1983). *Ways with words: Language, life and work in communities and classrooms.* Cambridge University Press.

Hirsch Jr, E. D., Kett, J. F., & Trefil, J. S. (1988). *Cultural literacy: What every American needs to know.* Vintage.

Henrich, J., Heine, S. J., & Norenzayan, A. (2010). The weirdest people in the world? *Behavioral and Brain Sciences,* 33(2–3), 61–83.

Hernández, R. D. (2018). *Coloniality of the US/Mexico border: Power, violence, and the decolonial imperative.* University of Arizona Press.

Kaul, S. (2021). Temporality and its discontents or why time needs to be retold. In S. Kaul (Ed.), *Retelling Time* (pp. 1–10). Routledge India.

Ladson-Billings, G. (2006). From the achievement gap to the education debt: Understanding achievement in US schools. *Educational Researcher,* 35(7), 3–12.

Ladson-Billings, G. (1995). Toward a theory of culturally relevant pedagogy. *American Educational Research Journal,* 32(3), 465–491.

Lefebvre, C. (2011). We have tailored Africa: French colonialism and the 'artificiality' of Africa's borders in the interwar period. *Journal of Historical Geography,* 37(2), 191–202.

Lemov, D. (2010). *Teach like a champion: 49 techniques that put students on the path to college (K-12)*. John Wiley & Sons.

Leonardo, Z., & Zembylas, M. (2013). Whiteness as technology of affect: Implications for educational praxis. *Equity & Excellence in Education*, *46*(1), 150–165.

Maldonado-Torres, N. (2007). On the coloniality of being: Contributions to the development of a concept. *Cultural Studies*, *21*(2–3), 240–270.

McCauley, R. N., & Henrich, J. (2006). Susceptibility to the Müller-Lyer illusion, theory-neutral observation, and the diachronic penetrability of the visual input system. *Philosophical Psychology*, *19*(1), 79–101.

Mignolo, W. D. (2009). Epistemic disobedience, independent thought and decolonial freedom. *Theory, Culture & Society*, *26*(7–8), 159–181.

Mignolo, W. D. (2011). The Global South and world dis/order. *Journal of Anthropological Research*, *67*(2), 165–188.

Mills, A. (2016). Colonialism in wizarding America: JK Rowling's history of magic in North America through an Indigenous lens. *The Looking Glass: New Perspectives on Children's Literature*, *19*(1).

Omi, M., & Winant, H. (2014). *Racial formation in the United States*. Routledge.

Ortiz, P. (2018). *An African American and Latinx history of the United States* (Vol. 4). Beacon Press.

Pasternak, S. (2020). Assimilation and partition: How settler colonialism and racial capitalism co-produce the borders of Indigenous economies. *South Atlantic Quarterly*, *119*(2), 301–324.

Paris, D. (2012). Culturally sustaining pedagogy: A needed change in stance, terminology, and practice. *Educational Researcher*, *41*(3), 93–97.

Payne, R. K. (2005). *A framework for understanding poverty*. aha! Process.

Pottermore. (2022, November 1). Wizarding World. https://www.wizardingworld.com/

Quijano, A. (2000). Coloniality of power and eurocentrism in Latin America. *International Sociology*, *15*(2), 215–232. https://doi.org/10.1177/0268580900015002005

Quirós, R. (2021). Algunas reflexiones en torno al rol de la cultura dentro de la investigacióncon motivo del décimo aniversario de The Weirdest People in the World? *PsicoInnova*, *4*(2), 48–61.

Ris, E. (2016). "The problem with teaching 'grit' to poor kids? They already have it. Here's what they really need." *The Washington Post*: 2016–2018.

Roediger, D. R. (1991). *The Wages of Whiteness. Race and the Making of the American Working Class*. Verso.

Rosa, J. (2019). *Looking like a language, sounding like a race*. Oxford University Press.

Rose, M. (2015). "Why teaching kids to have 'grit' isn't always a good thing." *Washington Post*.

Rothstein, R. (2017). *The color of law: A forgotten history of how our government segregated America*. Liveright Publishing.

Said, E. (1978). *Orientalism: Western concepts of the orient*. Pantheon.

Scribner, S., & Cole, M. (1981). Unpackaging literacy. *Writing: The nature, Development, and Teaching of Written Communication*, *1*, 71–87.

Segura, G. M., & Bowler, S. (Eds.). (2006). *Diversity in democracy: Minority representation in the United States*. University of Virginia Press.

Takaki, R. (2012a). *A different mirror: A history of multicultural America* (Revised edition). Back Bay Books.

Takaki, R. (2012b). *A different mirror for young people: A history of multicultural America*. Seven Stories Press.

Teen Vogue (2022, November 1). *(De)Colonized*. Teen Vogue. https://www.teenvogue.com/tag/decolonized

Thernstrom, A., & Thernstrom, S. (2004). *No excuses: Closing the racial gap in learning*. Simon and Schuster.

Tuck, E. & Yang, K. W. (2012). Decolonization is not a metaphor. *Decolonization: Indigeneity. Education & Society*, *1*(1), 1–40

Tuhiwai Smith, L. (2021). *Decolonizing methodologies: Research and indigenous peoples*. Bloomsbury Publishing.

Wilson, J. Q., & Kelling, G. L. (1982). *Broken windows. Atlantic Monthly*, *249*(3), 29–38.

2

WHAT IS RACIAL LITERACY?

Introduction

In his 2007 autobiography, Barack Obama wrote,

> The worst thing that colonialism did was to cloud our view of our past.
>
> (p. 434)

Looking into our past, or things from our past that linger on in our present, can be incredibly difficult, unsettling, and emotional. Striving towards the decolonial means, however, striving to do just that.

With that said, we want you to start this chapter by taking a deep breath, because we are going to talk about something that is essential to decolonization but is also the most taboo topic in our lives: race and racial identity. Race is and has arguably—certainly in our estimation—long been the most salient identity factor shaping life in the United States. That doesn't mean it is the most significant for everyone, day to day, or that it impacts everyone in the same way. But if we step back, and broadly survey our collective history, our social, cultural, and political present, points of tension in community cultural expectations, and the *de jure* and *de facto* systems, structures, and institutions of our post-colonial world, it is race—or more specifically, tension across perceived racial difference—as a dimension of identity that each of us in the United States (and world) experiences, more than any other, that shapes our lives. Racial identity profoundly shapes how we see ourselves, where we live, with whom we spend time, the languages and literacies we are fluent in, the types of stories we tell, the way we hear the stories of others, and how we read not just the word, but the world. And more to our point here, the critical foundation of all of this emerges in the developmental crucible of the middle grades.

This text is about decolonizing our middle grades literacy classroom, not fully unpacking the long, complicated, nuanced history of this thing we call 'race.' But if we have any interest in decolonizing our classrooms, nurturing ours and our students' racial literacies must be a central component of that work. So the point of this chapter is to answer some really important questions for decolonial classrooms and liberatory educators. Specifically, we hope to answer the questions: why race and coloniality?; why race and middle school?; and why race and literacy? When you're done with this chapter, it is our hope that you'll have a foundational understanding of race and coloniality that will

DOI: 10.4324/9781003290681-3

let you have something of a response to each of these questions, and to be in a position where you can put the ideas, suggestions, plans, conversations, and lessons we discuss in the other chapters into practice—because if we aren't ready to honestly engage with our racialized, decolonial identities, many of the liberatory lesson ideas and principles we suggest won't land in the ways they are intended.

During this chapter in particular, we encourage you to take your time. This is likely going to be a different definition of race than the one you are familiar with. If you encounter things here that are new or discomforting, we hope you will lean into it a bit, and keep reading, because understanding a bit about what race is and isn't, its context, and how it shapes our lives, and the lives of middle grades learners in particular, is critical to any effort to decolonize.

What Is Race? A Quick Primer for Decolonial Educators

What is race? This seems to most people like a simple question with a simple answer: Skin color (what we can better describe as phenotype), right? Well, not exactly. The answer is actually far more complicated, and far more complex than we might have previously considered. It is wrapped up in history, it takes turns in multiple directions, circles back on itself, and changes contextually. While we cannot cover all of this nuance, let's get a bit of essential context, because understanding race is essential to decolonial work.

A Brief History of Race

Let's start here: though we think of 'race' as something that has always been around (and certainly phenotypical variation has existed since the emergence of hominids), the story of this thing we understand as 'race' is actually only about 500 years old (Fredrickson, 2015). Keen observers will note that 500 years is also the duration of time since the beginning of European colonization—that same legacy we are now working to decolonize from. In very real terms, race and racism, and colonization and coloniality, are intertwined (Quijano, 2000, 2007). Race—and the creation of race as a concept—is the foundation of colonization's story.

Here's how the story goes: About 500 years ago, Europe was experiencing a considerable social upheaval. Older means of ordering the social world according to the divine right of kings and other markers of difference were beginning to fall apart as economic development and the first hints of the Enlightenment kicked in (Wilinsky, 1998). At the same time, Europe began to come into initial, or, in the cases of Africa and Asia, more substantial, contact with 'new' worlds, rich with resources. Tales of wealth and possibility abounded, but so did the reality that there were other people in these places, occupying these spaces of possible extraction. The question before these new leaders of Europe, essentially, was this:

If all men are created equal, as new Enlightenment philosophies suggested, how can we justify the conquest, enslavement, and exploitation that produces great wealth?

Especially given the fact that many of these 'new' peoples were as developed, if not more so, than Europe itself (at the time of first contact, the Mexica capital of Tenochtitlan, for instance, was larger than the city of London, more developed, with a stronger agricultural support system, and, as we mentioned previously, near universal public schooling), and some in Africa had been longstanding trading partners with Europe for years on a relatively equal footing, it was a tricky philosophical puzzle to figure out how to justify the economic and land grab that would be so lucrative.

The answer that Europe found was phenotype: these 'new' peoples that were being encountered were not just culturally different, they were *phenotypically* different as well, and it was this difference that became a marker for justifying their conquest. If their phenotype was different, then they must *be* different, and thus differential treatment, no matter their level of intelligence, culture, kindness, or development, could be justified (Quijano, 2000; Mignolo, 2003). And so the first mention of phenotypical difference being understood as *race* in our historical record occurs in the 1500s; coincidentally just as chattel slavery and serious displacement of indigenous Americans began (Fredrickson, 2015). So here's the point: *race, phenotype, is not some indicator of biological difference—it is a social creation from just about 500 years ago used to justify the human costs of colonization.*

It is well beyond our scope here to go into depth and unpack all of the complicated history of race that followed, but in large part you, dear reader, already know it, in broad sweeps—though the narrative you've been told is likely one that has (intentionally) decontextualized race from the origin of its quite literal creation. You're likely familiar with the transatlantic slave trade, the genocide of indigenous Americans, and the colonial scrambles for Africa, Asia, and Latin America. You surely know about things like the 3/5ths compromise, chattel slavery, the Civil War being fought over state's right to own slaves, the impacts of reconstruction and Jim Crow, and critical moments from the Civil Rights movement. Some folks may be aware of deeper cuts in that global history—*casta* systems used by colonial administrations, and efforts to exploit ethnic and community divisions through the redrawing of borders and promotion of some tribal groups as agents of the colonizers, or the racialized policies of the modern era, like the war on drugs, the War on Terror, or the militarization of the southern U.S. border. But the point is this: since colonization and coloniality began, the construction of race as a way to divide the world into Us vs Them has been a fundamental justification for inequality, abuse, and marginalization. If pursuing a deeper picture and more specifics of this complicated history is of interest to you, we offer a number of resources at the end of this chapter for further reading on the history of race as concept and idea.

This brings us to the answer to that initial question: What is race? Well, as we said, it isn't a biological or physiological reality. There is nothing inherent in phenotype that has any meaning about our existence as humans. In fact, you visibly see the lack of substance in this idea of phenotypical difference every day, because in an actuarial sense, there's more diversity within racial 'groups' than across 'races.' The ambiguity of phenotype, the wide variety of melanin concentration that we see daily, as well as the way racial 'categories' vary from context to context regionally and globally, shows us how arbitrary this thing is (Roth, 2012). But that doesn't make it any less *real*. Because of those choices, made 500 years ago, to ascribe meaning to it, phenotype, skin color, has become a common-sense way to understand and see difference in the world—not just physically, but in a multitude of dimensions, none of which have any basis in reality. Phenotype (arbitrary and varied as it is) accrued social, cultural, and political meaning; and even though it has changed, evolved, and adapted to new dynamics, those meanings still linger centuries later (Omi & Winant, 2014). Attitudes, stereotypes, and deep-seated misconceptions masquerading as common-sense beliefs are learned and passed along from generation to generation, retaining the significance of race, even as its artificial origins are forgotten. Racial categories and identities are perpetuated as assemblages of prejudices and biases, reinforced by social and political power, and cultural discourse (Puar, 2018). As Robin D.G. Kelley (2004) puts it, race is "not about how you look, it is about how people assign meaning to how you look." So simply put, today, in the 21st century, we can understand race as a socially constructed system of unequal human categorization, based around phenotype, that produces both social and material consequences that are very real, and very significant (Omi & Winant, 2014). So let's talk about what those social and material consequences are, and what they look like in the colonial classroom.

Race and Coloniality

We introduced the idea of coloniality in our last chapter, but let's dig in a bit deeper. We often talk about the consequences, or real impacts, of coloniality in three dimensions: the coloniality of being, the coloniality of power, and the coloniality of knowledge. These three dimensions, according to Quijano (2000), were all essential to the way that colonization, 500 years ago, sought to unsettle, disrupt, and usurp existing ways of being, living, and thinking in the Global South. And all of them were intertwined with the introduction of this idea of race; race became the new framework—intellectually, legally, politically, culturally—to understand and justify action in the world, giving colonizers wide leeway to dominate and take what they desired, and allowing indigenous communities little recourse to resist the ways their lives, communities, and land were being upended. Five hundred years later, sitting in our classrooms, what this means is that to be decolonial requires that we do our best to confront each of these dimensions, and, as a central piece of that, recognize how race is central to how they show up in our lives.

Coloniality of Being

Let's start with the coloniality of being. What we mean by this dimension is that the world our daily existence occurs in, the spaces and relations, have been impacted by colonial legacies. Colonization sought to change how people existed together in the world, and coloniality encourages us not to question the ways our lives and relationships remain segmented, distant, and detached from one another and the land. In some ways, this is the easiest to see. We live intensely segregated racial lives—though we might see folks of other races regularly at public facilities, by many measures, we are more segregated now, in our schools and communities, than before Brown v. Board of Education mandated integration (e.g., Rothstein, 2019; Thompson Dorsey, 2013). And we all live racialized lives that impact our connections to one another. We experience our racial identities—including how they might shift contextually (more on that later) each day in the way different people react, speak, and engage with us. BIPOC folks may likely immediately understand this feeling; knowing and feeling that behind many interactions, there is an affective distance between BIPOC folks and some white folks that is ontological, or rooted in how lived experience is understood (Muñoz, 2006). For white and white-passing folks, the process of experiencing race is actually alive and well, but it exists in the absence of having to feel or think about race, and the discomfort that comes from pointing that fact out (Bonilla-Silva, 2006). Essentially, that expectation of a non-racial existence is itself a racialized experience. In our world, shaped and impacted by coloniality, our BEING is shaped daily by our racial identity.

Coloniality of Power

Next, let's consider the coloniality of power. This dimension essentially captures the way that power lives in systems, structures, and institutions, and that the institutions we have all inherited are, necessarily, deeply embedded with colonial legacies. Five hundred years ago, colonial powers created systems of laws, governance, and cultural and political organization that, though shaped by the high-minded ideas of the Enlightenment, were also woven through with the ideology of race and European racial superiority. Among many, a classic example of this is our own U.S. Constitution, which at once argues for equality and equal representation, yet permitted chattel slavery and counted Black people as 3/5ths of a person. While (thankfully) time and incremental progress corrected the most egregious of these examples, like this one, many (if not most) of the underlying systems and structures that either expressly or tacitly permitted racial discrimination in the exercise of social and political power persisted; in many cases, mention of race was removed, but the source of the power imbalance—say, the way political representation and electoral boundaries were assigned, tax revenues distributed, housing appraised, or legal punishments calculated—was left untouched (Alexander, 2011; Rothstein, 2017). In our classrooms, this shows up in the deeply unequal school discipline statistics that appear year after year (Heitzeg, 2016; Skiba et al., 2014), the ways that BIPOC students are subjected to multiple opportunity gaps and an education debt (Ladson-Billings, 2006), the overwhelmingly white demographics of classroom teachers (NCES, 2022), and the ways in which school governance, from school boards to PTAs, fail to reflect the demographics of our communities. The result is a world in which abstract liberalism—or the idea that if things are fair in principle, even if clearly not in practice, that is good enough—thrives (Stoll & Klein, 2018). And so our world remains governed, largely, by systems that ensure POWER continues to benefit whiteness and perpetuate racial hierarchies whose origins stretch back to colonization.

Coloniality of Knowledge

Finally, we can reflect on the coloniality of knowledge, which involves the way certain ways of knowing, and certain perspectives and stories, are privileged over others. For us educators, the coloniality of knowledge is the most visceral, because we are aware of how powerful education can be. As settler-colonialism kicked off, and European powers sought to exercise control over indigenous populations, education became a powerful battleground for this. The Spanish burned nearly the entirety of the vast writings and documents of Mesoamerican cultures (Aldama, 2001). Residential schools established across North America to 'civilize' indigenous populations by stealing children from their families and robbing them of their language and culture operated well into the 20th century, and the full extent of the horrors which occurred there are still coming to light (Bombay, Matheson, & Anisman, 2014). Black and African slaves were disallowed from learning to read. And worldwide, European powers replaced indigenous and ancestral histories with European narratives that centered their arrival as the beginning of 'progress' and 'civilization' for those who were racially different, even in their own lands. Today, we see the coloniality of knowledge daily, when we pick up our textbooks, and look at the built-in biases in our curricula (those things we discussed in the previous chapter). These are the echoes of colonial book burning and residential schooling.

But the coloniality of knowledge also springs up in what knowledge we are dissuaded from exploring. What we are talking about is the taboo on directly discussing and confronting race, and the ways that when we do have to talk about it, we try to veer away, locating race and racism as an object of the past (solved by MLK, right?), a regional concern (often dismissing it as an issue for the U.S. South), or pivoting towards still uncomfortable, but less historically strained dynamics—talking about socio-economic class, for instance, or gender—as ways to not talk about race. Race, as we have mentioned, is foundational to the colonial story. And so coloniality is on full display every time race comes up, and, obeying the very intentional taboo, we veer away, rather than trying to grapple with what this KNOWLEDGE means for our lives in the past, present, and future.

All of this plays out in our classrooms, whether we intend it to or not. Our classrooms are, statistically speaking, profoundly segregated spaces; often even in a heterogeneous school, tracking re-segregates a desegregated student body (McCardle, 2020). Our schools are shaped by policies, systems, structures, and expectations that reinscribe racial inequities. And unless we are being incredibly intentional, our curricula perpetuate and encourage a taboo on exploring our knowledge and understanding of race and one another's racial lives through discussion. Across these three dimensions, in our schools and beyond, race accrues social, cultural, and political meaning, and this produces social and material consequences. Our discomfort with discussing race is a social consequence. Inequitable school discipline statistics and learning outcomes are material consequences. The increasingly segregated lives students will lead as they grow older and enter adulthood, leading to misunderstandings of one another's racial experiences, are a consequence that is both social and material. The list could go on.

As we talk here about decolonizing our classrooms, that necessarily means that we need to disrupt how race and racism play out in those classrooms, and how we talk about those big issues. We think this is a particularly valuable challenge to be exploring amidst a U.S. landscape that continues to take, and perhaps is increasingly taking, a reactionary approach to acknowledging the reality of race in our lives, even as its effects are quite clear. Problems simply do not go away because we ignore them.

Coloniality and race are intertwined, and decolonizing our classrooms cannot happen if we ignore race. We aren't going to be able to undo 500 years of social and cultural machinations in one school year, but if we understand the significance of race for our cultural and social lives and history, and how racial identity comes into being, we can help students challenge and question the 'common-sense' ways race is often presented, fostering positive racial literacies, and in so doing, making big strides towards liberatory outcomes.

Race and the Middle Grades

When we suggest centering discussions of racial experience with middle schoolers, as well as the importance of bringing up other dimensions of colonial inequity like gender, class, sexuality, etc. at this grade level, we are often met by the response:

> Why discuss this in middle school? Why burden students with these heavy topics? Surely these young students should just be left to be innocent kids as long as possible.

For the most part, the impulse that spurs these responses is grounded in some well-intentioned, but ultimately off-base, arguments and assumptions about middle schoolers. Specifically, that middle schoolers are too young to wade into such heavy topics; that they are colorblind, and not impacted by the political squabbles around race we adults are invested in; that their racial identities don't impact their young lives much yet; and that they are too immature to talk about race and will lose interest. Except—here's the important bit that applies to all these things—they aren't. We aren't just saying that as a retort; rather, that is precisely what the psychology of identity development tells us about this critical moment of human development. Let's look specifically at how race, or, more accurately, racial, ethnic, and cultural (REC) identity (Tatum, 2017) development—which we use rather than just racial identity because, as our historical discussion pointed out, race is contextual, and wrapped up with ethnicity and culture in complicated and inextricable ways—occurs.

Before we launch into this too deeply, though, let us first preface this by saying that what we will cover here is a brief summary and introduction to much more nuanced models and research on which there are literally whole books to explore. We are not claiming to be comprehensive here, but rather, to give you the summary context and base of information needed to understand, and explain, why talking about race, ethnicity, and cultural identity is absolutely critical to decolonizing your classroom, to literacy learning generally, and to supporting liberatory, ambitious academic outcomes for your students. As we explain all this, we'll be drawing on multiple models, all of which have their own unique terminology, and subtle and significant differences from one another, but generally speaking, all reveal a consistent story about REC identity: middle school and adolescence are a critical period when these ideas about ourselves, others, and the world begin to crystallize. So with that said, let's begin by looking at where REC identity starts for everyone: socialization.

As young children, all youth, like all adults, are immersed in a world of social and cultural messaging, or socialization—much of it related to race, ethnicity, and culture (Hughes, 2003; Simon, 2021). This includes obvious immersion like what shows up on TV, and what books and stories we encounter in schools, etc., and nowadays particularly, what's trending on social media. We can all be sure that the events, broadcast through both traditional mainstream media and social media outlets, of 2020's post-George Floyd protests, conversations, and identity crises had a profound impact on several generations. But these are, again, the obvious things. The cultural messaging we face also includes things that are far more subtle, and that we maybe don't even think about consciously as messages or lessons because they are just the fabric of our daily lives: observations of who we live around and what feels like normal cultural practices for us and for others; observations of social interactions and who has power in different spaces, as well as how and why that power is used; observations of who receives favorable treatment or interactions; observations of who our teachers and other role models seem to feel most comfortable around and who they gravitate towards. These messages are unspoken, unacknowledged, constant, and plentiful. They are complicated and contradictory at times. There is evidence that they begin as early as infancy, with the phenotypes of faces that children as young as three months old see being conditioned as normal, as 'Us.' And because they are broad and societal, and young children see the world locally (as opposed to being able to process abstract systemic dynamics), ultimately, for BIPOC youth, these messages add up to social conditioning—socialization—that suggests, without ever needing to expressly say so, that whiteness (as a cultural identity position) is normal, central, and desired.

To put these ideas of socialization into concrete terms, we can look to the most famous evidence of this early racial socialization that exists: the Clark Doll experiment. Now, chances are you may have already heard of this, but here is the quick recap: in the 1940s, researchers Kenneth and Mamie Clark (1940) conducted a psychological experiment to gauge the effects of segregation on children in which they had groups of young children, ages three to seven, choose between otherwise identical white dolls and black dolls based on a series of prompts, including "Which is the good/bad doll?" and which they would prefer to play with. The results were stark, and jarring. Overwhelmingly, the children identified the white doll as the 'good' doll, and the black doll as the 'bad' doll, and largely preferred the white doll. The Clarks' research would go on to be used as evidence of the deleterious effects of segregation on children during Brown v. Board and other trials, but it would also be repeated as an experiment with regularity through today (Powell-Hopson & Hopson, 1988). And through today, the same results that the Clarks found—that even young children, of all racial backgrounds, have internalized racial socialization that centers and preferentially values whiteness—continue to be replicated (Parsons et al., 2019). One need only jump on Youtube to see a number of modern examples of this experiment being rolled out, what these children's responses and unconscious biases look like, and how young the children involved are.

Though the results seem bleak, and might make us feel like racial inequity and unconscious bias are inevitable, that is not the point at all. Rather, considering the (continued) relevance of the Clark Doll experiment, both historically and in contemporary times, can help us as middle school educators to appreciate how embedded the cultural messaging, the coloniality, around race, truly is, and how it impacts the youth that enter our classrooms and ourselves. And if we can appreciate this first step of racial identity development, recognize that even before they have arrived in our middle-grades classrooms, students are immersed in racialized experiences, narratives, and perceptions, then we can also appreciate the importance of understanding the subsequent stages, and what the improved racial literacies we might offer can do. Now, with the baseline of socialization explained, let us consider what the subsequent stages of REC development look like for both BIPOC and white youth.

Racial, Ethnic, and Cultural Identity Development for BIPOC Youth

For BIPOC youth, the aforementioned socialization process all occurs in what Cross (1991, 1995; Cross & Fhagen-Smith, 1996; Ritchey, 2014) calls the pre-encounter stage; essentially, those years where we are, or are becoming, aware that REC differences are dynamics that exist in the world, and during which we may be consciously or subconsciously attributing meaning to them, but have yet to experience their social and material consequences in a profound, meaningful way. BIPOC youth know and can comprehend that race is a thing, that they and others have racial identities, and that these mean something, but the full weight and significance of those meanings—and thus the need to process, adjust, and grapple with that significance and consequences—has yet to arrive. So when does all that happen?

What comes next is the encounter or dissonance stage or moment (Bañales et al., 2020). Essentially, after a childhood absorbing societal messages and meanings, yet still living and thinking locally (i.e., limited to the scope of the world that young children can generally understand), children necessarily begin to be able to make more abstract connections to the world. Just like the way that younger children gradually learn about object permanence, adolescent children begin to appreciate and understand interconnection beyond themselves, their family, and their immediate community circle. In adolescence—middle school—ideas and the significance and consequences of those ideas begin to make sense (Tatum, 2017). And it is in this landscape and developmental turn that the next step in REC identity occurs, through what we might describe as an 'encounter' in which the full consequences of racial difference become clear. What we are talking about here is that moment when the messaging and meanings around our REC identity come to intersect with a realization of the social and material consequences of race. Essentially, it happens when BIPOC youth are ready, developmentally, to be able to make broader, more abstract connections between the racial messages they are processing and their lived experiences. This encounter moment can be a single, jarring incident—Michael still remembers, viscerally, his jarring moment of recognizing what being Latino meant in school—or perhaps a more drawn-out realization around things experienced countless times before. Either way, the result is that the encounter necessarily shatters the veneer of a colorblind world; it becomes clear that the socialization, the cultural messages, are not just happenstance, they are not just innocuous background noise, but rather, they are realities that have consequences, and that must be dealt with as part of daily life, impacting and shaping the choices, actions, and behaviors BIPOC youth will engage in as they navigate a racial world. And to reiterate, typically, because of the other developmental dynamics involved (ability for increased social abstraction), not because of any increased likelihood of exposure to racism, this racial encounter most regularly happens while students are with us, in the middle grades.

So what comes after the encounter? Again, there are many models (e.g., Brunsma et al., 2013; Constante et al., 2020; Nadal, 2004; Poston, 1990; Rockquemore et al., 2009), and some have more nuance to this stage, but we will keep it simple, suggesting that what happens next can be broadly summed up as coping. Coping can (and does) mean many things. For some BIPOC youth, coping will simply be an increased awareness and sensitivity to the socialization and cultural messages they continue to encounter. For others, this will be the start of what W.E.B. Du Bois classically refers to as double consciousness (Moore, 2005), or we might see in more contemporary terms as code-switching; learning that there is a clear distinction between Dominant, institutional culture, and our home or Primary cultures. This involves 'switching' back and forth between different codes or consciousness, and associated ways of being, one for the Primary culture of our home and family, and one for the Dominant, white culture, since being valued and successful in institutional settings, like schools, requires behaving, talking, acting, and speaking in ways that are acceptable to whiteness and white cultural norms. This bicultural existence is a continual negotiation, and can be exhausting (e.g., Darder, 2012). But if we think about these two coping positions—heightened awareness and double consciousness—as center points along a spectrum of possible reactions to the racial encounter, the coping mechanisms at the ends of the spectrum are critical to be aware of as well.

Oppositional Identity and Mimicry

At one end we have a dynamic that is often described as oppositional identity (Cross, 1995), or a coping mechanism that, confronted with the reality of racial bias and the prospect of continued racial injury, copes by embracing the most pronounced and perhaps, derided elements of that racialized identity as central to their REC identity performance, likely drawing the ire of culturally normative institutions. In our classrooms, we will have students who have much the same psychological coping reaction. Confronted with the realization that they will, as Homi Bhabha (2012) notes, be at best seen as "always the same but not quite, always the same but not white," they choose to reject participation in that game of code-switching and double consciousness, or seeking to appease cultural norms that continually undervalue them. If I am going to be criminalized and marginalized for my REC identity, the logic goes, then why not lean into it. To give some cultural referents, we are talking, here, about the identity position which Malcolm X, the Black Panther Party, or Che Guevara are often constructed as, defiant and uncompromising, or in more recent terms, the characterization of the character of Erik Killmonger/N'Jadaka from the film *Black Panther* (here's a lesson idea for you, in case you didn't pick up on the hint!). A student coping in this way is likely to be resistant and confrontational over anything related to the school or other institutions, to push against boundaries, to refuse to conform to institutional expectations and norms, and to reject deference to power. It

29

is that student in your class who, when told to follow some inane but innocuous school rule, adjusts their wardrobe or turns down their music to be just barely within the letter of the law, but in such a way that their intentional, uncowed resistance is clear.

At the other end of this spectrum is a coping mechanism that we, borrowing again from Homi Bhabha (2012), refer to as mimicry, but is also often described as Acting White (Cook & Ludwig, 2008), Assimilation, or sometimes as Covering (Yoshino, 2007). In this coping mechanism, confronted with the realities of racial bias, BIPOC individuals choose to cope by embracing and accepting, rather than resisting, the Dominant cultural norms of whiteness. It is an attitude, essentially, of 'if you can't beat them, join them' and manifests as embracing ideas and ideologies that might be self-disparaging, performing in ways that reject their community—even their family— culture and the practices of their racial peers, or aligning themselves with positions and people—sometimes as their spokesperson—who deny the validity and significance of race and bias, even in the face of evidence, possibly from their own lives. The cultural referents we can point you towards here are folks like politicians Ben Carson, Marco Rubio, or the numerous individuals of color who frequent cable news shows to proclaim the evils of affirmative action, welfare, immigration, or other talking points that support the coloniality of power (or worst of all, taco trucks on every corner! (Chokshi, 2016)). In lighter fare, the iconic character of Carlton Banks from the classic *Fresh Prince of Bel Air* sitcom is an excellent example of an individual pursuing mimicry, seeking white approval at the expense of his relationship with Black culture.

A student coping in this way may manifest as simply a dedicated, focused student who 'gets' and embraces schooling with some considerable fervor and may be uninterested in pursuing discussions of race and coloniality or dismissive of its significance. Or it may manifest as a student of color who aggressively takes positions that would seem out of sync with their REC identity, and possibly in contradiction to their own BIPOC peers. We aren't here to pass judgment, nor to dismiss the importance of academic excellence, or individuals' freedom of thought and choice (and, to clarify, academic excellence is not, itself, evidence of mimicry). But we would note that this coping mechanism, psychologically, is often associated with a hefty degree of internal colonization, or internal tension, insecurity, and self-abuse from feelings of inadequacy against the Dominant cultural standards and whiteness that exist (Fanon, 1952). While an important aspect of a decolonized, humanizing praxis is allowing individuals to come to their own conclusions and ideological positions, we would note that this coping mechanism often seeks to derail conversations around race, using their own REC identity as justification for this. This can be tricky ground to navigate, particularly for white educators who might feel conflicted resisting a BIPOC student's arguments to avoid discussing race, but we would stress the importance of insisting on the conversation, and reminding students that in language arts, our challenge is to explore, with evidence, what is significant to the narratives of others, as well as ourselves.

Ultimately, neither of these polarized coping mechanisms is terribly generative to decolonization or liberatory academic outcomes. Both exist, essentially, in reference to the dominance of coloniality, and the ongoing tension of racialization, and both reflect, unfortunately, underdeveloped racial literacies, and a lack of skill sets for making sense of one's own racial experience. Understanding them when we see them can help us plan for how, and what resources are needed, to support BIPOC youth as they cope with the aftermath of their encounter with the consequences of race.

In the end, BIPOC youth in middle school are, more than likely, grappling with an encounter experience, and then beginning to cope with what that means to them. BIPOC youth are not at all monolithic, and even as we sketch out these broad outlines, we should also appreciate the huge variance that will exist based on the differences between racial experiences, how gender, class, and region might shape things, and the normal idiosyncrasies that exist from person to person. But though there will be differences in timeline and in how it plays out, more than any other time in their lives, this is the moment to create space to grapple with what race means, how it works, and how we can understand it as it impacts ourselves and others. As literacy educators, we are uniquely positioned to support youth in this sense-making process.

Racial, Ethnic, and Cultural Identity Development for White Youth

First off, let's be clear: white students also have a REC identity (Tatum, 2017). Being white is not the absence of racial identity; it is a racial experience of its own. So as we look at the developmental process for white students, it looks similar, but a little different, because while BIPOC students are grappling with the marginality inherent in being racialized as BIPOC, white students end up needing to grapple (or not) with how they will relate to whiteness, and the dynamics of racial power that impact them in very different ways.

White People v. Whiteness

Now, before we explain the developmental stages for white youth in more depth, you'll note that we're talking about white people and whiteness separately. That's intentional. While this, too, is a topic upon which whole books exist, we want to encourage you to start thinking about what it means. Phenotypically speaking, white people are those whose skin is lacking in higher melanin concentrations. But just like BIPOC folks, skin tone varies considerably, even among ostensibly white people. Is a Southern European-origin individual with a darker complexion still white? Maybe not always in history, but in today's political estimation, yes. How about a person of Northern European descent who tans regularly, such that their observed complexion is regularly quite dark? Of course we would still understand this person to be white. This points to the limitations of phenotype, and the importance of thinking in complete REC terms—phenotype is only part of the story.

You see, whiteness is not just skin tone; it is ethnic and cultural as well. It is a social identity position that has accrued meaning over time, and which acts in some ways as a possession, a thing you can own (Jensen, 2020). Historically, we have seen that some groups can, through the luck of phenotype, or through the accumulation of wealth, social positioning, historical need, or other means, procure whiteness. Early Irish immigrants to the U.S., for instance, despite their white phenotype, were not initially offered the benefits of whiteness that (principally) Anglo and German communities held. The outbreak of the Civil War, and the subsequent need for troops, labor, and then law enforcement to control now integrated Northern cities, changed all this, and Irish communities were invited to embrace whiteness, and the wages—the cultural and social benefits—that came along with that social identity position. Over the course of history, we see this process of initial withholding, and then invitation, repeated with immigrants from southern and eastern Europe, some Jewish communities, some Cuban immigrants, BIPOC folks who can 'pass' as white, and, in recent years, some affluent segments of communities who would, at first glance, be identified as people of color (Roediger, 1991). While a white phenotype is an arbitrary designation, whiteness, a cultural possession that allows one exclusive access to Dominant culture, is a dangerous, and ongoing, colonial construction that some choose to adhere to.

Whiteness, this thing that some seek to cling to, is like a cloud, or a fog, that envelops too many of our institutions, and too many of us along with it. It obscures our vision of the past and present, silences certain knowledges and perspectives, and insulates us from dealing with (or feeling) some pressing social problems and challenges, and because that fog is all-consuming and clouding a host of opportunities for agency and power, whiteness makes it challenging, if not impossible, for someone on the outside to navigate in and make change. As we turn now to exploring the stages that white youth go through in their REC identity development, it is crucial to note that what we—and the models of identity development for white folks we discuss here—are getting at is that white people have a phenotype they don't choose, just like BIPOC folks don't choose their melanin concentration. Nor does anyone choose the ethnic and cultural histories and meanings that are ascribed to the ways they look, communities they belong to, and practices they engage in. But for white and white-passing folks, whether you choose to remain embedded in and committed to the social identity position of whiteness—a position that seeks to ignore race as a meaningful, and inequitable dimension of life, and protect the status quo of our lives—is a decision made almost daily (Wise, 2011), and which perhaps is first made during the formative years of middle school.

Stages of White Identity Development

The era of socialization for white youth is often discussed as the contact or acceptance stage (Helms, 1997). Amidst all the messaging that generally resonates with their racial, ethnic, and cultural lives and self-perceptions, and statistically in contexts in which they are more than likely interacting primarily with other white children and people, young white children are simply internalizing messages without recognition of their broader societal significance. Important also to note here is that for most white children the subtle messages reinforcing coloniality are developed under a veneer of intentional messaging about treating one another equally, which can be done either strategically and robustly, or, more likely, in colorblind ways that reflect against abstract liberalism: that things are fair and fine if we are just nice to everyone interpersonally.

But as the ability to think and make abstract connections emerges in adolescence, white children also come to confront the social and material significance of race. Just like the racial encounter for BIPOC youth, white youth experience, whether it is in a jarring instance or in a gradual confrontation, is a recognition that race impacts their world in profound ways that have shaped and continue to negatively shape the experiences of many people, and that they, as phenotypically white people, exist in relationship to these inequalities, suffering, and histories. This might be through an interpersonal interaction, the dynamics of a perhaps more integrated school, or possibly through contact with more direct narratives about racial experience, racism, history, and the world, but it presents white youth with the challenge of disruption and disintegration; their stable, settled visions of themselves as fair, just, equal individuals are now placed into direct conflict with the reality of a world in which people who looked like them made active, intentional choices to harm others based on their race. For an adolescent, this direct cognitive dissonance is challenging to navigate, and this stage is likely to provoke feelings of guilt, shame, confusion, and possibly anger as they work to come to grips with their social identity as a white person in a world in which white people created and benefited from systems of exploitation and suffering.

What happens with these feelings, and after these moments of disintegration, are, we believe, hugely up to the middle grades educators who are along for the journey (Kivel, 2017). Psychologically speaking, there are two likely outcomes (Helms, 2014). The first is the one we might expect, but certainly not desire: reintegration. Reintegration essentially involves white individuals, presented with all this cognitive dissonance, crystallizing their guilt, shame, and confusion into anger and resistance, rejecting more complicated understandings of race and inequality, and settling into the safe, colorblind self-perception that those early messages of treating others equally afford them. At best, reintegration leads someone to be ambivalent towards racial inequity and coloniality, taking up a position in which they seek to be colorblind, and simply avoid any and all engagement or discussion of race, so as to avoid grappling with its consequences. At worst, reintegration can lead towards increasingly toxic and reactionary positions—actually embracing and affirming racist and colonial rhetoric and positions as a way to insulate oneself from the emotional challenge of coping with what the benefits of whiteness might mean to one's own social position. This is, in some ways, a form of oppositional identity, or cognitive dissonance, a phenomenon in psychology we call abreaction, and an emotional coping strategy in which it is easier to reject challenging and complicated ideas than to deal with them.

The second direction things might go in involves retreat, emergence, and awareness. Essentially, in the face of their moment of disintegration and cognitive dissonance, a white individual might gradually retreat from toxic or problematic beliefs and narratives around race; essentially, they may recognize and pull themselves away from the unconscious biases they were exposed to, and begin to grapple with what their role in the world might be. In best-case scenarios, as youth (or adults) pull back from colonial narratives about race, they can simultaneously begin constructing a positive, healthy REC identity of their own that is not predicated on guilt or shame, but aware of the realities of race, their role in a broader racial landscape and historical context, and what action they might take to act in humanizing and more liberatory ways. Now while that all sounds really simple in a single sentence, it is, as you might expect, incredibly complicated, difficult work that can take a lifetime, can easily stall out as incomplete, or even come crashing down and fall back into reintegration.

Because of the colonial legacies in our worlds and the depth of socialization, talking about race and challenging students to embrace more nuanced and complicated understandings of racial identity and the world always risks what Felix Guattari (1995, 2000) warns is the "unbecoming" of the self. You, dear reader, may have even had some similar sensations and emotional reactions as you have begun reading this text, perhaps confronting ideas about race or history that contradict your longstanding, common-sense notions. Taken without adequate support, pacing, resources, and care, discussions of race with anyone, but particularly adolescents, and especially white youth, always risk unsettling foundational assumptions about ourselves, the world, our communities, and perhaps our loved ones (Evans-Winters & Hines, 2020). As we discuss in later chapters, the way you do this work must be intentional and driven by a sense of authentic care (Duncan-Andrade, 2022). It is critical that in the classroom when we challenge socialized ideas, we are providing texts and narratives that help build more robust racial literacies to support and guide student sense-making and not leaving them emotionally stranded and grasping for support without any alternative sense-making tools. And it is equally critical that our approach to decolonization is driven by urgency—urgency to end the harm that coloniality wreaks—but not hastiness. We must be intentional, thoughtful, and aware that transforming and unpacking a lifetime of socialization around race, ethnicity, and culture, does not happen completely in one lesson, one unit, one semester, or even one year. Our task is to lay a foundation for racial literacy and decolonial, humanizing thinking that will serve our students well into the future.

Building Racial Literacies as Decolonial Praxis

Now that we have a sense of the context of race, the ways it is central to coloniality, and how developmentally critical the middle grades are for REC identity development, let us circle back around to the core of our work: literacy. Knowing what we now know about identity development, we can recognize that our middle school literacy classrooms and instruction will become the foundation for the stories and narratives students come to see as normal, permissible, and valued. They will become the place where students will first learn to articulate and narrate their emerging identities as they relate to a broader, more complicated, abstract world and society. They will become the place where our students will acquire the skill sets and language in which they will first learn to TALK about different topics and ideas in the world, especially race, ethnicity, and culture (Orelus, 2020). As middle grades educators, we must ask ourselves this critical question: *Will our classroom be a place that continues the taboo of discussing race and difference, or one that breaks it?*

We know that there will be so many social and institutional pressures to keep up the taboo; from peers, from department chairs, from admin, from parents. We talk about navigating these in Chapter 10. But here, the one we want to touch on is the pressure you may encounter from students who are resistant or averse to discussing race and difference to maintain the taboo, perhaps because they are uncomfortable or because they do not want to make others uncomfortable by making missteps around this taboo topic. This is the most difficult pressure to navigate, because when we care for our students, we do not want to put them in positions where they are frustrated or uncomfortable.

That is understandable, but so is the reality that decolonization involves some discomfort. Change is not easy. So how do we challenge them, without putting them in unfair positions? We believe the answer comes in being intentional in supporting the development of their racial literacies.

When we talk about the idea of racial literacy (Sealey-Ruiz, 2021), we are talking about particular, intentional skillsets for discussing race, ethnicity, culture, racial experiences, racism and discrimination, and dynamics like coloniality. These are not things we just know, or can divine. As we have noted, we are, in fact, socialized to NOT have these skill sets and vocabularies and to lack the tools to more precisely discuss them. As educators, we have to build these new vocabularies, skills, and toolkits into our instruction, introducing new terms, sharing new practices for how we talk to one another, and normalizing vulnerable conversations about the scary, terrifying, taboo topic of race by talking about our own racial identities, by modeling how to bring up questions of racial experience politely and constructively, by pointing out and exploring questions of race, ethnicity, and culture in texts and materials where they might have otherwise been ignored. If we want students to become comfortable with navigating and exploring these big questions and big narratives in the world—things that are essential to decolonizing and creating a more liberatory, humanizing world—then we need to show them new ways to be in the world, new ways to approach knowledge, and new ways to think about power. If you are new to these words and terms, to the literacies our students will need, well, you have picked up some here, and we will offer some more strategies throughout this text. Regardless of where you are with your familiarity level, the challenge is to just keep trying with urgency, care, and intentionality.

RACIAL LITERACY VOCABULARY

A huge element of developing racial literacy is introducing the vocabulary to talk coherently and accurately about race. Make sure you feel comfortable defining and talking about the academic definitions of following terms—not their colloquial meanings—and feel ready to help your students understand them as well:

- Race
- Ethnicity
- Racism
- Prejudice
- Biases
- Systemic (i.e., systemic racism)
- Colorblindness
- Cultural racism

There are many other terms to know and explore that will help you, and your students, cultivate a racial literacy. Check the resources section in this chapter for more guidance on where to explore more comprehensive definitions of these terms beyond the pages of this book.

Making Decolonization Normal

Middle school and the middle grades are special. We know you know that, which is, presumably, why you're reading this text. These years that we have, as a society, constructed as adolescence are some of the most challenging, difficult, and formative years in anyone's life. What makes middle school so challenging isn't that students aren't ready for the big questions in life, but rather, that they absolutely are already starting to grapple with them, but rarely receive the respect and dignity that comes from being guided to engage with those questions, seeing their educators do so themselves, and being offered the tools and vocabularies to do so with confidence. Our choices of what kinds of inquiry and discourse we are going to support students to engage with are critical because middle school is going to shape their understanding of who they are, of who others are, of how we can talk about identity with others, of the significance of identity in our broader world. To put it succinctly, you, as a middle school literacy educator, are going to help shape how they will narrate stories of their own and others' experiences.

If we can make a recommendation as we head towards the rest of this book, it's to be thoughtful about what you are accomplishing in the developmental window we have. We aren't likely to get all of our students to be able to engage in deep, sophisticated racial analysis in literacy contexts, or to precisely explain the nuances of coloniality, identity, and whiteness (though some might!), but we can get them comfortable with talking about their own racial identities and comfortable with talking about others in humanizing ways. We can set the stage for a future in which these conversations can actually happen, in which the tools and vocabularies to do so effectively are present, and in which different stories and life-worlds can be respected and heard.

Decolonization/decolonizing racial literacy isn't about a big, flashy show, or reading the most edgy book on racial experience, or forcing students to constantly examine and read about the harsh realities of racial marginalization. Often, these intense approaches can turn students off, inadvertently reinforcing discomfort in discussing race. Rather, racial literacy, done well in the middle grades, is about normalizing deep listening and open, authentic, and accurate humanizing conversation around racial identity.

Questions to Consider While Planning for Racially Literate Praxis

1   What is my level of racial literacy? How comfortable am I speaking and writing about my own racial identity? Where can I seek resources to develop that myself?

2   How well do I understand the full breadth of racial identities in my classroom, and do I offer resources for all those folks to explore their identities?

3   What issues of race, ethnicity, and culture can I thread across every lesson? How can I make this a recurring, normal part of my instruction and classroom culture?

4   What resources and people in the community could help my students and I deepen our conversations about race, ethnicity, and culture?

Resources to Explore

Coming to Terms with Our Own Racial Literacies

Exploring and talking about race, and diving into the work necessary to build up our own racial literacies, can be incredibly challenging. We need help. We need support, and we need permission to take our time to wrap our heads around new ways to think about this most substantial element of American cultural, social, and political life. Take that time, approaching these resources with ease, but always with a sense of urgency:

- If you want the full picture of how REC identity plays out, you must read Beverly Tatum's *Why are all the Black Kids Sitting Together in the Cafeteria?* It is a classic, several-times-updated text for a reason. No one explains things as clearly and concisely and thoroughly as Tatum does in this book.
- As you continue on this journey, you'll want to explore more robust ways to think about race. We recommend Eduardo Bonilla-Silva's *Racism Without Racists*, as good a place as any to begin understanding what the racial landscape looks like in the 21st century, and locate meaningful, accurate definitions for the above terms. Depending on your racial identity, texts by Robin DiAngelo and Tim Wise that explore and unpack what whiteness, and being white, mean and mean in relation to work with diverse communities may also be helpful to you.
- As we noted, re-thinking race is difficult, emotional, even traumatic work that impacts us not just intellectually or emotionally, but spiritually and physically as well. With this in mind, and especially if you are finding grappling with these ideas challenging, we highly recommend you explore Resmaa Menakem's *My Grandmother's Hands: Racialized Trauma and the Pathway to Mending Our Hearts and Bodies*, a text which guides the reader through unpacking the ways race has impacted them on multiple levels.
- Finally, we encourage you to explore the *Race: Are we so different?* online resource (https://understandingrace.org/) both on your own, and as a potential resource to direct students towards. This extensive resource is affiliated with a traveling museum exhibit which we also highly recommend you visit, and take your students to, if it is accessible. We have done this with different groups of students in different contexts and states, and found it to be a powerful learning experience accessible to youth each time.

References

Aldama, A. J. (2001). *Disrupting savagism: Intersecting Chicana/o, Mexican immigrant, and Native American struggles for self-representation.* Duke University Press.

Alexander, M. (2011). *The new Jim Crow: Mass incarceration in an age of colorblindness.* The New Press.

Bañales, J., Hoffman, A. J., Rivas-Drake, D., & Jagers, R. J. (2020). The development of ethnic-racial identity process and its relation to civic beliefs among Latinx and Black American adolescents. *Journal of Youth and Adolescence, 49*(12), 2495–2508.

Bhabha, H. K. (2012). *The location of culture.* Routledge.

Bombay, A., Matheson, K., & Anisman, H. (2014). The intergenerational effects of Indian Residential Schools: Implications for the concept of historical trauma. *Transcultural Psychiatry*, *51*(3), 320–338.

Brunsma, D. L., Delgado, D., & Rockquemore, K. A. (2013). Liminality in the multiracial experience: Towards a concept of identity matrix. *Identities*, *20*(5), 481–502.

Chokshi, N. (2016). Taco Trucks on every corner: Trump supporters immigration warning. *New York Times*. https://www.nytimes.com/2016/09/03/us/politics/taco-trucks-on-every-corner-trump-supporters-anti-immigration-warning.html

Clark, K. B., & Clark, M. P. (1940). Skin color as a factor in racial identification of Negro preschool children. *Journal of Social Psychology, S.P.SS.SI. Bulletin*, *II*, 159–169.

Constante, K., Cross, F. L., Medina, M., & Rivas-Drake, D. (2020). Ethnic socialization, family cohesion, and ethnic identity development over time among Latinx adolescents. *Journal of Youth and Adolescence*, *49*(4), 895–906.

Cook, P. J., & Ludwig, J. (2008). The burden of "acting White": Do Black adolescents disparage academic achievement? In J. Ogbu (Ed), *Minority status, oppositional culture, & schooling* (pp. 307–329). Routledge.

Cross, W. E., Jr (1991). *Shades of black: Diversity in African-American identity*. Temple University Press.

Cross, W. E., Jr. (1995). Oppositional identity and African American youth: Issues and prospects. In W. D. Hawley & A. W. Jackson (Eds), *Toward a common destiny: Improving race and ethnic relations in America* (pp. 185–204). Jossey-Bass/Wiley.

Cross, W. E., Jr & Fhagen-Smith, P. (1996). Nigrescence and ego identity development: Accounting for differential Black identity patterns. In P. B. Pedersen, J. G. Draguns, W. J. Lonner, & J. E. Trimble (Eds), *Counseling across cultures* (pp. 108–123). Sage Publications, Inc.

Darder, A. (2012). *Culture and power in the classroom: A critical foundation for bicultural education*. Paradigm.

Duncan-Andrade, J. M. (2022). *Equality or equity: Toward a model of community-responsive education*. Harvard Education Press.

Evans-Winters, V. E., & Hines, D. E. (2020). Unmasking white fragility: How whiteness and white student resistance impacts anti-racist education. *Whiteness and Education*, *5*(1), 1–16.

Fanon, F. (1952). *Black skin White masks*. Grove Press.

Fredrickson, G. M. (2015). *Racism: A short history*. Princeton University Press.

Guattari, F. (1995). *Chaosmosis*. Power Publication.

Guattari, F. (2000). *The three ecologies*. Continuum.

Heitzeg, N. A. (2016). *The school-to-prison pipeline: Education, discipline, and racialized double standards*. ABC-CLIO.

Helms, J. E. (1997). Toward a model of White racial identity development. *College student development and academic life: Psychological, intellectual, social and moral issues* (pp. 49–66). Routledge.

Helms, J. E. (2014, June). A review of White racial identity theory. In *Psychology serving humanity: Proceedings of the 30th International Congress of Psychology* (Vol. 2, p. 12).

Hughes, D. (2003). Correlates of African American and Latino parents' messages to children about ethnicity and race: A comparative study of racial socialization. *American Journal of Community Psychology*, *31*(1–2), 15–33.

Jensen, R. (2020). Whiteness. In S. Caliendo & C. McIlwain (Eds), *The Routledge companion to race and ethnicity* (pp. 25–32). Routledge.

Kelley, R. D. G. (2004) In C. Phelps (Dir). *Race—The Power of an Illusion*. [Film] Prod. by Larry Adelman, 2003. 3 parts, 56 mins. each. (California Newsreel, Order Department, Box 2284, South Burlington, VT 05407; 877-811-7495; www.newsreel.org [Sept. 13, 2004]).

Kivel, P. (2017). *Uprooting racism: How white people can work for racial justice*. New Society Publishers.

Ladson-Billings, G. (2006). From the achievement gap to the education debt: Understanding achievement in US schools. *Educational Researcher, 35*(7), 3–12.

McCardle, T. (2020). A critical historical examination of tracking as a method for maintaining racial segregation. *Educational Considerations, 45*(2), 4.

Menakem, R. (2021). *My grandmother's hands: Racialized trauma and the pathway to mending our hearts and bodies*. Penguin UK.

Mignolo, W. (2003). *The darker side of the Renaissance: Literacy, territoriality, and colonization*. University of Michigan Press.

Moore, T. O. (2005). A Fanonian perspective on double consciousness. *Journal of Black Studies, 35*(6), 751–762.

Muñoz, J. E. (2006). Feeling brown, feeling down: Latina affect, the performativity of race, and the depressive position. *Signs: Journal of Women in Culture and Society, 31*(3), 675–688.

Nadal, K. L. (2004). Filipino American identity development model. *Journal of Multicultural Counseling and Development, 32*(1), 45–62.

National Center for Education Statistics. (2022). Characteristics of Public School Teachers. *Condition of Education*. U.S. Department of Education, Institute of Education Sciences. Retrieved 11/1/2022 from https://nces.ed.gov/programs/coe/indicator/clr

Obama, B. (2007). *Dreams from my father: A story of race and inheritance*. Canongate Books.

Omi, M., & Winant, H. (2014). *Racial formation in the United States*. Routledge.

Orelus, P. W. (2020). *Unschooling racism: Critical theories, approaches and testimonials on anti racist education*. Springer.

Parsons, S., Collins, T. Z., & Cox, R. D. (2019). Race and color in Louisiana: An update on the Clark and Clark doll experiment. *Journal of Race & Policy, 15*(1), 24–53.

Poston, W. C. (1990). The biracial identity development model: A needed addition. *Journal of Counseling & Development, 69*(2), 152–155.

Powell-Hopson, D., & Hopson, D. S. (1988). Implications of doll color preferences among Black preschool children and White preschool children. *Journal of Black Psychology, 14*(2), 57–63.

Puar, J. K. (2018). *Terrorist assemblages: Homonationalism in queer times*. Duke University Press.

Quijano, A. (2000). Coloniality of power and eurocentrism in Latin America. *International Sociology, 15*(2), 215–232. https://doi.org/10.1177/0268580900015002005.

Quijano, A. (2007). Coloniality and Modernity/Rationality. *Cultural Studies 21*(2–3): 168–178. https://doi.org/10.1080/09502380601164353.

Ritchey, K. (2014). Black identity development. *The Vermont Connection, 35*(1), 12.

Rockquemore, K. A., Brunsma, D. L., & Delgado, D. J. (2009). Racing to theory or retheorizing race? Understanding the struggle to build a multiracial identity theory. *Journal of Social Issues, 65*(1), 13–34.

Roediger, D. R. (1991). *The wages of Whiteness. Race and the making of the American working class*. Verso.

Roth, W. (2012). *Race migrations: Latinos and the cultural transformation of race*. Stanford University Press.

Rothstein, R. (2017). *The color of law: A forgotten history of how our government segregated America*. Liveright Publishing.

Rothstein, R. (2019). The myth of de facto segregation. *Phi Delta Kappan, 100*(5), 35–38.

Sealey-Ruiz, Y. (2021). Racial literacy. A policy research brief. *National Council of Teachers of English*.

Simon, C. (2021). The role of race and ethnicity in parental ethnic-racial socialization: A scoping review of research. *Journal of Child and Family Studies, 30*(1), 182–195.

Skiba, R. J., Arredondo, M. I., & Williams, N. T. (2014). More than a metaphor: The contribution of exclusionary discipline to a school-to-prison pipeline. *Equity & Excellence in Education, 47*(4), 546–564.

Stoll, L. C., & Klein, M. (2018). "Not in My Backyard": How abstract liberalism and colorblind diversity undermines racial justice. In D. Embrick, S. Collins, & M. Dodson (Eds), *Challenging the Status Quo* (pp. 217–240). Brill.

Tatum, B. D. (2017). *Why are all the black kids still sitting together in the cafeteria? And other conversations about race in the twenty-first century*. Basic Books.

Thompson Dorsey, D. N. (2013). Segregation 2.0: The new generation of school segregation in the 21st century. *Education and Urban Society*, *45*(5), 533–547.

Understanding Race (2022, November 1). *Understanding Race: Are we so different?* https://understandingrace.org/

Wilinsky, J. (1998). *Learning to divide the world: Education at empire's end*. University of Minnesota Press.

Wise, T. (2011). *White like me: Reflections on race from a privileged son*. Catapult.

Yoshino, K. (2007). *Covering: The hidden assault on our civil rights*. Random House Trade Paperbacks.

Part II

IN PRAXIS/TRAVESIAS

After we have engaged in unlearning, Anzaldúa notes, we enter what she calls a state of Nepantla, being between two things, spaces, or identities. This isn't some fixed position, but a description of a process. Once we have unlearned the old knowledge that constrained and limited us, once we have identified that there are new ways to be in the world and with one another, new identities to explore, we begin to cross into new terrain, new possibilities. And these *travesias* are important, because once you learn how the world might be, you can never really go back. Freire also noted that we cannot stop after we create new knowledge. Instead, we must transform our world through action or praxis.

This part introduces ways we can take action. Each chapter emphasizes a quality of decolonized classrooms and provides lesson ideas and ways of thinking that will help you to enact these qualities. We begin in Chapter 3 by focusing on the importance of nurturing introspection in our students, as well as ourselves. We examine ways to reflect upon ourselves as individuals and ourselves as a part of larger communities. Chapter 4 shifts to ways we can connect humans together. Through connection, we can help our students build empathy, which is the foundation of decolonized instruction—the ability to see and appreciate each other for what we bring to the learning environment. In Chapter 5, we challenge the notion of expertise, particularly as it is typically presented in school. We urge students to identify and develop their own expertise, as well as to tap into the resources within their communities. Digging into meaningful questions, Chapter 6 points to the problematic ways questions are often used in schools and demonstrates ways to help students develop their own questioning skills so that they are prepared to continue the decolonizing work we begin in our classrooms. Chapter 7 questions what it means to be normal and ways to push beyond the constraints normality presents. We delve into the importance of multilingual classrooms, whether language differences stem from the presence of multiple languages like Spanish, Mandarin, or English or from different dialects like African-American Vernacular English, in Chapter 8. And finally in Chapter 9, we explore how decolonized classrooms work toward cultural change rather than cultural stagnation. We hope these ideas and perspectives on praxis will offer you new roads and possibilities or travesias that will have you thinking and re-thinking your instruction in new ways, so you can't (and wouldn't want to) go back to the old, colonial ways that schooling would have you enact and behave in the classroom.

DOI: 10.4324/9781003290681-4

3

DECOLONIZED CLASSROOMS... NURTURE INTROSPECTION

Introduction

As we consider the role of introspection in decolonization, we turn once again to Gloria Anzaldúa who famously wrote:

> The struggle has always been inner, and is played out in outer terrains. Awareness of our situation must come before inner changes, which in turn come before changes in society. Nothing happens in the "real" world unless it first happens in the images in our heads.

This inner struggle was visible to Michael when he had the opportunity to see a 7th-grade classroom conduct a Socratic Seminar around their reading of *To Kill a Mockingbird*. As the dialogue got rolling, the level of the conversation was impressive. Students talked analytically about the ways the characters were exhibiting racism. They talked about the unfairness of structures that led to Tom's prosecution, and the responsibility of the community for one another. The conversation was so robust, academic, and astute that a casual observer might have been impressed that these were middle-school students. Yet here was the thing: all of these ideas about racism, structural bias, and community culpability were discussed in the *past* tense and from a *distance*. Specifically, the conversation, though rhetorically advanced, positioned racism as something that had 'happened *then*,' but was over now, a contrast to the present. And it positioned racism as a *Southern* problem, a cultural issue of regional concern, in those few much maligned post-confederate states where the specter of chattel slavery still hung over Black folks' lives, and the 'backward' culture of Southern Whites.

Now, this classroom was located in a city in the Western U.S. known for its progressive politics. It was staffed by strong educators who would—with good reason—have considered themselves progressive and anti-racist, and students who were willing to read and discuss the issues in texts like *To Kill a Mockingbird*. But it was also a city and a school where tracking and *de facto* segregation were quite pronounced. Sure, some students of color were sprinkled among the Honors and Advanced classes, but for the most part, there was a color line in the school no one discussed. And the city itself was beset by issues of housing, transit, and educational equity for the communities of color who

DOI: 10.4324/9781003290681-5

worked the service jobs in the primarily white town. These were not necessarily intentional, malicious actions, but rather, classic systemic tensions that reflected the lingering malaise that grows out of coloniality when it is ignored. In short, racism and coloniality were not things past, and they were not regionally limited to the south; they were occurring right then, there, in that moment, in a town uneasy, or unwilling to look inward. As a result, the instruction and engagement with *To Kill a Mockingbird* had failed to explore the realities of race in the daily lives of their students and educators, and in so doing, it had failed to invite the students to engage in introspection. It had not done the internal work necessary to disrupt coloniality.

Complicated Racial Landscapes

As we learned in the last chapter, middle school youth are grappling intensely with questions of identity, especially around race, and trying to make sense of how they and their identities fit into a larger, more complex world. Engaging in meaningful, productive, and well supported instruction that gives them the opportunity to critically explore who they are is a crucial piece of literacy learning. Remember, these are the years in which middle-grades students will learn how to narrate their own lives, how to discuss and engage with the lives and identities of others, and how to connect broader social stories and narratives to their own experiences and realities. If we want to decolonize our classrooms, we must make room for the inner work of honestly engaging with our realities and the tensions and contradictions in their lives and worlds. While issues of coloniality and racism are systemic or structural issues, not individual issues that can be remedied by correcting interpersonal actions, they do manifest themselves in our inner lives and worlds. Recall that we are deeply socialized around issues and ideas of race, and more than that, the tension of race and marginalization looms over our social worlds in such a way that no individual can escape it. We may try to pursue emotional or personal distance from the impacts and realities of racism, but this will always be an impossible task, and without productive engagement, coloniality and racism fester—regardless of your racial, ethnic, and cultural identity—and manifest as unresolved trauma that impacts us mentally, emotionally, and even physically (Menakem, 2021). Ibrahm Kendi (2019) uses the metaphor of metastatic cancer to capture these dynamics, and we find this analogy apt not just for racism, but for coloniality generally, and the ways it manifests as misogyny, homophobia, eurocentrism, and more. We cannot resolve any trauma, any illness, by ignoring it. We have to look inward, examine the causes and effects, in order to heal. That may sound intense, but doing this work, and having fun while doing so, is absolutely possible in the middle-grades classroom.

Reading Instruction to Trace Community Histories

One strategy to nurture introspection—especially around race and ethnicity—is to connect and link our reading instruction to the exploration of community and community histories. As we noted in the previous chapters, coloniality and the impacts of the racial marginalization that go along with it are pervasive. As such, there is not a community anywhere in the world, and certainly not in the United States, where there is not a racial history and story, and very likely, an array of social stories or social narratives that accompany that history, alternatively preserving or seeking to cloud the way race, class, and other dynamics impacted that community. That includes whatever town, neighborhood, or community you are sitting in reading this text; and we encourage you to take some time, personally, to reflect on and dig into the racial stories and dynamics of your school and community yourself (see Chapter 11).

What all this means is that every text we read, particularly texts that recount the stories of tension and marginalization around issues within communities, whether they are an individual character's story or community ensemble narratives, are invitations to explore corollaries in our local settings. Doing so allows students to dive deeply into introspection, asking and answering questions about why their communities look the ways they do, as well as giving them compelling motivation to explore the social narratives they have come to experience and accept as natural and common sense. Such opportunities are especially compelling to middle-school youth who, as we have discussed in previous chapters, are just beginning to get a grasp of a world beyond themselves, and linking the examination of major concepts and social issues, like race, to local stories allows them to connect to students' real lives and lived experiences, offering compelling motivation to engage meaningfully in the task.

There are an array of middle-grades novels and stories that are perfectly suited for this task, and while we discuss different ways you might organize teaching novels in Chapters 4 and 6, here we want to present an approach to supporting reading instruction—connecting fiction with community-based inquiry—that can be applied however you choose to organize the text selection in your room, but always with an eye for introspection around race and ethnicity, or other dimensions of colonial marginalization like class, gender, sexuality, ability, etc.

Step 1: Know the Narratives That Are and Are Not Discussed in Your Students' Communities

The place to start with this reading instruction strategy begins even before you get to the teaching. Specifically, you need to begin by knowing a bit about your school and students' communities, and what sorts of social stories and narratives are present. When we talk about social stories, we are talking about the broadly held community narratives that explain, rationalize, justify, uplift, and reinforce a community's image of itself. More often than not, these community narratives are also linked to majoritarian stories, or even broader socio-political stories that justify the existing social hierarchy, affirm the position of the Dominant culture, and reinforce the norms and workings of society as common sense.

The trick is, of course, that everything about our social worlds did not just 'happen.' There are long histories of choices, shaped and constrained and directed by the pressures of coloniality, that led to our communities looking the way they do today. With this in mind, knowing what sorts of social stories are told in the community, and what stories are not, can be incredibly valuable for selecting texts that will resonate with your students.

Here, we do not just mean the obvious, like 'race isn't discussed.' Maybe not, but the question would be, how and where is it not discussed? Really what we hope you will reflect on are more specific, tangible questions and themes impacting your community, and which necessarily involve different layers of marginalization to explore. For instance, is community change/gentrification impacting your community? How about housing tensions, or segregation? What about variances in income levels, or in-school performance levels? Maybe policing and public safety are big concerns? Or environmental issues and pollution? You get the point.

So for this first step, figure out what are pressing issues, if and how they are discussed, what the popular narratives around them are, and then you will be positioned to pick texts that will invite comparison and analysis.

Step 2: Choose Texts Where the Community Story Is Just as Rich as the Character's Story

So, you have a sense of what narratives permeate your community and will be compelling for students to explore. Now, you need to choose a text (or texts) that lines up with this. Our recommendation is to select a text around two criteria: first, make sure it invites challenging engagement with identity questions of race, class, gender, sexuality, immigration status, etc. (or multiple of these dimensions!). Second, make sure that the community story is just as rich and complex as the story of the protagonist, and it invites and echoes and parallels some of the concerns you found in considering community needs. What we mean by this is to think not just about the plot as it centers around the protagonist or other characters, but as it implicates broader systemic issues and dynamics in the community in which the story takes place and how that might invite your students to read the word as a transition to reading the world. Our goal in this particular reading activity is to encourage our middle-grades youth to use literature as a way to develop their burgeoning engagement with a broader, more complex world. We want to position them as historical actors, and create a reading environment that encourages students to pay close attention to the macro-level social dilemmas in the text as a way for them to pay close attention to the social dilemmas in their own lives and communities.

There are, of course, a vast number of texts that can be used to accomplish this goal. If there were tensions of gentrification in our setting, we might give Pablo Cartaya's *The Epic Fail of Arturo Zamora* a try. If students are struggling to understand the complexities faced by people who were displaced from their communities and forced to find asylum elsewhere, you might pick up *The Boy at the Back of the Class* by Onjali Q. Raúf. While *To Kill a Mockingbird* would not be our choice, if it was part of your curriculum, you might use this text to help students explore present-tense echoes of community segregation. Particularly if your hands might be tied in terms of what texts you can teach, we encourage you to think about how you can draw out systemic connections with the texts you must teach, finding ways to bring a decolonial lens to what might be more colonial texts. In any event, the social dilemma and narratives in your school community do not need to line up precisely; the key is simply that your fictional text choice plants a seed for exploring and reading the world in the same way they have read the word.

Step 3: Setting Up the Challenge of Systemic Inquiry

The next step is, essentially, to set up the challenge. This is, we think, rather straightforward, though you will want to be clear and student friendly in your messaging. We might frame the task something like this:

> We read a story in which the characters were dealing with [insert the relevant social dilemma here]. How does [the aforementioned social dilemma] appear in your life and community? Explore the history of that issue in our community, how it has changed, and how it impacts us today.

Like any research project, students will need support identifying a topic, narrowing its focus, and making connections to the original text. Because we are encouraging them to engage in systemic introspection around questions and history that may be altogether new to them, and questions of race around which they are likely still quite uncomfortable openly discussing, you, as educator, will want to model several examples for them. We suspect you will find that students will want to veer away from the systemic and the racial dilemmas, and towards social challenges that feel safer and more comfortable. This is a natural response, reflecting the way adults often deflect towards issues of class or gender rather than discuss race. But recall from our previous chapter that to develop racial literacies, our challenge is to make the uncomfortable, comfortable. While you certainly should not force students into particular directions of inquiry, be steady, confident, and encouraging in guiding them to explore questions and dynamics for which they are still finding their feet and vocabularies.

Step 4: Be Transdisciplinary in Your Approach

Alright, you have reflected on narratives in your local community, and chosen a text (or texts) that invites students to engage in introspection around race and themes and narratives in their community. Now what? We think a critical next step is to think about your instruction in transdisciplinary ways. What does transdisciplinary mean? You have likely heard interdisciplinary, or engaging multiple disciplines, before, so what makes transdisciplinary different? Essentially, what we are talking about here is a true blending and blurring of the lines between disciplines, not just interjecting another discipline in here or there for a mini-lesson.

We are encouraged in school to stay in our lanes, and stick to our subjects, because of all the pressures we may face over our benchmarks and assessments and standards. But learning for youth does not happen in a silo, and more than that, this silo-ing of knowledge, of placing boundaries around things that can be known, is deeply colonial. Understanding and comprehension in reading are nuanced and multifaceted. We know that when a student picks up a text seeking to comprehend it, they process what they read through their schema, or contextual and ideological understanding of the world, in order to make sense of it. That schema does not exist or see itself in a silo, limited only to English Language Arts-related content. It draws on our full wealth of knowledge, and distributes the information from a text back across that full breadth of knowledge. In order to grow our comprehension, our schema requires nurturing and cultivation, and as educators, we can do that by continually feeding additional context and complementary information to our students that will expand and grow their schema, allowing them richer and more nuanced comprehension as they continue reading. In short, we need to infuse our instruction around a text with contextual instruction beyond our subject area that will help enrich comprehension. Did you select a text that looks at gentrification? Then infuse your instruction with historical context for neighborhood change and housing segregation. Does your text explore issues of environmental racism? Prep yourself to teach some rudimentary air-quality science or food-desert economics to your students.

While complex histories full of nuance and contradiction may be beyond what we can accomplish in the limited scope of our single classroom, that does not mean we should pull back from or ignore the importance and significance of weaving context throughout our instruction. We encourage you to see yourself as a transdisciplinary educator, rejecting the silo-ing of topics and knowledge, and making sure that your instruction gives students all the context they need to transform their schemas for understanding, and read in deeper, richer ways.

Step 5: Encourage Students to Explore Archives and Outside Materials

While we set this up as a lesson around a novel, at its core this is a research project. Starting with a novel, and another character's story, provides a safe introduction to exploring systemic challenges in a fictional setting, and thus a constructive way to segue into introspection on the systemic biases and coloniality in our own lives and worlds that aligns developmentally with where students' racial literacies are (as opposed to just launching into a research project on systemic challenges).

In Step 4, we encourage you to be transdisciplinary in your teaching, weaving in content and instruction that will help students understand content and concepts they read, even if those ideas do not neatly fit into the English Language Arts silo. With this in mind, we also will note that encouraging systemic racial introspection successfully, like any research for middle schoolers, will involve you providing students with an array of resources, archives, articles, and sources to explore. In fact, if done well, the local element of this project can make this task even more challenging and stimulating, because you will need to identify specific, locally relevant resources—things like local papers or local historians—rather than relying on more easily available, but less specific, national sources (looking at you, Wikipedia). Pulling local newspaper articles, statistical snapshots of demographics or other relevant statistics over time, and generally creating data sets students can use to cross-check different perspectives on events can be incredibly powerful in helping them critically analyze social stories. Should time permit, you might also more robustly extend the research element of this activity and consider including community interviews—something we talk more at length about the benefits of in Chapter 5.

No matter what archives and resources you procure, the challenge is to ensure that students are not just reading the words, but the world. We must encourage students to put what they have learned into critical conversation with our text, and other information, exploring what social narratives people in their community tell themselves and others. We want to guide them to consider: How do the stories we have discovered line up with the demographics of the time? Do official recollections of events align with informal reporting of them from the community? Is there anything else we found that was not part of the official institutional narrative? Asking these sorts of questions, and encouraging students to critically assess both official sources and unofficial or informal ones, to find things that were different, or omitted, can be a powerful, introspective exercise in understanding how complicated social narratives around race, marginalization, and difference can be.

We will not pretend this step will be easy. But we cannot stress enough how important and impactful keeping things local is as a task of developing racial literacy and engaging in introspection around systemic issues. Taking the extra time to find these resources will help students remain anchored, and, in the long run, recognize the ways in which their community has a racial narrative that they are a part of.

Step 6: Create Opportunities to Discuss the Past-in-Present

Ultimately, this project is setting you and your students up for the opportunity to engage in introspection and to discuss what Patricia Hill Collins (2005) calls past-in-present racism. However you choose to wrap things up—as a five-paragraph essay, a presentation, a poster, or something more creative, transdisciplinary, and experimental (see the mixtape idea in Chapter 4, or the protest art activity in Chapter 9)—what will make learning meaningful is ensuring that you are drawing the conversation with each student, and the class as a whole, back to the systemic issues and social narratives in the community. Making sure you are asking the key questions: How did what you found parallel what we read in our story? What differences did you see in the narratives told in the community? How has the story changed? How do events from the past shape the way things are now?

As you assess how things go, we encourage you to keep in mind developmental appropriateness for analyses. It is not likely our students, with limited background knowledge, context, and ability to process extensive outside reading sources, are going to produce incredibly complex analyses of gentrification or food deserts or housing segregation in their local contexts on their first try. But they will make some connections. They will see how folks in their communities tell stories about themselves, and how these stories do and do not line up with one another. Be proud, excited, and supportive of even small systemic analyses, for these are the first steps towards decolonial thinking.

Writing Instruction to Practice Our Self-Narration

In our discussion of reading to engage in introspection, you may have been thinking: why not memoir, or character-focused texts? If we want students to see examples of introspection, shouldn't we have them engage with memoir-esque texts where characters spend a lot of time thinking about their personal identity? Well, we could not agree more! We're thinking here about texts like Michael's personal favorite, *Bless Me, Ultima* or the graphic novel *Almost American Girl* by Robin Ha. The inward-looking elements of these texts are wonderful models of personal introspection around identity, as we will discuss in a moment, and you could potentially modify the above unit idea to focus more on personal identity experiences. But it is also the case that there are more layers to introspection than just the individual. Reflecting on community trends and introspection to help students understand and explore the systemic elements of marginalization, rather than just a focus on the personal, is crucial to disrupting the socialization we receive that encourages us to see identity and marginalization as just personal problems. That said, there is of course a place for that more personal introspection in our decolonial classroom. It is just that it is not the only place we do introspection. So let us talk about where we most recommend personal identity introspection: in regular, consistent writing instruction and opportunities.

As we explored in the previous chapter, no matter who our students are, they have a burgeoning racial identity and racial story. They have a cultural world and practices that exist in some relation to dominant and marginalized cultures in our society and communities. They have family histories and narratives that shape their understanding of identity, ethnicity, gender, sexuality, class, and more. And yet they rarely have opportunities to name these things, unpack, and discuss them, in no small part because of socialization and cultural messaging that they should not do so, and that being colorblind and ignorant of our own and others' experiences with racialization is more polite and productive than actually talking about our experiences.

This idea of putting our heads in the sand is, of course, deeply colonial to our knowledge and our being. If we do not talk about our racial identities and experiences, then the tensions they produce when their social and material effects play out widen the chasms between us, reinforcing colonial biases, and keeping the logic and power of coloniality clicking along for another day. It is for this reason that intentionally engaging our identities is so powerful, and so critical; the simple action of learning how to narrate and make sense of our complicated, nuanced, racial and cultural experience disrupts the coloniality of power, of knowledge, and of being, bringing us closer together by ensuring we understand ourselves, and where one another are coming from. Writing about our own identities is a path to better communicating with ourselves, and eventually, with others. With all this in mind, we cannot suggest strongly enough that writing opportunities focused on and supporting the exploration of identity—in its many dimensions—is a critical element of decolonial literacy instruction.

Step 1: Make a List of Cultural and Identity Elements and Help Students Learn This Vocabulary

In the previous chapter, as we discussed racial literacy, we pointed out that a huge element of developing racial literacy involves supporting students' (and our own) vocabulary acquisition and comfort with the discourse and vocabulary around race, ethnicity, culture, and identity. Simply put, we do not often take the time to teach students the vocabulary necessary for them to accurately, confidently, and respectfully, be ABLE to narrate their lives and world. Too often, we launch into discussions of these tense issues, and possibly ask students to write about them, assuming they know the words, and are comfortable with them, even as we struggle to voice them, and question ourselves over our racial utterances. So step one here is both simple and complex: teach students the vocabulary necessary to discuss race, ethnicity, culture, and identity accurately and comfortably.

To do so, you will need to ensure you have consulted and explored the resources necessary to name and define things for students. Can you clearly, in student-friendly language, explain the difference between racism (a systemic condition, independent of any individual, linked to social power) and racial prejudice (an individual bias around race held by a single individual)? Obviously, if we struggle with this task, we would be hard-pressed to expect our students to immediately grasp it. Remember that they are subject to a huge degree of socialization that both conditions them away from talking about their racial, ethnic, and cultural identities, but also offers up erroneous, colloquial understandings of key terms that add more confusion than clarity.

With all this in mind, as you move through your school year, make a list of every term related to race, ethnicity, culture, gender identity, sexuality, class, ability, disability, identity, etc., and make sure that, as these become relevant, you are intentionally and directly teaching them to students, clarifying their definitions, dispelling misconceptions and colloquial understandings, and modeling your own comfort in talking about them. Students may still struggle and feel uncomfortable taking up some of this vocabulary, but by demystifying it, and setting it into a developmental, learning context, you create the conditions for them to begin using it as an essential element of experience, not as loaded, taboo language and terminology.

Step 2: Provide Students with Prompts that Test Their Perspectives

Obviously, encouraging students to write about identity begins with prompts that challenge them to explore their identities. Thus, a crucial element to encouraging student introspection is to ensure that we are, as we discuss further in Chapter 6, asking them to engage with challenging prompts and questions. This can be more complex than it initially seems. We do not want, especially early in a school year, to be too 'on the nose,' asking questions a bit too directly and in ways that might put students still developmentally flirting with making sense of race off the task. We equally do not want to be too obtuse, asking questions so vague or removed from our interests in racial, ethnic, and cultural experience that they allow students to avoid the topics altogether.

We also think that modification with a decolonial eye can be an excellent way to save some labor; a quick internet search will yield countless 'daily journal'-type prompts. Draw from these, but as you go, modify them to be more specific to racial, ethnic, and cultural identity elements. For example, we just found this one:

What is something that made you laugh today?

That is a fine question, but generic, and potentially a bit shallow. But a quick edit helps you create something a bit more incisive and revealing:

What is something that made you laugh, but someone from a different cultural world might not have understood as funny?

You may still want to tweak that a bit, but you get the idea—a generic question is transformed, and now challenges them to both reflect on cultural differences and locate their own cultural world.

Only you will know your students and your community, and thus how to tailor questions to get at those things most relevant to the community generally, and to particular trends and themes that come up in your classroom over time, as well as the students' developmental readiness for more direct prompts. But as you plan out writing prompts, make sure that you build towards some of those core, big questions that invite students to purposefully speak to who they are and how they see themselves in racial, ethnic, and cultural terms.

Step 3: Help Students See Consistency and Divergence in Their Lives

One thing that we feel is universal about strong instructional praxis, and which we have mentioned several times already, is the importance of modeling skills, thinking, and practices. Because the types of questions we are asking students to engage with in a decolonial approach to teaching are likely to be so new, even a bit jarring, it makes clear, intentional instructional modeling all the more critical, so that students can see YOU working with the ideas and doing the type of decolonial thinking you will be asking of them. Remember, these are patterns of thinking students likely have never seen before in a school setting.

With this in mind, YOU will need to model writing about YOUR OWN identity clearly, and often, and with a particular focus on helping students get past flat or reductive conceptions of race and culture. Make sure that you show them how your racial identity meets expectations and how it does not. Show them how you exist in consistency with the cultural expectations of your identity and where you diverge from those cultural expectations. Show them how you can locate yourself proudly around your identity, even if your experience is more complicated than what might be observed. Essentially, helping students to see consistency and divergence in racial, ethnic, cultural, and other dimensions of identity, and how to speak about these confidently, and plan to discuss them in well-organized writing, falls on you!

Step 4: Share Examples of Other Folks Narrating Their Identities

Going back to our discussion of memoirs and character-driven texts, we are particularly fond of texts like *Brown Girl Dreaming* by Jacqueline Woodson, *Apple: (Skin to the Core)* by Eric Gansworth, or for older middle schoolers, *All Boys Aren't Blue* by George M. Johnson. All of these, and many more, feature authors grappling with the kinds of identity questions that are certainly facing our students as well; being pulled between different worlds, feeling like they don't quite fit in, sensing that who they are is perceived differently by different groups of people, curious about how they fit in to their own cultural worlds, or already seeing the code-switching that happens between one cultural space and another.

But we can only read so many novels a year, and if we have other goals for those novels, shorter readings can also be powerful ways to explore all of these same questions. NPR's long-running series *This I Believe*, as well as the *Story Corp* project provide easily accessible, tighter exemplars of individuals narrating their beliefs, values, culture, and identities. Collections like *Colonize this!* and *How does it feel to be a problem?* include powerful, short memoirs of individuals narrating their racial identities and experiences. Beyond all that, given the growth of media and interest in identity in recent decades, searching digital magazines and periodicals will unearth even more examples of both everyday people, and sometimes public figures and celebrities, writing about their racial, ethnic, and cultural identities and experiences in ways students will likely find compelling.

As with any writing, seeing exemplars—including your own modeling—allows students an opportunity to see the way others think and write and translate those practices into their own writing. Also as with any genre, you may see students lean towards mimicry of the style and tone they saw in the exemplar, and for this reason, we encourage you to offer students an array of exemplars that capture the breadth and depth of racial, ethnic, and cultural experience, paying particular attention to not just show racial identity reflection as a somber, dreary task of recounting pain and marginalization, nor as something taken so lightly it begins to feel unimportant.

Step 5: Make Sharing Identity a Routine

The final step we want to suggest you take is, essentially, to engage in this process with regularity and with regular opportunities to share. Revisiting personal introspection matters not only because youth need time to continue to develop their skill sets and vocabulary for discussing identity, but also because there are so many elements—of culture and of identity—to explore. And more than that, all of the positive impacts of personal introspection are amplified by the opportunity to talk about oneself with others, and to have regular, consistent exposure to the narratives of others, their experiences. Learning about others necessarily pushes us to reflect further on ourselves, fostering more introspection, but also empathy and understanding.

In more practical terms, regularly engaging in personal identity introspection, and sharing with others about it, is also crucial for the development of racial literacy. By interacting with the stories of others, we learn how others want to be seen and named, how they wish to narrate themselves and why, and enrich our understanding of the vocabularies that exist to relate to one another. And while narrating our identities, and participating in the sharing of stories, allows you to support youth to develop their racial literacies and humanize others, it also provides opportunities for you to engage in that critical decolonial task of facing challenges to elements of identity that need to be critically questioned. Regularity of process and the creation of sharing spaces with clear norms for conversation around identity offer ample opportunities to gradually engage with perspectives that are less humanizing, teasing them apart over time, rather than feeling the weight—and potential political challenge—of trying to fix someone's unconscious biases all at once.

Pushing Past Racial Discomfort

Make no mistake, engaging in introspection generally is challenging, and engaging in introspection around racial, ethnic, and cultural identity is harder still. It will not be easy to guide your students to develop their racial literacies, to embrace systemic reflection, or work through years of socialization. As we mentioned in the previous chapter, talking about race can lead students into tricky and challenging emotional and affective terrain. Your task is akin to helping folks navigate through an incredibly treacherous landscape, full of pitfalls, rocks, cliff edges, dangerous rushing water, and thorny plant life. It is tough. You will come out with some scrapes and scratches. But getting through it leads to a far more positive space—open, inviting, and full of possibility.

But the reality is that you will see resistance to this journey show up in many ways, from many students, and often in ways that you do not expect and from folks who might surprise you. These responses might range from simple disinterest and disengagement, to more extreme pushback and hostility at being asked to reflect on identity, race, and culture. So varied are the possibilities that we cannot hope to offer explanations or directions on how to respond to each variation here. What we can say is this: to be patient, caring, and understanding in your responses and reactions to students, and be attentive in your listening practice. Remember that students are working through years of socialization, and engaging with new ways of being and honest ways to name themselves can be scary. No matter who we are, or how willing we are to try, closing the emotional and personal distance between our intellectual selves and the social and material impacts of racism and coloniality (i.e., confronting these realities in our lives) is difficult. Showing that you are listening, and challenging students to listen, is critical to fostering racial literacy and empathy.

As you challenge students to engage in introspection, to explore their own identities, and the realities of race, ethnicity, culture, and coloniality in their communities and lived experiences, we hope you will be patient with them, and with yourself. Work with urgency, but not with haste, sensitive to their developing selves, and modeling the type of kind, humanizing approach to navigating identity, difference, and learning that you hope they will carry forward from your classroom.

Challenge in Practice

Ms Ruiz teaches at a suburban middle school across the hall from Ms Patino, a teacher of about the same age, who joined the school in the same year. Throughout her school and department, Ms Patino has become known as combative, difficult to work with, and resistant to trying anything new, experimental, or that she is unsure about in the classroom. Moreover, she has repeatedly said things in staff meetings that show a misunderstanding around the challenges that marginalized students, particularly students of color and LGBTQ students, might face as they navigate school, and an unwillingness to engage with some of the educators and staff in the school community who are passionate about these things. Privately, she has expressed confusion about racial and queer issues to your department, including that she just doesn't understand why talking about identity is such a big deal to people.

This year, Ms Patino is assigned to teach a few sections of 7th-grade ELA, which is the course Ms Ruiz has been teaching with great success the last two years. They have been directed by their department chair to ensure that throughout the year, they need to collaborate so that their curriculum, pacing, and objectives are aligned as comprehensively as possible. In her first planning meeting with Ms Patino, Ms Ruiz lays out her plans, which include several new books relevant to their school community that will necessarily invite students to engage with and reflect on racialized experiences, LGBTQ perspectives, and several key projects that involve multimedia, digital, or multimodal products, and community engagement. Presented with these plans, Ms Patino becomes frustrated and flustered, and wonders why they can't just teach classic texts they already have materials for—left over from retired and departed teachers—and focus on essay writing. She continues to complain that Ms Ruiz' plans are too much work to make happen, and she won't stay to plan beyond contract hours, so they need to stick to easier activities, texts, and assignments.

What are Ms Ruiz' options? What can she do to maintain the ambition of her curriculum, and navigate a relationship with a colleague insecure about teaching in culturally proactive ways?

Questions to Consider While Planning for Introspection

1   How can you begin the year by centering and grounding introspection as a core classroom value?
2   Where examples are there of your community engaging in meaningful introspection? Are there organizations that are engaged with forgotten or marginalized histories whose work could serve as a model for your students?
3   What are the dynamics or challenges of identity that I most need to model for my students? How can I practice doing so? Are there other community members I could enlist who could also model racial, ethnic, and cultural introspection?

Resources to Explore

Looking Inward to Understand One Another

Nurturing introspection is difficult, delicate work. You will need tools to consider how you navigate racial conversations, as well as models and exemplars of other folks in the world exploring these questions to show students that there is purpose and possibility in doing so. The following resources can support you with these tasks:

- Glenn Singleton's *Courageous conversations about race: A field guide for achieving equity in schools* (2014). This text is an excellent primer for how to navigate conversations around race in humanizing ways, especially if doing so is new to you.

- *Everyday antiracism: Getting real about race in school* is a collection edited by Mica Pollock that offers a wide range of short, accessible articles on an array of topics that are of great use for guiding the different twists and turns racial introspection might take us on.
- What Our Communities Tell Us: Student-Led Ethnographic Research (2021) by Alice Dominguez provides a road map for how to approach the sort of community introspection work we describe above.
- The This I Believe series by NPR (https://thisibelieve.org/) provides decades worth of powerful, personal, introspective reflections from everyday (and more famous) individuals that can serve as excellent examples of written introspection.
- Similarly, Story Corps (https://storycorps.org/) has yet another archive of introspective stories, framed around conversations. Not only are there excellent examples of introspection that invite more systemic reflection—check out the "Facundo the Great" story—but it offers the opportunity to contribute as well.
- The edited collection *Colonize this!: Young women of color on today's feminism* by Hernandez and Rehmann, and Bayoumi's collection of stories in *How does it feel to be a problem?: Being young and Arab in America* are wonderful resources to draw examples of the way other young people have engaged in introspection around their own lives, identities, and communities.

Assessment Alternatives

When we think about decolonizing assessment to encourage introspection, the thing that strikes us is less the means for assessment, and more the way it is done. Across our other chapters, we will talk about some different strategies for assessing proficiency, practices for reviewing student work, and question the merits of grading. Here, we want to ask you to reflect on the values you bring to that work.

Specifically, as we discuss further in the next chapter, schools are set up to distance teachers, and their lived experiences, from those of students—especially students with historically marginalized racial, ethnic, and cultural identities. So when we think about how you assess introspective work, activities like those discussed here, the thing we want you to think about is how honestly and earnestly you are actually reading and engaging with what they have to say. Are you spending just a few moments quickly looking over their writing products? Assessing by eyeballing how much and how well structured a submission is? We get it. Time is tight, and responding fully to students is laborious. But if we want to commit to encouraging and fostering introspective, and cultivating the development of racial literacy, we must make time to respond fully and engage intentionally with what students write when they are writing introspectively. That means reading it closely, and responding personally to each student. In their work, they may be working through intense questions, and possibly problematic misconceptions. As challenging as it will be, we need to take the time to engage with those racial misconceptions, otherwise our students' racial literacies will not develop. That will be challenging. You will need to be delicate and thoughtful, and it will take time. So make that time. You won't be able to do this for every assignment or task, but when you ask students to be introspective, especially about race, culture, and identity, make sure your assessment is personal and substantial.

Technology Spotlight

In the section of this chapter suggesting ideas for writing lessons, we urged you to engage in personal reflections and journaling around aspects of our identities. But who says that needs to be just in written, essay format? With an array of tools now widely available, digital storytelling can be a way in which students reflect on, create, narrate, and share their identity experiences and narratives, allowing them to pull together more than just linguistic resources to capture the complexities of their identity, and truly show, through images and media, who they are. Supporting and encouraging reflection on the choices made in digital storytelling—asking why a particular image was chosen, how a song or color makes them feel, why that emotion was important to convey through the design or transitions—can also help students imagine how to translate the affective, socioemotional dynamics and sensations they produce in a digital, multimedia format into words when the time comes.

References

Anzaldua, G. (1987). *Borderlands/La Frontera*. Aunt Lute.

Anaya, R. (2022). *Bless me, Ultima*. Penguin.

Bayoumi, M. (2009). *How does it feel to be a problem?: Being young and Arab in America*. Penguin.

Cartaya, P. (2017). *The epic fail of Arturo Zamora*. Viking Books for Young Readers.

Collins, P. H. (2005). *Black sexual politics: African Americans, gender, and the new racism*. Routledge.

Dominguez, A. (2021). What our communities tell us: Student-led ethnographic research. *English Journal, 111*(2), 42–48.

Gansworth, E. (2020). *Apple:(skin to the Core)*. Chronicle Books.

Ha, R. (2020). *Almost American girl: An illustrated memoir*. Blazer & Bray.

Hernández, D., & Rehman, B. (Eds.). (2019). *Colonize this!: Young women of color on today's feminism*. Hachette UK.

Johnson, G. M. (2020). *All boys aren't blue: A memoir-manifesto*. Farrar, Straus and Giroux (BYR).

Kendi, I. X. (2019). *How to be an antiracist*. One world.

Menakem, R. (2021). *My grandmother's hands: Racialized trauma and the pathway to mending our hearts and bodies*. Penguin UK.

Pollock, M. (Ed.). (2008). *Everyday antiracism: Getting real about race in school*. The New Press.

Singleton, G. E. (2014). *Courageous conversations about race: A field guide for achieving equity in schools*. Corwin Press.

Raúf, O.Q. (2018). *The Boy at the Back of the Class*. Hachette.

Story Corps. (2022, November 1). *Story Corps*. https://storycorps.org/

This I Believe. (2022, November 1). *This I Believe Essays*. https://thisibelieve.org/

Woodson, J. (2016). *Brown girl dreaming*. Penguin.

4

DECOLONIZED CLASSROOMS...
CONNECT HUMANS TO ONE ANOTHER

Introduction

Humanity. It's something most assume is a given, that no matter our differences, we are all human. But Junot Diaz (2009) problematizes this assumption:

> You guys know about vampires? ... You know, vampires have no reflections in a mirror? **There's this idea that monsters don't have reflections in a mirror**. And what I've always thought isn't that monsters don't have reflections in a mirror, it's **that if you want to make a human being into a monster, deny them, at the cultural level, any reflection of themselves**. And growing up, I felt like a monster in some ways. I didn't see myself reflected at all. I was like, "Yo, is something wrong with me? That the whole society seems to think that people like me don't exist?"

And unfortunately, the way we teach literature often erases a significant portion of our students—or skews representation so much that our students still cannot see themselves reflected within the classroom.

Years ago, Robyn came across an 8th-grade classroom where the teacher had assigned the novel *Tom Sawyer* (Twain, 1962). Each day, students sat at their desks, which were arranged in evenly spaced rows, and listened to the book being read to them on tape. Periodically, this routine was interrupted by a quiz designed to ensure that students were following along in the book. The silence in the room was remarkable—punctuated only by the sound of the narrator's voice. This class, the teacher believed, was a very well behaved class. The class, we maintain, was one disconnected from each other and the teacher. It was one that perpetuates normative schooling and culture. They were reading the book (although many were not), not because it reflected the experiences of the students in the class—not even the white ones—but because it was (and is) considered a classic. Classics, the argument often goes, provide readers with cultural touchstones— but those cultural touchstones often perpetuate norms of whiteness. Further, this classroom embraced only one definition of success: the successful passing of reading quizzes that had only one correct answer. There was no space for dialogue, for critiquing, for connecting to others' human experiences.

DOI: 10.4324/9781003290681-6

Abolishing Zero-Point Thinking

Creating classroom spaces and practices that isolate our students from each other, that discourage human connection, furthers zero-point thinking (Castro-Gómez, 2005). In this specific classroom, the students were presented with a narrow view of the novel—that of the teacher. The teacher directed the study of the novel, highlighting specific values and belief systems that came from a very Western-centric perspective. And the novel itself, while sometimes lauded as a criticism of slavery and the treatment of Blacks at the time, still perpetuates a very white-centered viewpoint, with the character of Injun Joe serving as a disparaging representation of Indigenous peoples and other reinforcements of stereotypes, even as it critiques larger political systems. Without providing space for dissection of these treatments of characters, for conversation that can problematize ideas within the novel, students walk away with distinct images of different racial and cultural groups. And these flattened stereotypes discourage students from making connections to others who have different lived experiences from themselves. For middle-school students who are often still in the egocentric stage of development, still trying to connect with a larger and more complicated world, it is important that we shift their focus away from themselves and toward others. Emphasizing human connection assists our students as they move toward a more collective understanding of the world and allows us to begin extricating ourselves from the coloniality of being that shapes how we see and position ourselves and one another. The examples in this chapter provide ways to emphasize collectivism and human connections while assisting students in developing their reading and writing.

Reading Instruction to Nurture Interconnection

One way to nurture human connection is by providing students with the opportunity to engage in dialogue about novels in ways that matter to them. Building knowledge together around a common text can provide students with opportunities to see books—and by extension, the world—in different lights. Literature circles (Daniels, 2002) have long been a staple in many middle level ELA classrooms. Through literature circles, students have opportunities to explore the questions they have about novels together. They encourage students to work together to develop projects around the themes of the novel, allowing them to build connections with one another when structured well.

Literature circles can also serve as a vehicle for helping students see beyond the single (Eurocentric) story that Adichie (2009) cautions against. Often, our students have had singular exposures to different communities of people, prompting them to believe that everyone within a community looks and acts the same. Further, students' exposure to literature about marginalized communities often focuses on issues such as racism and violence. Although well intentioned—and needed to draw their attention to problems in the world—only focusing on these kinds of stories also skews students' perceptions of the lives of people who identify differently from them, reinforcing the coloniality of knowledge. As author Nic Stone (2020) posits through reading the stories of people who are traditionally othered, we can build connections: "Because the more we see

Black people *living*—loving and doing and being and feeling and going on adventures and solving mysteries and being the heroes—the more we come to recognize our shared humanity" (para. 23). Through literature circles, students can be exposed to multiple stories that can help them recognize the complexities of people.

Step 1: Select Texts that Nurture Connections

Designing literature circles using the work of authors who identify with underrepresented groups means that we must look outside the canon. This is a necessity if we want to decolonize our classroom. Reading outside the canon resituates whose voices are valued, whose cultures are valued. Coloniality is continually reinforced by constructing people, places, and cultures as Other. When we select literature that focuses solely or primarily on White culture, we Other all other students. This is harmful to our students from marginalized communities because they understand their value as outside the community norms. This impacts how they see themselves, how they relate to others, and who they can be in the world. It is harmful to our white students, as well, because it feeds their understandings of the systems that currently exist in the world.

Alfred Tatum (2008) argues that teachers should use what he calls *enabling texts*. Although much of his research examines how to elevate Black boy readers, his recommendations can be extrapolated across marginalized youth. Enabling texts should focus on the collective, promote mental well-being, reflect an awareness of the world, and guide students towards ways of being, doing, thinking, and acting. When selecting texts for literature circles, it is important to keep these characteristics in mind. If the intent is to show multiple ways of being within a community, to celebrate how people live, love and act within a community, teachers should also focus on a single identity marker, whether it's racial, cultural, gender, etc., so that students start to recognize the heterogeneous nature of those communities. It is also important to use contemporary books because the problems and joys of communities are continually changing. This means that as language arts teachers, we need to be continually reading and researching books to add to our instruction, to be dynamic with our plans, and to be willing to phase out texts that no longer speak to our students. And finally, we must recognize that we cannot stop with just one literature circle—students need to see texts from diverse authors throughout the curriculum and year.

Step 2: Provide Students with Opportunities to Explore Selected Titles

After selecting the literature circle texts, providing students with time to explore the different books is important to the unit's success. Students, like any reader, connect to different genres, different themes, different settings, different writing styles in different ways. It is important that students have a say in which books appeal to them. Finding a connection with the book, whether it's because students enjoy participating in the same activity as the main character or they have an interest in the theme of the book, increases the likelihood that students will engage with the book. There are various ways to effectively introduce the selections to students. Showing personal enthusiasm for a book through book talks can build excitement around the titles. Embedding book trailers on class websites provides students with the opportunity to explore the books at their own pace. Simply having the books available in the classroom allows students to pick up and read sections, giving them a sense of what the entire book looks and feels like.

Using the tea-party reading strategy can also be an effective way to get students interested in learning more about books (Beers, 2002). In a tea party, students are given slips of paper that include quotes from the text. Quotes should provide insights into characters, themes, plot events, and setting, without giving away the story. Once each student has a slip of paper with a different quote on it, they socialize with their classmates as if they were at a tea party. Students find a partner, and each partner shares their quote. They then spend a few minutes chatting about how their quotes might connect in the book, speculating about what the story might be about. Once they've finished their short conversation, students find a new partner and repeat the process. With each new discussion, they bring with them the knowledge from previous discussions, which can build their curiosity about the story. Tea parties are particularly effective with middle-school students who need to have opportunities to productively move around the room and engage with their peers. Multiple tea parties can be used to introduce each of the books, and students can then choose the books they find they are most curious to learn more about. We would further note that while this approach has long been called 'tea parties,' we encourage you to reflect on what will resonate with your students as a name for this activity—would the idea and context of a tea party even make sense to them?—and convey that the purpose is mingling, sharing, and getting to learn from others.

Step 3: Introduce Discussion Protocols that Encourage Interconnection

As mentioned, literature circles have long been used in middle-school classrooms. Yet most often, they are structured very traditionally following the structure popularized by Harvey Daniels in his book *Literature Circles: Voice and Choice in the Student-Centered Classroom*, which was first published in 1994. The problem with this structure is that it's too formulaic, focusing students on singular elements by assigning students different, limited, roles such as word wizard, literary luminary, or connector. This provides students with a task to complete, but it doesn't encourage them to really delve into larger themes and ideas within the novels, nor does it foster holistic reader identities within our students. To disrupt stereotypes and reimagine the world, it is important that we teach students how to engage in reflective discussions around issues and experiences that help them better see beyond unknown words or surface connections. This is not to say, however, that we leave students to discuss their books in unstructured ways. Rather, we can look at different discussion protocols that encourage students to look at books in different ways and through different perspectives.

The following discussion protocols offer more authentic discussion: Save the Last Word for Me and the 4 As Text Protocol. In Save the Last Word for Me, students come prepared for the discussion with quotes, including page numbers, that stood out to them while reading the text. Depending on group size and time for discussion, you can vary how many quotes they bring, while also asking them to bring 'back-up' quotes in case others have identified the same quotes. Within the protocol, one student shares their quote but does not provide an explanation as to why they brought it to the discussion. The rest of the group each takes turns responding to the quote, sharing their interpretation as to what it means and why it is important. Once each person responds, the student who brought the quote to the discussion explains why they thought it was important to share. This process continues until all students have shared their quotes. This protocol encourages students to see other perspectives around the same idea, increasing the likelihood that they will recognize different ways to interpret the world. It also teaches them how to draw upon specific events within the book to guide their discussion.

When using the 4 As Text Protocol, students focus their discussion around the questions: What Assumptions does the author of the text hold? What do you Agree with in the text? What do you want to Argue with in the text? What parts of the text do you Aspire to? Through this protocol students hear other perspectives, while also learning that texts are complex. We can both like and dislike elements within a text, just as we can like and dislike characteristics of people. By looking at both feelings, we can make a better judgment about how we feel about the work (or people) as a whole rather than focusing on one element that initially jumps out at us. The protocol also asks students to consider the worldview of the author and ways they want to learn and grow from the text. These are important skills to develop when learning how to connect with people. More information about how to structure these protocols, as well as other protocols, can be found at https://nsrfharmony.org/protocols/.

In addition to these formal protocols, teachers can create their own protocols by asking students to consider texts through different lenses. One way that can be particularly effective is to ask students to identify the characters' vulnerabilities, strengths, and needs. This helps draw students' attention to the challenges people face within existing structures, while also drawing their attention to the strengths. Reading about characters through these lenses helps to humanize them, which helps to combat the single-story narrative they may have previously been influenced by.

When conducting literature circles, teachers can use one protocol throughout or they can vary protocols across weeks. This decision should be based on the needs of students. Some students might initially need more structure, so threading the same approach to discussion across all discussions can help scaffold them toward different ways to engage in dialogue. Other students who are more comfortable interacting with each other may benefit from the challenge of looking at their books through different lenses. In any case, and whatever the lens or structure used, we encourage you to ensure that you have tweaked and added elements pointed towards critical engagement with the lived experiences of marginalized peoples and the examination of power in the texts. These elements are unsurprisingly often absent from on-offer structures, but essential to creating a learning environment that will question coloniality and the single story in texts.

Step 4: Design Experiences that Assist Students in Connecting Across Books and to the World

Literature circles are effective in helping students develop a deeper understanding of a book because students are collaboratively building knowledge together. If we also want to use them to help students see multiple stories about people from the same identity marker, we cannot just stop after they've studied their own novel. We also must build in experiences that encourage students to make connections across their books. Like any unit we design, there are multiple ways to accomplish that goal. Here, we share two possibilities.

Two-voice poems are poems written in three columns, with the outer two columns representing the different perspectives of two different people or characters and the middle column representing the spaces where their perspectives converge. These poems focus on exploring two different approaches to viewing the same topic. For example, a poem might be written from a parent's and a child's perspective about effective discipline. In many ways, they will have different views of what works and what doesn't, as well as why it does or doesn't work. These ideas are represented in their respective columns. But there will be moments when their views are similar, and these moments are captured in the middle column. Two-voice poems can be used in multiple ways. When considering how to help students make connections across books, partnering two students who read different books and tasking them with creating a two-voice poem can be an effective strategy. Here, they must discuss their books and identify a topic they feel their characters might approach in different ways. Through the writing of the poem, they can identify the characters' similarities and differences, which helps them to see the complexity of humanity within any given group.

Another potential avenue is to have students from different literature groups work together to speculate on 'what if?' questions: What if the two characters met? How would this meeting change the trajectory of the story? How would one character support another? How might one character challenge another? The questions are endless, but by engaging in these conversations, they begin to imagine different worlds through the vehicle of literature. And once they become comfortable speculating about different worlds in fiction, it becomes easier to prompt them to speculate 'what if?' around our existing world. Engaging students in this kind of conversation can be done in small moments through simple conversation. Students can also engage in larger world-making by adding in research or creating products such as videos, podcasts, or posters that share their speculations with a wider audience.

Writing Instruction to Foster Empathy

Too often, writing is seen as an individual endeavor. This, however, is a very colonial view. In Indigenous cultures, storytelling is a community experience (Chan, 2021). It is a way to share histories, to connect to others, to heal. Through story, we can help our students connect with others, and in doing so, we foster empathy for others. But writing stories to foster empathy looks different from a typical lesson on plot structure. Unlike colonial structures that expect an exposition that neatly introduces the story, rising action that builds to a climax, and falling action that results in a satisfactory ending, Indigenous stories focus on the heart, on the people, and on the spirit of the story. Storytelling is meant to teach us something as humans. It can be prolonged, can seem disconnected in its telling, can lack a clearly defined ending. Most importantly, it centers the humans telling the stories. So what might that look like in a middle level class-room? First, it means designing an experience that requires students to listen to, engage with, and capture the stories of people outside the classroom. It requires students to begin with a burning question that cannot be neatly answered. It prompts teachers to reconsider what writing looks like and to value new ways of constructing meaning. The Investigation Mixtape is one such way to bring storytelling that fosters empathy into the classroom.

Step 1: Identify an Important Question

Middle-school students tend to be curious. And as early adolescence tends to be a social stage of development, many are eager to interact with people and ask their questions. Middle school is also a time when students are transitioning from a self-centered per-spective to one that is more considerate of others. As a time of transition, many stu-dents benefit from experiences that support developing empathy. Inspired by Ibram Kendi's (2021) episode "The Juneteenth Mixtape" from his *Be Antiracist* podcast, the Investigation Mixtape requires students to talk to people from a variety of backgrounds in order to gain new perspectives. In the Kendi episode, he was curious about how peo-ple perceive Juneteenth, so he tasked his producer with asking people from a variety of backgrounds about the holiday. Middle-school students can mimic this process by asking their own questions about things they are curious about.

To start, provide students with opportunities to listen to podcasts such as Kendi's that provide multiple perspectives around the same question. Discuss the kinds of questions that are asked and the kinds of answers they solicit. Then, help students begin to brain-storm questions they are curious about. Show them how to frame open-ended questions and to think widely about things that have made them wonder. Questions can be very broad: What inspired you? Or they may be more specific: Why is it important to travel? Remind them that the best questions are the ones that have no single answer. And because many middle-school students still think concretely, you may need to work with them to mold their curiosities from concrete ideas, such as What is the best thing you ever made with Legos? to more open-ended ideas, like What is the best thing you have ever created? It is also important to remind them that when they ask questions like these that only require one-word answers, following up with a simple 'why?' can help people dig more deeply into their answers.

Step 2: Collect People's Answers

After students have settled upon and refined their questions, send them out to collect answers. If you have flexibility in your schedule and location, you can take students out to public spaces to ask their questions, but it will likely be a task that they will need to do on their own. There is flexibility in how they approach this task. Approaching strangers in public spaces is one way to collect a variety of answers, but it is important to talk with students about how to safely do so. They can also ask people they or their families know, but if they choose this approach, it is important to remind them that they need to talk to people from a variety of backgrounds with different experiences. Only gathering answers from people who think like them means they will create echo chambers that simply affirm their own beliefs. We develop empathy when we learn the stories and perspectives of others, so it is important that we reach outside our comfort zones and find people who will challenge our thinking. It is important to explicitly discuss why we want students to talk to new people and to help them brainstorm where and how to find these people.

When collecting stories, students may be tempted to take notes. After all, schools tend to privilege written information and notes are often emphasized when gathering information. Yet, when we are constantly looking at our paper or our computer screen, we are distracted from the stories others are telling us. Prompt them to leave their notebooks or computers behind and have them simply record the stories on their phones or other recording devices. Remind them to make sure to get permission from whoever they are talking to, but that once they start recording, they should actively listen to the answers they are receiving. And while they may start with one simple question, let them know that it is okay to ask more questions as they engage in conversation.

Step 3: Listen and Reflect Upon What Students Have Learned

Create space and time in your class schedule for students to listen to their recordings. At this time, encourage them to listen closely to each answer and jot down the main ideas, memorable quotes, and questions they have while listening. Demonstrate how to listen to the recordings multiple times, noting different aspects of their answers each time. The more we listen, the more we understand what is being said.

Once students have listened to their recordings and captured the ideas and moments that stood out to them, prompt them to reflect upon what they've learned. What are some 'a-ha!' moments or things they had never thought of before? Where did they find moments of agreement and how did those moments support their previous thinking? Where did they find moments of disagreement and what is at the root of the disagreement? Are there places where they can find common ground?

Step 4: Develop a Podcast

Using their reflections and recordings, demonstrate to students how to pull everything together into a podcast. Like traditional writing pieces, students need to begin their podcasts with an introduction, consider how they will transition between recordings, and summarize their ideas. Encourage students to begin their podcasts by sharing the story behind their curiosities. What prompted them to explore the question? Explore different ways to transition in audio texts. While they might choose to talk between recordings, reflecting upon each answer, they might also use music, other sound effects, or even purposeful moments of silence to signal a transition. Finally, ask them to use their reflection over the recordings as a whole to form their conclusion. What did they learn from this experience? What are they thinking about in regard to the question now that they have multiple answers? What new questions did this experience prompt?

There are multiple digital tools students can use to compile their recordings and add their own commentary. Computer-based software, such as Garage Band and Audacity, offers multiple tools to help students mix, overlap, and fade sounds. They can also be more complicated than some online tools like Anchor and Soundtrap. In Anchor, for example, students can drag and drop recording, directly record their own voices, insert copyright-free music, and rearrange each element until they are satisfied with their final product. The flexibility of tools such as these allows for students to receive feedback and revise easily without re-recording their entire podcast. And engaging in a writing process that encourages students to draw from others' stories, to listen to stories multiple times, and to create their own understanding about their questions during the process provides the support middle-school students need as they work toward developing empathy.

Building a Holistic Ecology in the Classroom

Individualistic communities are uniquely colonial. Decolonizing our classrooms means that we break down the emphasis on the individual and build a holistic ecology that emphasizes the interdependence of humans. Creating an atmosphere that nurtures a reliance on one another to move learning forward can be challenging. Competition is ingrained in Western culture—we only have to examine popular culture's emphasis on sports and reality television to realize how influential competition is on the decisions we make daily. But within competitions, there are always losers. And when we emphasize individualism in our classrooms, we nurture competition, meaning that we are setting some of our students up to be losers in the classroom. And often, the losers are the students who have been historically marginalized.

Recognizing and emphasizing that there are multiple ways of knowing and sharing can help build a more holistic classroom ecology. Rather than focusing on what students *cannot* do, holistic classrooms help students identify what they do know and create opportunities for them to share their knowledge in new—and often more complex— ways. And because the emphasis is on interconnectedness, a holistic classroom encourages students to learn from each other. The learning experiences described in this chapter help build an interconnected, holistic classroom ecology. Through a focus on an array of literature from different identity markers, we expose students to ways of knowing that are different from their own. Honoring the voices in these texts provides students with a broader and deeper understanding of where knowledge comes from, helping to shift mindsets from the Other to the collective. Allowing students to compose digitally, as well as through the written word, values other modes of expression and taps into other talents. Celebrating new talents provides all students with pathways toward discovering their roles in the classroom community.

Through literature circles, we provide opportunities to build collective knowledge as students interrogate the books and each other together. When multiple voices come together around a shared experience, we prompt individuals to consider perspectives they may have missed if left to interpret it on their own. This holds true in literature circles, as well as in the mixtape, which provides students with a way to tell stories that matter to the collective rather than the individual. Literature circles are just one way to build connectedness using the Indigenous practice of circles. Establishing a classroom grounded in restorative practices builds community, and the circles that are the foundation of restorative practices can also nurture students' listening skills.

Many mistakenly believe that restorative practices are only used as a response to harm. However, restorative practices are actually proactive approaches to building community. In fact, 80% of the restorative-practice continuum is proactive because when we build community, we have fewer instances of harm. While we cannot adequately cover the intricacies of restorative practices here, we can highlight the tenets that guide them. First and foremost, restorative practices subscribe to the social discipline window that emphasizes doing things *with* people as a way to build community and buy in, rather than doing things *to* people, which is more punitive in nature, or *for* people, which is permissive and doesn't teach people how to do things on their own. When we work *with* our students, they build social capital and confidence in themselves and others as learners.

Creating a culture of fair process is also a vital aspect of a holistic, restorative classroom. Restorative practices refer to a fair process as one that engages, explains, and clearly sets expectations. Through engagement, students are involved in the decisions made that impact them—and it's more than perfunctory. Teachers genuinely listen and take their ideas into account. When explaining, teachers make sure to explain the reasoning behind decisions and address how people will be impacted by them. When there is this kind of transparency in the classroom, students are more likely to accept a decision even if they don't like it. And expectation clarity means that students not only understand why a decision has been made, but what teachers expect them to do in response.

The social discipline window and fair process all require students to learn how to listen to each other in order to make decisions and clarify roles. They also require students to learn how to clearly articulate their own ideas and feelings, strengthening their speaking skills in ways that are not always focused upon in the classroom. The third tenet of restorative practices, affective statements, aligns even more closely to developing students' (and teachers') speaking skills in that they teach students how to interact with each other in honest ways. Through affective statements, students learn how to identify and articulate their feelings about something that has occurred and to name the impact of that event. This makes communication more concrete. Rather than talking in general statements like, "I thought you did a good job on your podcast," affective statements offer concrete feedback such as, "I found myself asking so many questions when I listened to your podcast because you interviewed such an interesting person."

Finally, there is a continuum of restorative practices that emphasizes the proactive nature of circles. Within the 80% proactive approaches, restorative practices emphasize affective statements, affective questions, small impromptu conversations that notice when others are doing good things or that proactively address small problems before they escalate, and different forms of proactive circle discussions like check-in circles, norm-setting circles, and discussions around academic content. Responsive circles that bring together people who have had conflict and formal conferences that develop plans of action make up the reactive restorative practices. In addition to these circles, listening circles can be used to respond to community harm, whether it is harm that has been done in the classroom or school or harm that is more globally occurring in the world. Through listening circles, students learn to listen closely to others' stories and to develop and strengthen their empathy toward others. For more information about listening circles, as well as other aspects of restorative practices, see the International Institute for Restorative Practices' website found in the Recommended Resources section.

Challenge in Practice

Mr Smith is in the middle of his second year of teaching 8th-grade ELA in a suburb of a large city. Having grown up in the city schools, which were populated by students from a wide array of racial, cultural, and economic backgrounds, it has been an adjustment for him to work in a school populated by primarily white students. Committed to introducing his students to new perspectives, Mr Smith designed a literature circle unit using books written by Black authors that feature Black characters. Knowing the importance of showing a wide array of experiences, Mr Smith chose novels that explore young love, time travel, grief and loss, racial conflict, and growing up. The unit has been going well, with students engaging in rich conversations about their novels during their small-group discussions and making connections across novels in their weekly whole-class discussions. Now, they are excited to create book trailers to introduce their books to the wider school community.

On Tuesday during his planning period, Mr Smith is called to his principal's office. The principal has received a parent complaint about one of the books in the unit. It seems that the parent discovered the book while cleaning their child's room and was shocked to discover that the school was requiring a book that featured voter suppression and police brutality. Further, it appeared that the parent had printed flyers protesting the book and had distributed them at a Little League baseball game the previous night. Not wanting to stir up controversy around race in the community, the principal wants Mr Smith to stop teaching the book immediately. Mr Smith is devastated and knows his students will be, too.

What are Mr Smith's options? What might he have done differently to prevent this outcome?

Questions to Consider While Planning for Human Connections

1 How can you be transparent in your communication with students, parents and other community members?
2 How can you create classroom experiences or events that allow students to begin to build trust with and connect to the community?
3 Who might be a resource to build bridges between the school and the community? How might you invite them into your decolonizing efforts?

Resources to Explore

Connecting Through Restorative Practices

A holistic classroom ecology that nurtures reading for interconnections and writing for empathy can be supported by integrating restorative practices into your classroom environment. While we touch upon restorative practices in this chapter, restorative practices are more complex than we can cover in this book. For more information on restorative practices, check out the following resources:

- The International Institute for Restorative Practices (iirp.edu) is a group of researchers who study and implement restorative practices around the world. Their website provides an overview of restorative practices, as well as resources for K-12 schools.
- The Schott Foundation for Public Education is dedicated to connecting philanthropists to activists to further their mission "to develop and strengthen a broad-based and representative movement to achieve fully-resourced, quality PreK-12 public education." They have developed a restorative practices toolkit to introduce educators to restorative practices, as well as to provide guidance on implementing these practices at classroom, school, and community levels: http://schottfoundation.org/resources/restorative-practices-toolkit
- This blog post from the Teaching Channel shares three approaches, as well as additional resources, for making a shift to restorative practices in the classroom: https://www.teachingchannel.com/blog/restorative-conflict
- This video, posted by the Festival of Literary Diversity (FOLD) Canada, features a panel made up of Dwanna Nicole, Christianne Paras, Udoro Gatewood, and Jermaine Williams who discuss "Decolonizing Education and the Role of Restorative Justice in Schools": https://www.youtube.com/watch?v=nfmAd6iDUPI.

Assessment Alternatives

School assessment practices favor the individual over the collective, reinforcing disconnection and the coloniality of knowledge. Assessments are typically designed by the teacher, given to the student, and then scored by the teacher. Points are added up and turned into percentages that are then translated to letter grades, which can then be used to compare students to other students in the class. This practice likely sounds familiar to you as it is repeated over and over in classrooms across the United States. And this practice, like so many others, is a result of the colonization of school and society. It nurtures competition, with one sector of students eager to come out on top, another sector deciding that the game is rigged against them so they refuse to play, and another sector caught somewhere in the middle.

And while we acknowledge that a complete abandonment of grades is not something one teacher can accomplish on their own, there are ways that teachers can de-emphasize grades in the classroom. One way to accomplish this is to emphasize feedback, allowing students to use feedback to continually refine their ideas and work. In doing this, it is also important to shift the feedback gaze from resting solely on the teacher toward the collective community. Feedback protocols can be created so that peers can help each develop their work in meaningful ways. Keep feedback simple, prompting the creator of the work to sit quietly and listen while peers examine their work and answer questions such as: What is the author's purpose? What specific details do you see that help accomplish the purpose? What specific details could be improved to support this purpose? This simple questioning technique keeps peers focused and allows the creator to listen to the feedback and focus on aspects of the work that are working and those that need revisiting.

Experts and community members who have experience in aspects of the students' work can also be invited in to visit with students about their work. For example, if students are writing a narrative, authors from the community might be invited in to read through their narratives and provide suggestions to students. Or, if students are creating advertisements, marketing and advertising experts might be invited in to listen to students pitch their ideas and help them refine them. Parents and guardians can also be a valuable part of the feedback process. Set aside days when you invite them to come and talk with the students, using the protocol that you would use during peer feedback days. By inviting multiple perspectives into the classroom, students begin to see feedback as an important part of the learning process rather than something that one person—the teacher—does to them.

Technology Spotlight

Today's digital landscape provides opportunities for teachers to connect their students to others from inside the classroom walls. Video conferencing tools such as Zoom, FaceTime, or Google Hangout all allow people from around the world to connect with students in real time, providing opportunities to collectively build knowledge that did not exist in years past. Other tools, such as Flipgrid, allow for connecting to others when it is not possible to connect in real time. When students are provided with the opportunity to see the people they are interacting with, rather than just reading emails or other messages, they are better able to make connections and create relationships that will sustain learning.

References

Adichie, C. N. (2009, July). *The dangers of a single story* [Video]. TED Global 2009. https://www.ted.com/talks/chimamanda_ngozi_adichie_the_danger_of_a_single_story?language=en

Beers, K. (2002). *When kids can't read: What teachers can do*. Heinemann.

Castro-Gómez, S. (2005). *La Hybris Del Punto Cero: Ciencia, Raza E Ilustración En La Nueva Granada (1750–1816)* [*The Hubris of the zero point: Science, race, and illustration in New Granada (1750–1816)*]. Pontificia Universidad Javeriana.

Chan, A. S. (2021). Storytelling, culture, and Indigenous methodology. In A. Bainbridge, L. Formenti, & L. West (Eds), *Discourses, dialogue and diversity in biographical research* (pp. 170–185). Brill. https://doi.org/10.1163/9789004465916_012

Daniels, H. (2002). *Literature circles: Voice and choice in book clubs and reading groups*. Stenhouse Publishers.

Diaz, J. (2009) https://www.nj.com/ledgerlive/2009/10/junot_diazs_new_jersey.html#comments

Kendi, I. (Executive Producer). (2021, June 16). The Juneteenth Mixtape (No. 5) [Audio podcast episode]. In *Be Antiracist with Ibram X. Kendi*. Pushkin, https://www.pushkin.fm/podcasts/be-antiracist-with-ibram-x-kendi#episodes

Stone, N. (2020). *Don't just read about racism—Read stories about Black people living. Cosmopolitan.* https://www.cosmopolitan.com/entertainment/books/a32770951/read-black-books-nic-stone/

Tatum, A. (2008). Toward a more anatomically complete model of literacy instruction: A focus on African American male adolescents and texts. *Harvard Educational Review, 78*(1), 155–180.

Twain, M. (1962). *The adventures of Tom Sawyer.* Airmont Books.

5

DECOLONIZED CLASSROOMS... POSITION EVERYONE AS EXPERTS

Introduction

As we noted in a previous chapter, Django Paris and H. Samy Alim (2014) caution that

> For too long, 'access' and 'equity' have centered implicitly or explicitly around the question of how to get working-class students of color to speak and write more like middle-class White ones.
>
> (p. 87)

We just have to look at the books featured in most school curricula to see this. Recently, we were doing a search for commonly taught middle-school novels, and we came across Books-a-Million's 6th–8th Grade Common Core Reading List (n.d.). Of the 40 books listed, only five were written by non-white authors: Soman Chainani, Laurence Yep, Sherman Alexie, Langston Hughes, and Sharon Draper. None of these authors are Hispanic, and the almost singular representation of the other racial and cultural backgrounds increases the chances that students will, as we mentioned in the previous chapter, walk away from their literacy learning with the singular story that Adichie (2009) warns us about. Further, of the 35 white authors, 23 are men. Thus, the implicit message conveyed to educators—and the larger society—is that white males are the primary conveyors of knowledge.

Disrupting Colonial Expertise

Positioning whites as experts is foundational to reinforcing the coloniality of knowledge. In doing so, we position those who are not white as 'less than,' and when expertise is devalued, this can lead to those from marginalized communities feel inferior to others. While this feeling of inferiority may be subconscious, it shapes how our students see themselves, contributing to the "coloniality of Being" (Maldonado-Torres, 2007). And at the middle-school level, when students are in the midst of identity making, it is vital that we disrupt this messaging. As teachers striving toward a decolonized classroom, we must shift our epistemology away from the White Gaze and toward a new emphasis on who can define what knowledge is and how it counts. The examples explored in this chapter demonstrate ways we can shift expertise away from an exclusive Western perspective and toward an inclusive vision of everyone as experts.

DOI: 10.4324/9781003290681-7

Reading Instruction to Validate Youth Expertise

Middle-school students have a lot to say. Too often, in our quest for managing the classroom, we don't provide them with opportunities to speak. And the more we put books that they cannot connect to into their hands, the less they see their ideas as valuable. One of the hallmarks of many literacy classrooms is the reading workshop. Reading workshop can be a powerful tool for increasing reading engagement as it allows students to choose the books they want to read rather than requiring everyone to read the same book. Choice in texts provides all students the opportunity to connect to literature. As a widely accepted instructional strategy, reading workshop can provide teachers with an avenue for more purposefully disrupting the notion and veins of coloniality around expertise and for positioning students as experts in the classroom.

Step 1: Provide Students with Opportunities to Explore Their Identities

Before students can recognize their expertise, they must identify who they are, what they know, when they act in certain ways, where they like to be, why they make the choices they do, and how they demonstrate to the world their individuality. Providing middle-school students the space and structures that allow them to make these identifications is a necessary first step. There are multiple ways to do this. Concept maps such as the one illustrated in Figure 5.1 can help students visualize how their attributes,

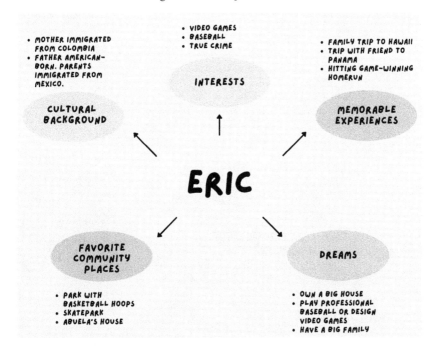

Figure 5.1 Concept maps such as this can be used to aid students in visualizing how their experiences, interests, and backgrounds make them unique individuals.

interests, experiences, and community interconnect to make them a unique individual. Traditional "I Am" poems (see Figure 5.2) can encourage students to pause and reflect upon different personal characteristics in a more structured way. Simply giving students time to brainstorm a bulleted list can help, too.

"Where I'm From"

I'm from the sunrises and sunsets in Morelia,
From enough sunshine and rain,
That could contain answers in the sky,
If you stare for hours.

I'm from a fierce mother,
And a vulnerable father.
Who carry four chicklings under their wings,
Until they're ready to fly on their own.

I'm from "ponte las pilas!" and "vete al huevó!"
While they screamed across the hall,
And as I learned what authoritative parenting is.

I'm from panaderias and fruterias,
Filled with different colors and flavors,
That opened a new culture around me,
And would once enchant me with wonder.

I'm from a diverse school,
Where students isolated themselves by ethnicity.
Where I learned the true definition of microaggressions
In my own classes.

I'm from diaries that could make a tower,
Filled with fragments of myself.
From small drawings and long paragraphs,
That I never wish to revise.

I'm from the books and movies I critique,
From the pauses and unpauses of scenes,
Wishing I could write or direct my own,
But knowing I have one life to complete.

~ Dulce Urueta Tapia

Figure 5.2 An example of a "Where I'm From" poem written by one of Michael's students.

Step 2: Assist Students in Researching and Selecting
Books that Connect to Their Lived Experiences

In a typical reading workshop, students are tasked with finding a book that interests them and given time to read the book in class. Teachers often support their efforts to find books by talking about titles they found interesting or they discovered while researching new titles or talking to students, colleagues, or friends. There is nothing inherently wrong with any of these practices. However, helping position students as experts requires students and educators to be more mindful of how they go about selecting and reading books. Rather than asking students to simply choose a book that looks interesting, have students return to their identity explorations and research books that have specific connections to them. As a teacher, read their identity explorations prior to the book selection process and locate books that connect to your students. Read excerpts from these books aloud. Provide students with links to book trailers. Pull these books from your shelves and put them on display around the room. Take students to the library after prepping the librarian with a list of identity markers and students' interests. Give them time to research on their own—and consider adding titles they discover to your classroom library. While you do this, be careful not to unintentionally reinforce limited notions of identity for students. While there is something incredibly profound and important in ensuring students have opportunities to read books that feature stories from their cultural world, we similarly do not want to foreclose on or assume that a certain identity position or racial, ethnic, or cultural background will translate to interest in a certain text. Rely on what your students tell you about who they are to guide them, not the suppositions we hold that may unintentionally and without malice limit their agency.

Once students have selected a book that embodies an aspect of their identities, have them write down their reasons for selecting the book. What specific aspects appear to connect to their lived experiences and/or interests? What do they know about this lived experience or interest prior to reading the book? Give them time to free-write. Let them discover their own expertise. Then, ask them to jot down a few questions they have prior to reading the book. What do they hope to learn? Convey to them that whether the book is fiction or nonfiction, we can always learn something about the world. Then give students time to read, prompting them to think about the questions they've asked, but not requiring them to answer those questions while reading. Help nurture the joy of reading through uninterrupted reading time.

Step 3: Create a Venue for Sharing Student Expertise and New Discoveries

Once students have finished reading their books, have them reflect upon what they learned about the experience or interest that initially drew them to the novel. What similarities and differences did they discover when considering their own lived experiences? How would they answer the questions they posed? What advice do they wish they could share with the characters in the book? What do they want to share with others in the community? Ask them to reflect upon these questions and any others that occur to them in a notebook or a digital journal. But don't stop at this reflection. Too often, students are asked to share their knowledge solely with the teacher. As we discussed in Chapter 3, sharing only with the teacher creates a teacher/student dichotomy rather than an inter-connected classroom. Creating a venue where students can share their discoveries about their books, as well as their own stories, can build the interconnectedness of the class-room, but it can also position students as experts on the book and their own lives.

As with almost any goal in the ELA classroom, this can be accomplished in multiple ways. We share two suggestions here. First, consider creating a class book blog and have students compose entries that summarize the book they read, but more importantly, that discuss the aspect of the book that drew them to it from their own lens of expertise. Have students practice writing skills that best apply to the purpose they have identified for the entry. Perhaps they want to critique the way the aspect is presented in the book—this provides an opportunity for them to read mentor texts and learn how to construct an effective critique. Perhaps they want to promote the book for its accurate reflection of the experience—here, students have an opportunity to learn about persua-sive techniques. The key here when we think about decolonizing the classroom is that students are the experts, not only on the book and accompanying experience, but also on the skills that are most important for them to learn at that moment. The most impor-tant aspect of a blog is that it shifts the audience away from the teacher and toward the broader community. Provide the rest of the class time to read the posts and comment or question in the comments section. This can create a community of readers who support each other. It can introduce other students to books they might also connect to or to books that allow them to learn more about others. Once the blog has been developed, consider asking the school and/or community librarian to link to it from their library websites, encouraging a broader audience to learn from students' expertise. And con-tinue building the blog throughout the year.

Another approach to sharing student expertise is to reimagine the concept of the living museum. Traditionally, living museums privilege the expertise of others (and can sometimes awkwardly position Global South figures, stories, and knowledge). In a social studies classroom, this often looks like students taking on the persona of a historical figure and presenting their research from that figure's perspective. In an ELA classroom, this might look like students assuming the persona of the author or a character in the book. One of the problems with this approach is that it forces students to make assump-tions. If visitors to the museum ask questions, students can only rely on what they know from the texts they read and their personal assumptions to answer the questions. Even if their answers are factual in nature, students still interpret them through the lens of their own experiences. However, if we reimagine the living museum and have students create displays that privilege their own expertise and experiences while sharing the novels they read, we reinforce the message that students are experts, as well. Further, encouraging students to acknowledge and identify ways that their perceptions and infer-ences may be limited humanizes others and helps students develop dispositions to resist colonial appropriation of knowledge. Displays can also be personalized so that students build an exhibit in a way that makes sense to them. They may bring in personal belongings, create original artwork, or compose writing to share. A living museum experience can build confidence in students as experts as they are able to engage in dialogue with community members about their experiences—and they don't have to make assumptions about others because they are telling the stories of their own lived experiences alongside the retelling of the novel.

Writing Instruction to Sustain Community Literacies

Research is an important part of writing, and research papers have long been featured assignments in ELA classrooms. Learning how to research is an important skill for students to develop. Students learn how to locate facts to support or disrupt opinions. They learn how to synthesize ideas from multiple sources. They learn how to uncover new ideas. For all these reasons and more, research can be a powerful force within the classroom. Yet, the power of research is often stifled in education where writing—and researching—tends to stay isolated in the classroom, with students relying upon online tools to research work written by outside experts. And in a system that had been built upon white expertise, more often than not the experts they consult and cite are white. For our students from marginalized communities, this continues to cement the internalization of the Other identity and way of Being, which can be particularly harmful at the early adolescent stage of development. Shifting research away from relying solely on online and print texts can help students value the expertise found in their communities. The following is one way teachers can reinforce the understanding that valuable research can be done within students' own communities.

Step 1: Center the Research Around Issues That Matter Within the Community

Decolonization requires an emphasis on community rather than the individual. Often in marginalized communities, others seek to define the community for them, which can result in a deficit-based view of the community. And when there is a deficit view, it is easy to dismiss the expertise of those who make up the community. Sustaining a community means researching and writing about communities in asset-based ways. It means that even when communities face challenges, community members identify ways their assets can help address these challenges. Decolonized classrooms work to leverage this kind of asset-based problem solving.

Start by helping students identify the assets and challenges within the community. By doing so, we situate the students as experts in their communities and assist them in locating the issues that need to be researched rather than giving them a topic. Again, this builds the interconnectedness of the classroom community while also shifting the notion of expertise away from the unknown Other. Ask students to start by identifying 15 assets and 15 challenges they see in their communities. This can be done together by taking a series of community walks as a class or it can be assigned as homework. Have students take photographs to capture their observations. Once students have individually collected their lists of assets and challenges, come together as a class to categorize and identify themes within their research. Listing and sorting helps students to learn how to synthesize their research. It also helps them to develop a research mindset that is used by qualitative researchers—that of pattern finding. Through discussion, work with students to narrow their ideas to one theme within the asset list and one theme within the challenge list. These themes will become the foundation of the research project.

Step 2: Identify Community Experts

Experts about a community can be—and should be—found within the community. Thus, rather than asking students to go online and research the asset and challenge the class identified, have each student identify at least one person in the community to interview about the asset and challenge. Think about ways the asset can be used to address the challenge. Work together, as a class, to develop a list of questions they hope to answer through their interviews. Once the questions have been compiled, brainstorm a list of experts within the community who can answer some or all of the questions. This list might include specific names of people that individual students know and it might include general categories such as professions, hobbies, or interests. For example, if the class has chosen to focus on community spaces such as a park or garden, some students may have friends or family members who are expert gardeners or who have spent quite a bit of time within those spaces. Their names can be added to the list. Then, the rest of the list might include city planners, greenhouse companies, or landscape designers. In the moment, students may not know the individuals who make up these categories, but the categories give them a place to start when trying to locate an individual.

Step 3: Create Time and Space for Interviews

Once you have developed your lists and students have identified who they want to interview, carve time into your schedule for those interviews. If possible, invite the community members into your classroom so that students can conduct the interview during the school day. If they are not available to come to the classroom, set up teleconferences through technologies like Zoom or Google Hangout that allow students to interview community members virtually. Make sure students video record their interviews to be reviewed and used by the rest of the class at a later date. By providing students time to conduct these interviews during class, you are recognizing that middle schoolers do not always have the means to reach experts in the community on their own time, but you are also demonstrating the importance of the research and affirming the expertise of the community.

Step 4: Develop a Plan for Bringing Students' Ideas Together

Through the collaborative research process, students should have a deep pool of information to pull from to create a final product that shares their discoveries. Rather than asking students to watch all of the interviews that were recorded, ask each student to provide a summary of the information they gleaned from the interview. In the summary, students should include key ideas, two to three quotes that stand out to them, and further questions the interview prompted within them. This approach can broaden their summary writing skills beyond a simple recounting of facts. Once students have written their summaries, share them with the rest of the class and work together to repeat the process of categorizing the information and finding themes across interviews. For example, they may discover that more than one expert helped to define the challenge, shared positive experiences within the space, and had ideas for creative solutions to the challenge. These themes can be used to structure and organize the final project.

The final project can take on many forms, depending upon the time and resources you have available to you. Here, we propose using the videos collected during the research process to develop a class documentary that shares the story of the community. Although a documentary is a lengthy process that will take considerable class time, developing a documentary allows for students to learn the standards that are expected as part of an ELA classroom while doing so in a meaningful way. To begin, use the themes identified during the class brainstorming session to divide the students into working groups. Each working group will focus only on one of the themes. Together, have the groups use a storyboard template to sketch out their portion of the video. While creating their storyboards, they can reference the videos the class has already collected and identify other videos that need to be collected. This additional video might include follow-up questions with previous interviewees, new questions to new experts, or simply video footage of their community. As they are planning, remind them to be mindful of how their portion of the video supports the telling of the story of the community's asset and challenge. Once students have completed their storyboard, ask them to write a script that can be used to narrate the film.

Step 5: Produce the Final Project

Once groups have developed their initial ideas, come together as a class to share their ideas. Discuss the sequencing. How will each part come together to create the whole? Co-develop an outline for the entire documentary and create a shared folder using a tool such as Google Drive or OneDrive where students can share their storyboards, scripts, and other content. Help students tweak their storyboards and scripts according to the class discussion and then have each group work to develop their portion of the documentary. Make sure to build in time before they start filming to practice with apps and tech tools so that students understand what they can and cannot do with the different tools.

While students are working on their documentaries, make sure to build in time for mini-lessons. Although students will be composing through images and sound, they will still need lessons around topics we typically see in writing instruction. Spend time helping students develop a title that is short and catchy. Prompt their thinking by asking questions such as: What is the purpose of my documentary? Are there any words or phrases surrounding this subject that would make a catchy title? Are there any symbolic words that represent the subject matter? Is there a quote or part of a quote from one of my interviews that would work as a title?

Introductions can be difficult for students, whether in writing or in film. This means that you will want to work with them to develop an introduction that will draw the audience into the documentary, as well as inform them what the documentary will be about. Make sure they identify the community challenge they will be addressing. Teach them how to pose a driving question that the documentary intends to answer and then prompt them to develop a one-sentence answer to their question. This will keep them focused as they not only develop the introduction, but also as they film the rest of the documentary. Help students identify their target audience and then consider what the audience needs to know in order to understand the main points in the film. And make sure they provide context about their communities in the opening scenes. Rewriting community narratives means that students need to highlight the expertise and assets of the community from the start. Similarly, you will want to demonstrate to students how to frame transitions so that they not only connect the ideas between scenes but so that they also reinforce the asset-oriented narrative they are composing.

In addition to structural support, you will want to help students identify other elements they may need to consider adding to their documentaries in order to help tell their stories. Ask them to consider aspects of the community they want to film to serve as a background while they narrate parts of the story. Prompt them to go back to their planning sheets and identify quotes and texts that help them make their points. Have them listen closely to each interview and determine if there are points where the audience would benefit from subtitles. Make sure they consider the role music and other sounds can play in setting the tone and telling the story. And if possible, consider bringing in community members to watch and critique, to mentor, to provide general support. The more the community is involved in the process, the better students can see that expertise permeates the community—it is not something that is just found in books and online spaces. The process of working with the community to identify problems, but more importantly to propose a solution, assists students in becoming experts themselves. This experience will position students to recognize the power of their own voices and stories.

Closing the Cultural Gaps Between Ourselves and Our Students

When we narrowly define whose expertise matters in the classroom, we widen the cultural gap between teachers and students, between students and students. This chasm has been described as ontological distance—the gap that exists between our identities and lived experiences of the world and those of our students (Domínguez, 2017). Positioning everyone as experts can help close this distance, but that means we must put mechanisms in place to discover expertise. Discovering expertise means that storytelling among the community—both within and outside of the classroom—must become the norm rather than the exception. The more we hear the stories of our students and their families and friends, the better we understand our students and the funds of knowledge (González et al., 2006; Vélez-Ibáñez & Greenberg, 1992) they bring to the classroom.

The tradition of storytelling has long been valued in Indigenous communities. By listening to stories, we learn about the perspectives and experiences of others, and we prepare our minds for new learning. Storytelling distributes expertise by shifting the narrative—whoever is telling the story is the expert in the moment. This makes book selection an important aspect of what we do. Who do we want our students to see as experts? Do we want them only to read novels by white authors, implicitly sending the message that these authors are the only experts that matter? Encouraging students to find stories that connect to parts of their identities allows students to value the expertise within themselves, and it also allows them to find experts they may not have discovered within traditional literature instruction. And while reading these stories is an important part of the ELA classroom, as well as their own identity development, listening to stories provides opportunities for even stronger cultural and community connections.

Creating the documentaries described in the previous section is one way to develop a culture of listening to stories. Producing documentaries privileges storytelling while also teaching students skills such as researching, organizing the story in a coherent way, and elaborating on ideas for the audience. These are important literacy skills for middle-school students to learn if we want them to be effective communicators. Documentaries, however, can take up a lot of time. There are other approaches to gathering stories that teach students about the value of listening to community experts and that can also prepare them for creating documentaries later in the year. One such approach has been inspired by the Human Library (humanlibrary.org), a project from Denmark that positions humans as books that can be checked out. Human books are storytellers willing to talk about their personal experiences so that readers can ask important questions and engage in dialogue about issues the participants may find uncomfortable. Teachers can recreate this experience by inviting community members to be books that are available for students (and ourselves) to check out, and can be intentional in their decolonial effort by making sure that the options and diversity of the living library you create challenges the centricity of white experience and perspectives. Human books, along with hours of general availability and methods of contacting them, can be listed on a class website for students to check out. This catalog of living stories provides students with people to go to when they have specific questions about a topic or when they are just curious and want to learn new things. And it reminds us of the knowledge and expertise that exists beyond ourselves.

If we want to continue to create a culture of distributed expertise, however, we can also build the library together with our students. Invite students to consider people in their lives who have stories to tell about topics such as discrimination, race, religion, sexual orientation, class, gender identity, lifestyle choices, disability, and any other aspect of life. Who do they know that have experiences that others can learn from? Who might be willing to share those stories? Work with students to identify these people and to develop questions that encourage the storytellers to share their stories. Ask students to record those interviews so that each recording can become a book for a digital human library. Students can provide summaries of their books, as well as key quotes, so that visitors to the library can select stories that they want to learn from. And while co-creating a human library teaches student curators about the value of listening to a single story, providing the rest of the class time to check out and 'read' stories from the library can provide opportunities for closing cultural gaps as the learning community regularly engages in the art of listening to stories.

After providing students with multiple opportunities to listen to and engage with the stories in the library, teachers can help students recognize the impact these stories have had on their understanding of the world by asking students to create an epiphany project. An epiphany project is one where students identify an 'a-ha!' moment, a moment of insight or discovery, that they had as a result of listening to one of the books. This project can be as big as a presentation or as small as a short reflection, but asking students to identify such a moment draws their attention to what they've learned and the new connections they've made. Providing students with time for reflections helps ensure the moments don't go unnoticed, increasing the likelihood that students will see the value in learning from others' stories.

These learning experiences challenge zero-point thinking by clarifying other cultures' knowledge systems through stories from the perspective of those with lived experiences rather than through a lens of whiteness. When we see what matters to humans with lived experiences that are different from our own, we begin to develop empathy and not sympathy. We expand our knowledge about the world, which can shift ideologies and nurture a classroom ecology that shifts our understanding of expertise by looking across people to understand that knowledge is not absolute. Rather, knowledge is shaped by lived experiences. And when we recognize that everyone's lived experience matters, it opens up the world of what counts as knowledge and who can be an expert.

Challenge in Practice

Mr North, a 6th-grade ELA teacher, has just ended the school year on a high note. Hired by his principal because of his student-centered pedagogy, Mr North spent the year continuing to refine his lesson designs. He made connections to the community and started a Human Library. Students used the library to help them identify areas within the community they wanted to further research. They started exploring video composition, creating short videos about their research, inspiring Mr North to work toward longer documentaries next year. And students were reading books written by authors representing a wide array of racial, cultural, gender, and sexual identity groups during their reading workshop time. Mr North is excited about how responsive his students were and eager to spend the summer planning for more approaches to decolonizing his classroom.

Despite his success with his students, Mr North has had to spend much of the year justifying his work to the district curriculum director. While his principal is supportive of his approach, the curriculum director keeps insisting that Mr North use textbooks and boxed curricula, which Mr North recognizes as perpetuating deficit-oriented teaching and colonized practices. So far, he has been successful in sustaining his efforts, but fears that the curriculum director may try to force him to use the materials she has selected. This fear is amplified when he learns that he is required to attend training on a new reading program purchased by the district—a training that will prevent him from attending the restorative practices training he had been excited to attend.

What are Mr North's options? How can he work to ensure that he can continue to teach students in ways that are responsive to them as humans?

Questions to Consider While Planning to Position Everyone as Experts

1 Where can you find fissures in your curriculum when faced with mandates that are not responsive to students' experiences and expertise? How can you embed responsive pedagogy even when you must teach using curriculum or practices that are not in students' best interests?

2 How can you build relationships with your administrators so they respect your expertise in your content, as well as your students?

3 How can you learn more about your community in order to discover expertise you can share with your students?

4 What will you do when you don't know the answers to all students' questions? How can you be comfortable with not knowing?

Resources to Explore

Sharing Expertise Through Storytelling

- Humans of New York was a photography project started in 2010 by Brandon Stanton. What started as a New York-based project has expanded around the world, connecting humans through story: https://www.humansofnewyork.com/

- As explained previously, the Human Library originated in Denmark in 2000 as a way to help people confront stereotypes. Visiting its online site can help students imagine what a Human Library might look like in a school setting: https://www.humansofnewyork.com/

- As of the writing of this book, the C-SPAN, a non-profit media outlet for public service, sponsors a yearly contest for student documentaries. Each year, the StudentCam competition posts a question designed to help students think critically about issues that impact society. Not only can their site provide mentor texts for student documentaries, but you may also consider having your students participate in the contest, giving them a platform to share their expertise: http://www.studentcam.org/

- The New York Film Academy offers tips for students who are interested in making films: https://www.nyfa.edu/student-resources/10-tips-for-making-more-polished-student-films/

Assessment Alternatives

Assessment is often something teachers do *to* students. We have specific goals for what students need to learn—goals set by our own beliefs, as well as through district curriculum and other policy mandates—and we design assessments to make sure that students have met our goals for them. Yet we know from our work in restorative practices that when we work *with* people, the positive impact is much greater. Students are more likely to be motivated to learn when they have a say about what they are learning, as well as how they are performing toward their goals.

One of the benefits of engaging students in personal goal setting is that this equips them with skills that will translate beyond the classroom. And it's an easy process to incorporate into language arts classrooms. Goals can be both short term and long term, with students setting weekly or unit goals, as well as semester- or year-long goals. Students can create short-term goals in collaboration with the teacher by examining the purposes of their units of study and identifying the skills, processes, and products that need to be developed to meet each purpose. For example, when creating a documentary, students might determine that the most compelling documentaries tell the story from a wide variety of perspectives, so they might set a goal of finding five people from various backgrounds to appear in their films. Because the students have set this goal themselves, they see the reason behind the goal and are more likely to strive toward reaching it. Goals can also be written more broadly. For example, students might look across their writing and determine that they need to expand their ability to invite people into their work, thus they might set a goal to work on their introductions. This could be a semester- or year-long goal that they look to each time they compose a new work, whether in writing or multimodally.

Providing students with the power to write their own goals respects them as experts in their own learning. It invites students to reflect upon their purposes for learning, the areas they feel confident in, and the areas they feel they need to continue to develop. Goal setting creates an iterative process where students are constantly examining their work through the lens of their goals. As a part of this process, students also refine their goals as they meet them or as they discover their goals didn't quite capture the work they needed to do. And when students are experts in their own learning, they are often better positioned to determine their progress in our class than we, as the teachers, are. This makes self-assessment a vital part of the learning ecology. Through self-assessment, students can make adjustments to their learning goals and provide input to teachers about the grade they have earned. Students can draw upon self-assessments to craft a grade justification that can guide teachers as they determine grades to report on progress reports and report cards. Not only do grade justifications position students as experts in their learning, they also teach students how to draw upon evidence to support their arguments and how to advocate for themselves as humans.

Technology Spotlight

Video composition is another way for students to share their expertise—and to capture the expertise in their communities. Fortunately, there are many free and inexpensive options available to students. If students have small projects that simply require uploading video and images, video creation tools like Adobe Express, Animoto, or Lumen 5 utilize drag-and-drop technologies, have an array of templates, and provide royalty-free music, making them easy for students to quickly start composing. For more sophisticated video composition, such as what might be required for projects like documentaries, Adobe Premiere Rush, iMovie, and WeVideo are current technologies that allow for layering of elements within a multi-track editing system. While these tools require more time to learn, once students get the hang of them, they can be powerful educational technologies.

References

Adichie, C. N. (2009, July). *The dangers of a single story* [Video]. TED Global 2009. https://www.ted.com/talks/chimamanda_ngozi_adichie_the_danger_of_a_single_story?language=en

Books-A-Million. (n.d.). *8th Grade Common Core Reading List for Middle School*. https://www.booksamillion.com/feature?cat=common-core68&oxdate=073013#

Domínguez, M. (2017). "Se Hace Puentes Al Andar": Decolonial teacher education as a needed bridge to culturally sustaining and revitalizing pedagogies. In D. Paris and H. S. Alim (Eds), *Culturally sustaining pedagogy: Teaching and learning for justice in a changing world* (pp. 225–245). Teachers College Press.

González, N., Moll, L. C., & Amanti, C. (Eds.). (2006). *Funds of knowledge: Theorizing practices in households, communities, and classrooms*. Routledge.

Maldonado-Torres, N. (2007). On the coloniality of being: Contributions to the development of a concept. *Cultural Studies*, *21*(2–3), 240–270.

Paris, D., & Alim, H. S. (2014). What are we seeking to sustain through culturally sustaining pedagogy? A loving critique forward. *Harvard Educational Review*, *84*(1), 85–100.

Vélez-Ibáñez, C. G., & Greenberg, J. B. (1992). Schooling processes among US Mexicans, Puerto Ricans, and Cubans: A comparative, distributive, and case study approach. In T. Weaver (Ed.), *Handbook of Hispanic Cultures in the United States: Anthropology*, 270–280. Arte Público Press.

6

DECOLONIZED CLASSROOMS...
ASK CHALLENGING QUESTIONS

Introduction

An Arapaho proverb states,

> If we wonder often, the gift of knowledge will come.

Yet the kinds of questions we often ask our students don't provide much space for students to wonder.

Several years ago, Robyn attended a national literacy conference where a middle level author was a featured speaker. Because the conference was largely populated by teachers, the conversation turned to how teachers could integrate her book into the classroom. Not surprisingly, given the emphasis on standardized reading programs, one popular computerized reading program came up. All these years later, the exact program escapes her, but she suspects it was Accelerated Reader, given its popularity at the time. But which program doesn't really matter because too many exist (of course, one is too many!). As she was talking, the author begged teachers not to reduce her book to this test. The richness of her characters, the intricacies of the plot, the complexities of the community, all were forgotten in the questions students were asked to answer. In fact, the questions on this particular text were so irrelevant to the story that she, the author who created the story, failed the quiz. It was a moment of realization for all of us—if these details were such inconsequential pieces of the story that the author couldn't recall them, was this a test of comprehension of text or compliance with what schooling wants us to do?

Challenging Reductive Knowledge

Reading programs like Accelerated Reader and Reading Counts are popular instructional approaches. These programs are used during independent reading and award points to students after they complete a reading quiz. On the surface, these programs seem to solve many of the challenges with reading instruction: they provide choice, which research shows to be motivating; they provide students with a task to complete at the end of each book, which can build accountability for unstructured time; and they provide data about the accuracy of students' answers, which can be construed as assessing comprehension. Unfortunately, reading isn't as simple as these programs make it seem.

DOI: 10.4324/9781003290681-8

One of the issues with these kinds of programs is the kinds of questions they ask. Rather than providing complex questions that truly assess deep understanding, these programs focus on small details within the text—functioning more as 'gotcha' questions than as true comprehension assessments.

Aside from the problematic questions these quizzes ask, we also find the books they are reading within the programs to be problematic when we consider decolonizing our classrooms. According to a custom report pulled from the Accelerated Reader website, of the 100 most popular books read in grades 6–8 across the United States, only 13 were written by BIPOC authors. And of these 13, only four were published in the last decade: *Ghost* by Jason Reynolds, *New Kid* by Jerry Craft, *The Crossover* by Kwame Alexander and *The Dragonet Prophecy* by Tui Sutherland. To be clear, the books on the list are not problematic. Instead, what *is* problematic is the lack of diverse representation on the list. This indicates that middle-school students are still widely exposed to literature by white authors, and that this lack of exposure (coloniality of knowledge) is further *institutionalized* by these popular programs. And more than that, they are being encouraged to see reading comprehension as a regurgitation of plot and character details. This reductive approach to what counts as knowledge is equally a part of coloniality, for it robs students of the ability to look, think, and analyze the texts they read and the world around them more deeply and critically. Providing students with books written by a diverse array of authors that present more contemporary problems gives students opportunities to wrestle with bigger questions—questions that not only help them develop the critical literacy skills needed for deep comprehension, but that also teach them about the world, cultures, and society. This chapter provides approaches for teaching students how to ask these kinds of questions while reading, as well as while writing and listening.

Reading Instruction to Get at Big Ideas

Developmentally, middle-school students are starting to see themselves as individuals, which means they are trying to figure out what sets them apart from others—while at the same time trying to fit in with their peers. This desire to figure out who they are and what they are interested in means that middle schoolers like choice. Choice is what makes programs like Accelerated Reader appealing, and it's why instructional strategies like reading workshop and literature circles are effective. Yet, there are benefits to having all students read the same book. If we stay away from the traditional reading quizzes at the end of each chapter and shift to using a common text to inspire inquiry, we can engage in rich discussions, connect to each other, and ask challenging questions that allow us to arrive at a deeper understanding of the world.

Step 1: Select a Book that Sparks Questions

We read for many reasons. Sometimes, it's to laugh or escape. And that's an important reason. It's one of the reasons reading workshops are so important—they nurture a love of reading. At times, we read for information and for new perspectives. As we have explored throughout the pages of this book, Indigenous communities recognize the power of learning about the world through storytelling. Reading a book together as a class can assist students in creating dialogue around and looking for answers to questions that hold meaning to them as citizens of the world. But this means that we must be very purposeful in the books we select for whole-class reading.

Books that spark questions often connect to students' lived experiences but provide new ways of thinking about those experiences. For example, students may engage with social media regularly outside school, which means that a book that focuses on the impact of bullying through social media might be a good choice because the book can connect to their lived experiences but also problematize how social media can be used—resulting in questions that can have a direct impact on students' lives. At times, however, the best questions arise when we identify books that address gaps in students' knowledge. It is in these spaces that we can build students' socio-cultural knowledge by exposing them to books that prompt questions around social issues and cultural practices. For example, students who live in the middle of the United States may know little about the realities of immigration. Introducing a book such as *Indivisible* by Daniel Aleman can prompt questions about the human impact of immigration policies students may have never considered before. Similarly, students who have largely lived in urban spaces might benefit from learning about the challenges faced in rural spaces like Appalachia through Jeff Zentner's book *In the Wild Light*. Selecting a book that doesn't provide answers, but rather prompts multiple avenues for questions is vital for helping students get at the big ideas that will deepen their comprehension about the book, but more importantly about the world.

Step 2: Design Experiences that Allow Students to Make Connections Between the Book and the World

Research (e.g., Bartlett, 1932) has long shown that the more connections we can make to our prior knowledge the more likely we are to retain our learning and the more deeply we understand our new learning. This means that as we design our instruction, we must build in opportunities for students to make connections as they are reading. Reading quizzes at the end of each chapter won't accomplish this goal. Rather, we should consider providing short supplemental non-fiction texts about topics within the book for students to connect to in some way—or better yet, have our students find those texts. We might think of ways to bring in community members to answer questions about questions raised in the book. We might offer approaches to making personal connections through activities such as journaling or blogging. We might create space for small-group conversations. There's no single way to approach this connection building—in fact, we encourage you to find three to four approaches for each novel study. The important thing to remember is to create experiences where *students* are making the connections for themselves. The teacher cannot make the connections for them or students will not learn how to work with ideas in texts in ways that will lead to the development of challenging questions.

Step 3: Assist Students in Developing Questions that Challenge Their and Others' Thinking

Colonized schooling has largely led to an abandonment of students' questions. Children who begin school full of curiosity quickly learn that school is not a place for their own questions. Rather, it's a place where they are expected to answer the questions that others find important. As a result, by the time they get to middle school, many of our students don't know *how* to ask questions. At times, they seem to lack curiosity. But this lack of curiosity is a facade meant for school. If you followed that same indifferent student home, you'd likely find them asking questions around their interests and hobbies, whether it's how to defeat a villain in a video game, which outfit will create the most impact at a party, or what's going to happen next in their favorite streaming series.

Often, students resist asking questions in school because they don't believe their questions will matter or they're afraid of the response their question might receive. This means that we, as teachers, must spend the time needed in class to assure them their questions will lead to a search for answers and that it's a safe space to ask all questions. It also means that we must assist our students in re-learning how to ask the questions that invite investigation. We cannot assume that they will know how to ask these questions. Instead, we must design mini-lessons and other experiences that allow them to explore the elements of questions that evoke multiple perspectives and to practice developing their own questions. For example, a mini-lesson on interrogative statements can be used to help students explore how different question statements produce different kinds of answers and knowledge. This helps them understand the ways that the framing of questions can lead to specific kinds of answers, to bias.

Once students feel comfortable asking questions, prompt students to use the ideas in the novel they studied, as well as in the accompanying learning experiences, to design questions they want to further explore. Give them the space to take the questions in whatever direction they choose. For example, if students were reading Zentner's *In the Wild Light*, they might have questions about the impact of poverty on opioid addiction, about inequalities in schooling opportunities, about how to cope with grief. It is important to let them take the lead rather than having a predisposed idea for what they will study. This ownership of their learning teaches them the value of questions and encourages them to continue to ask questions after leaving our classrooms.

Step 4: Allow Students to Discover Answers and Design a Product to Showcase Their Learning

As discussed previously, one of the reasons students abandon questions is because they have been taught in school that their questions don't matter. The KWL strategy that is often used in literature instruction often reinforces this idea because it asks them to identify what they want to learn but those questions often go unanswered as the unit follows the teacher-designed path, regardless of what students had indicated curiosity about. For students to believe that their questions matter, time must be built into the curriculum for students to explore their own answers and teachers must be willing to change their plans to follow their students' lead. As teachers, we can guide students toward resources that will assist them in their searches by showing them how to use research databases, how to better utilize internet search engines, and how to identify individuals in the community who they can reach out to for interviews. We can also model for them the iterative process of questioning—how answers to one question often lead to many more questions. And importantly we can show them that their questions matter by actively including them in our instruction even if that means scrapping what we had planned. In teaching them about the complexity of finding answers, we deepen their learning around ideas.

Although one of the important lessons of asking challenging questions is that the cycle of questioning is never truly complete, it is also important to help students identify when they've done enough exploration and are ready to share their new understandings with the world. Again, when possible, it is important to provide students with the opportunity to determine how they want to share their knowledge. By allowing students to determine the best product, they can engage in audience identification, as well as their purpose for sharing. Do they want to inform, persuade, or even just entertain others? Do they want to share their learning within the class community as something to build upon, with the school community as something to shape the school culture, with their local community as a way to spread new ideas, or even with the world community as a way to promote social change? When they know their audience and purpose, students can determine the product they want to create to accomplish their goals. Seeing the transformation of their questions to products to be shared with a larger audience reaffirms to students that they are the experts in their learning and that their expertise matters.

Writing Instruction to Engage with the World

Writing is a form of thinking. It is a form of questioning. In its beginning stages, whether in its traditional form of words on a page or in less traditional forms that integrate other modalities such as images and sounds, writing requires us to sift through the possibilities by asking ourselves questions such as *what if?* What if we focus on a specific topic? What if we shift our audience? What if we try a different genre? Before we put the words, images, and sounds together in a cohesive product, we are brainstorming possibilities, and if we limit our wonderings to the singular audience of the teacher, we limit the questions our students will ask themselves, and in turn, we will limit their potential solutions. When we widen the landscape of possibilities by expanding our audience, we also invite students to deepen their questions as they draft their ideas. Writing to a known entity such as the teacher leaves less room for questioning. Students tend to know teacher expectations through verbal interactions, written rubrics, and previous experiences. Writing for a wider, more authentic, audience forces students to consider the expectations, experiences, and interests of their audience. It requires them to consider how their ideas will be received as they are drafting, often causing them to shift their thinking during the process.

Limiting students' audience to the teacher also prevents them from learning how to engage through writing with others. And it is through engaging with others that we begin to break down the barriers that have been put in place through colonization. Engaging with others through writing means more than getting feedback while drafting and revising. It means that students have opportunities to publish their writing to the larger world, demonstrating the power of writing to shape ideas and thinking. Posing provocative questions and solutions to an authentic audience allows students to engage productively with society around social and cultural dilemmas and divisions. Productive engagements can break down barriers, can create fissures in foundations, can impact systems. Composing op-eds, opinion pieces that are published in newspapers and magazines, is one way we can use writing instruction to demonstrate to students the power of posing challenging questions to the larger world.

Step 1: Assist Students in Selecting Social or Cultural Dilemmas They Care About

Middle-school students are beginning to become more aware of the world around them. Family values, community experiences, cultural traditions, social media, and popular culture are just a few of the spheres of influence that are shaping their identities. At times, there are so many different competing interests that students are not exactly sure where to start when identifying an issue they feel passionate about. Strategies that allow students to sift through their experiences and values can assist them in getting started. If you have students explore their identities as described in Chapter 5, students can pull from those explorations here, as well. You can also provide students with time to explore current events and issues that are commanding people's attention. This can be done by having students explore a variety of media outlets using the Ad Fontes Media Bias Chart (https://adfontesmedia.com/), which will provide them with multiple perspectives around issues while also educating them about media bias and factual reporting. In Chapter 7, we suggest another strategy—building radical consensus—that can work as an excellent iteration, or precursor, to this step and lead students into the rest of this task with complex and humanizing perspectives on the things that matter to them and others in their community.

Step 2: Structure Experiences that Allow Students to Explore Different Perspectives Around Their Self-Selected Causes

Writing informed opinions pieces means that students need to have an awareness of the varying perspectives around a topic, as well as how words can be used to imply positive and negative meaning. When students first begin to explore the complexities around issues, they will often be tempted to seek out the sources and ideas they already know. Helping them reach beyond perspectives they are comfortable with and examine perspectives that might make them uncomfortable is an important part of educating our students. This doesn't mean that we are trying to tell students how to feel about an issue, but rather that we are asking them to consider multiple sides in order to frame their own opinions. Gathering stories is an important part of discovering new perspectives, and we offer multiple ways to collect stories throughout this book. Here, we offer an approach that can be used alongside the Ad Fontes Media Chart.

To begin, teach students about the difference between denotation and connotation and explore how words that may have similar meanings can convey completely different messages. Brainstorm example pairings so that students can get a sense of how language is used to shape perspectives. For example, if we say that we bought inexpensive souvenirs at the amusement park, we think of small items like cups or magnets that can be used to capture our memories at the park. This paints a positive picture. However, if we say that our friends brought us cheap souvenirs, the image in our heads is of something made up of flimsy materials and not worth buying. This creates a negative message. And yet, if we look up both words in a thesaurus, we'd see them side by side. It's important for students to pay attention to word choice when they read messages, and when they consider how they are composing their own messages.

Once students have identified the issue they want to explore, prompt them to return to the chart and identify three to six news outlets that range across the chart. This chart identifies ideologies of media outlets, as well as their use of facts versus opinion. By starting with a minimum of three outlets, students can examine the issue from the perspective of an outlet on the left, the right, and in the middle. Adding more outlets can prompt them to look at more than one outlet across the spectrum. After students have identified the media outlets to explore, have them search for stories that pertain to their identified social or cultural dilemma and select one from each outlet. Then, have them read through each article, noting the different perspectives, as well as the way the language works to convey positive, negative, and neutral denotations. Consider creating an organizer where students can document different words and phrases that help structure the message, as well the ideas, facts, and details that support the arguments being made around the issue.

Step 3: Help Students Identify a Target Audience and Venue

Examining the messages about their selected topics across media outlets will help students formulate their own opinions about the issue. While students may not know exactly what they want to say about the issue right away, this exploration will likely help them identify who they want to speak to. Assist them in articulating who their audience might be, who needs to hear the messages they want to convey around the issue. Remind them that their voice matters. It's often adults who frame conversations around topics that will ultimately have a greater impact on youth. So taking the time to consider their audience is essential to making change.

Determining the audience also means that students must consider the best venue for their op-ed. While some of the outlets they researched might be viable options, it is often more difficult to be published in larger publications. Thus, it is important to also consider more local outlets. Students can also research online publications or blogs that accept opinion pieces. At times, there will be platforms that actively seek out youth writing, so encourage students to research those options as well. As they are researching, remind them to consider their target audience and whether or not they are likely to reach that audience through the outlets they are exploring. Once students have a venue in mind, they can begin analyzing op-eds published in that venue, which can guide them as they construct their own.

Step 4: Work with Students to Develop Thought-Provoking Questions

Writing op-eds means that we frame arguments that attempt to convince our audience to make a change, whether it's rethinking their positions on an issue or prompting them toward a specific action. Developing thought-provoking questions can assist students in searching for answers that help them develop arguments that provide unique perspectives, and building these op-eds from consensus-building activities (see Chapter 7) can be an excellent way to ensure this happens. Further, thought-provoking questions can also be integrated into their writing, prompting their readers to consider the issue in new ways. When we begin to see issues in different ways, we are often more open to hearing arguments when they are presented to us.

Often, students' questions will start very literally, and they will need assistance in developing questions that prompt them to think in new ways. We often return to speculating around the question, *what if?* Here, as with other learning experiences, providing students with prompts that encourage them to explore *what if?* can help them begin to engage in thinking that encourages the development of thought-provoking questions. You might start by showing them two seemingly disparate pictures and ask them to consider what would happen if the two images were part of the same story. We have found that games like Dixit or The Detective Club have cards that feature beautiful artwork that can engage students in this kind of thinking. Give them time to brainstorm ways to connect different cards. This can be done through writing or simply through shared storytelling. Once students have had the opportunity to speculate connections, work with them to ask questions that can connect their own topic to items or ideas that seem to be disconnected at first glance.

Step 5: Facilitate the Writing of the Op-Ed Pieces

Using the mentor texts that students identified when looking for their venue and the questions they posed to guide their thinking, students can begin crafting their op-eds. Like any writing piece, op-eds need a hook to draw readers into the article, an argument that guides their decision making, evidence to back up their arguments, and a conclusion that provides something for the reader to think about. In op-eds, the conclusion also provides a call to action. It is also important to demonstrate to students the importance of acknowledging opposite views about the issue and providing counterarguments. Depending upon their writing experiences, it is likely that you will need to provide mini-lessons to help them effectively craft their arguments. Let their needs guide you as you determine the kinds of supports you should offer. It is also important to provide time for the entire writing process including drafting, feedback, revisions, and edits.

Step 6: Send the Pieces to the Targeted Venue

An op-ed has no impact if it is simply shared with the teacher or even the class. Publishing, or at least submitting writing, in public spaces demonstrates to students the power of our voices. Once students have completed their op-ed articles, demonstrate how to submit them to their target outlets. This will also allow you to demonstrate how to write an email or cover letter that summarizes their work for an editor. Having students submit the pieces on their own teaches them how to advocate for their own work rather than having others do it for them. Make sure before they submit, however, that you obtain their parents' or guardians' permission.

Making Classroom Literacy Consequential

Making literacy consequential means demonstrating to students the importance of asking challenging questions. While questioning might lead to inquiry and guide students toward researching questions that matter to them, it is also important for students to ask questions that challenge the texts they encounter. Incorporating critical media literacy into your curriculum can help students learn the questions to ask. Doug Kellner and Jeff Share (2019) have spent years researching and developing theories of critical media literacy, resulting in a framework that draws from multiple theories to guide teachers and students toward six questions to ask about media texts:

1 Recognizing that knowledge is socially constructed, the first question to ask is **WHO** are all the possible people who made choices that helped create this text?

2 Knowing that all texts are constructed of language with specific rules of grammar and semantics, we next should ask **HOW** was this text constructed and delivered/accessed?

3 Understanding that different audiences receive messages differently, we must ask **HOW** could this text be understood differently?

4 Realizing that all messages and mediums have biases that either support or challenge belief systems and power structures, it is important to ask **WHAT** values, points of view, and ideologies are represented or missing from this text or influenced by the medium?

5 Acknowledging that all texts have a purpose, we must ask **WHY** was this text created and/or shared?

6 Accepting that media messages are never neutral, we are obligated to ask **WHOM** does this text advantage and/or disadvantage?

Teaching students to ask these questions when they encounter new texts helps them become skeptical consumers. When we are skeptical consumers, we are more likely to recognize messages that perpetuate colonizing practices, and when we recognize those ideas, we are more apt to explore alternate practices that are inclusive of all our students.

All texts—whether written, audio, video, or still images—can be approached through a critical media literacy stance. In fact, we advocate for introducing critical media literacy early in the academic year so that students begin to get into the habit of reading (and creating) texts through this lens. Reading instruction, whether through literature circles, whole-class novels, or reading workshop, can thread these questions throughout the unit. Students can have these questions in front of them when they are researching topics of interest, using them to guide their selection of sources, whether they are found online or they are people they interview. Critical media literacy can also be an effective approach to listening instruction.

Podcasts can provide texts that engage students in sustained listening, a skill that is often neglected in language arts classrooms. Through podcasts, particularly those that are serial in nature, students can engage in problem solving and reflection. For example, true crime podcasts like *Serial* that attempt to solve a crime by providing new evidence across episodes can encourage students to track the evidence and form hypotheses about the crime. One approach is to collect evidence as a class on an evidence board and have students develop arguments about who perpetrated the crime using evidence from the podcast. The questions from Kellner and Share's framework can help students uncover biases in not only the podcast itself, but also within the investigation.

Podcasts can also serve as powerful texts that challenge existing power structures and prompt students to ask difficult questions about society and its values. Through podcasts, students can learn how to frame difficult questions because podcasts are often created around questions that challenge social norms. For example, the podcast *Sounds Like Hate* from the Southern Poverty Law Center asks why everyday people become involved in extremism and how we can help disengage them from hatred. National Public Radio (NPR) hosts multiple podcasts that focus on different aspects of social life, including *Code Switch*, which examines how race impacts society, and *Caught*, which explores the mass incarceration of youth. The series *This American Life*, which has been broadcast since 1995—before podcasts became a staple text for millions of people— brings together stories around different themes each week, providing a rich resource from which to draw questions.

Kellner and Share's critical media literacy framework provides students with the questions to start their exploration. The six questions help students begin to consider the humans behind the creation of texts and how humans—through texts—perpetuate or challenge colonizing systems. Podcasts can model ways to explore challenging questions by demonstrating how to consider multiple perspectives around a theme and how to continue to develop new questions as you uncover the answers to your original questions, as well as new information. By engaging students in this kind of questioning, literacy becomes consequential because students learn how to ask the questions that shape what we value in society, as well as the questions that can move us toward change.

Challenge in Practice

Mx Johnson teaches 7th-grade ELA in a small rural school. Seeking to diversify their students' understanding of different cultures, they have chosen a book written by an Indigenous author featuring an Indigenous protagonist. The book blends elements of fantasy and Indigenous myths to create a mystery the main character must solve. Despite their excitement about the book, Mx Johnson is worried that their students may not give it a chance because the students' previous experiences reading about Indigenous Peoples is limited to their history textbooks, which paint a very flat and unflattering picture of Indigenous communities. They also noted that several students seem disinterested in reading anything, so they want to design their lessons to help students be accountable to the reading.

As a part of their lesson design, Mx Johnson developed reading quizzes for students to take every two to three days to demonstrate they were keeping up on their reading. Mx Johnson feels these quizzes will help bolster students' grades because they ask questions about characters and plot that should be easy to answer if students completed the reading assignments. In addition, Mx Johnson developed a series of questions to guide student discussions. On Friday, Mx Johnson is excited to hold the first discussion about the book. They post the questions on the board so students can see them and then proceed to ask each question one by one. Mx Johnson is quickly disappointed by their students' lackluster participation. Only a few students raise their hands when Mx Johnson asks the questions and the rest of the class seems bored and disinterested. To make matters worse, as Mx Johnson grades the reading quizzes at the end of the day, they discover that many students do not seem to be reading the book. They're not sure what to do to get students to read the book. They're sure that once they get into the story, they'll really enjoy it.

What are Mx Johnson's options? What might they have done differently to prevent this outcome?

Questions to Consider While Planning for Challenging Questions

1   How can you design a reading experience that motivates students to read because they are curious rather than because they are told to read?
2   How can you create classroom experiences that privilege students' questions rather than teachers' questions?
3   What resources do you need to help students develop their questioning skills? How can you scaffold their questions so that they challenge preconceived ideas?

Resources to Explore

Supporting Students' Development of Challenging Questions

Although children begin school as curious beings, the structure of schooling often strips them of their curiosity and leaves them looking for questions that have simple, correct answers. Thus, asking meaningful questions does not always come naturally to middle-school students. As teachers, we can design activities to spark students' curiosities and help them rediscover their ability to wonder and ask questions. The following resources can assist with these goals:

- The Right Question Institute (https://rightquestion.org/) focuses on assisting people across ages and experiences to develop better and more effective questions. They have developed the Question Formulation Technique as a concrete way to help teachers and students (or anyone) develop their divergent and convergent questioning skills.
- Project Zero from the Harvard Graduate School of Education developed a Thinking Routines Toolbox that provides ways to scaffold and support student thinking. When students become more aware of their thinking and how to think differently, questions will naturally emerge: http://www.pz.harvard.edu/thinking-routines.
- Through discussion, students begin to engage with each other and pose questions. When listening to other perspectives, students have opportunities to challenge each other's thinking. Discussions do not always happen naturally, so discussion protocols

can assist students in developing their conversational skills. The National School Reform Faculty has collected, refined, and created more than 200 protocols that teachers can adapt for use with their students: https://nsrfharmony.org/protocols/.

- In "How to Cultivate Curiosity in Your Classroom," Amy L. Eva of the Greater Good Science Center at the University of California, Berkeley, shares dimensions and types of curiosity, as well as ways to encourage curiosity in the classroom: https://greatergood.berkeley.edu/article/item/how_to_cultivate_curiosity_in_your_classroom

Assessment Alternatives

As we've discussed throughout this chapter, teaching students how to ask meaningful questions is a process that needs to be scaffolded. There will be a lot of trial and error as students practice forming questions, so normalizing the idea that developing questions—and learning, in general,—is a process that includes taking risks and experiencing failure is vital if we want to develop this skill in students. This means that we cannot attach grades to students' questions. The moment we attach grades to their questions, they will fall back into a routine of writing questions for the teacher and not for themselves. That does not mean that we shouldn't build in some form of assessment of their questions—if we don't, they will never learn how to dig deeper and form the questions needed to challenge systems. Building in purposeful approaches that encourage students to respond to each other's questions and that encourage self-reflection around their questions can accomplish this goal.

Several strategies exist that can assist students in formulating and assessing questions. In their book *Hacking Project Based Learning: 10 Easy Steps to PBL and Inquiry in the Classroom*, Ross Cooper and Erin Murphy describe question carousels as a way to push students toward asking questions about topics that they don't know the answers to. Conducted in three rounds, groups of students work together to formulate questions and then identify the best of the questions. In the first round, groups identify a problem or idea they want to explore and write it on a piece of chart paper. The groups then rotate so that they are examining a different group's topic. Students are given an extended amount of time to write as many questions as they can about the topic. It's important to give them plenty of time because this encourages them to keep digging once the easy questions have been posed. For the third round, groups rotate to a new paper. Here, they examine the questions the previous group posed and identify the critical questions. Which questions will best assist the group in exploring their problem or idea? After identifying the critical questions, the original group starts their research with the critical questions as their guide.

Similarly, the Question Formulation Technique (QFT) described in the previous section takes students through a series of steps to develop and refine a series of questions and then prompts them to prioritize the questions that will best assist them in their work. This approach, unlike the question carousel, prompts self-assessment of questions rather than peer assessment. Project Zero has also developed the Creative Question Starts protocol to help students identify important questions. It merges the self-assessment of QFT with the peer assessment of question carousels by having students brainstorm a series of questions using question stems and then identifying one question they would like to discuss with the rest of the group. This approach helps students begin to self-identify their strongest, most interesting questions, but then work together with peers to continue to develop the question—or to spawn more questions. In addition, the final step of this protocol encourages students to reflect upon what they learned from the group after discussing the question, further strengthening their understanding of the impact of good questions.

While these approaches might not be considered traditional assessment, they can be more powerful than what students typically experience during formative assessments because they teach students skills that can translate globally, while also providing them feedback. Consistently engaging with students around these types of self- and peer assessment will strengthen their questioning ability. And strengthening their questioning ability will result in stronger, more meaningful work in other aspects of the class.

Technology Spotlight

Currently, technologies like Kahoot! and Blooket that encourage game-style questioning are popular in classrooms. While these technologies may be fun, they encourage surface-level questioning, as well as competition that can actually harm students' learning by making them more reluctant to take risks. This is particularly true for quiet students. There are, however, technologies that do encourage students to ask deeper questions and help students who tend to be quiet have a voice. Backchanneling uses instant messaging technologies like the stream in Google Classroom, Padlet, or Yo Teach! to encourage students to engage in conversation and ask questions about information happening in the front channel. The front channel is any type of live information such as a speaker, a video, or even a small-group discussion. Using a backchannel, students can capture their thinking in the moment and ask questions that clarify, connect, or even challenge the ideas being presented to them. Through backchanneling, students learn that questioning and thinking never stop, which encourages them to be more mindful of their questions as they occur.

References

Aleman, D. (2021). *Indivisible*. Little, Brown Books for Young Readers.

Alexander, K. (2014). *The crossover*. Houghton Mifflin Harcourt.

Bartlett, F. C. (1932). *Remembering: A study in experimental and social psychology*. Cambridge University Press.

Cooper, R., & Murphy, E. (2016). *Hacking project based learning: 10 easy steps to PBL and inquiry in the classroom*. Times 10 Publications.

Craft, J. (2019). *New Kid*. Quill Tree Books.

Eva, A. L. (2018, September 25). *How to cultivate curiosity in your classroom*. Greater Good Magazine. https://greatergood.berkeley.edu/article/item/how_to_cultivate_curiosity_in_your_classroom

Kellner, D., & Share, J. (2019). *The critical media literacy guide: Engaging media & transforming education*. Brill.

Reynolds, J. (2016). *Ghost*. Atheneum Books.

Sutherland, T. T. (2012). *The dragonet prophecy*. Scholastic.

Zentner, J. (2021). *In the wild light*. Crown Books.

7

DECOLONIZED CLASSROOMS...
DISRUPT NORMAL

Introduction

Maya Angelou once said,

> If you are always trying to be normal, you will never know how amazing you can be.

Yet too often, we cling to the comfort and familiarity of the normal when we design instruction—even when we think we are trying new things.

A while back, Michael was supporting a 7th-grade humanities course where the educator, a very committed advocate for marginalized students, had set out to design a year that added a decolonial spin to her course, infusing her curriculum with perspectives, messaging, and supplementary materials that challenged a Eurocentric world history narrative and asking students to think critically about marginalization in history and stories. The trick was, this intentionality was not necessarily filtering down to the students. Why? The answer was fairly clear if we looked at what that shake-up of curriculum and praxis *had* impacted, and what it had *not*.

For instance, one day we were meant to be exploring some content related to meso-American civilization and cultural achievements. Victoria, a Chicana student in the class, was exactly the student that a lesson like this could have been incredibly exciting for. It was an opportunity for her to see her own history and cultural practices in a new light and to locate herself as part of a tradition of historical actors with agency and vision. Yet nothing we did during this unit offered this to Victoria because rather than explore compelling questions or inquiries around this content, she spent several days in a row taking structured Cornell notes on the material, individually and quietly, before taking another two days to put together slides for a formulaic Google presentation that was collectively submitted by her table-group, using one-to-one computers. For her component of the presentation, she just picked a random fact to explore, as she had for every unit prior, and collaborated only by adding her information to the Google Doc shared with other students, but never actually interreacting with them at all. In conversation, Michael struggled to get Victoria to identify anything from the texts they were studying—even where there were explicit connections to her own cultural world and local Chicanx histories—that she found compelling. In her words, she was just, "gonna do this chapter, then the next one, then the next, and get my points."

DOI: 10.4324/9781003290681-9

Even though Victoria had been presented with critical, diverse, and compelling materials and content, any real substance or decolonial potential had been drained from it as it had been placed back into the normal rhythms, practices, and routines of schooling and teaching. Nothing changed here from *the way school had always been done*, and the way it had always been done *never worked* for students like Victoria. Changing the cultural contents (what is in our curriculum) does nothing to move us towards decolonization if we keep doing things (our pedagogy and practices) normally in the same ways that coloniality has dictated for our schools to work for years.

A New Way to Think of the Banking Method

Something we have seen endlessly in our work as teachers and teacher educators is the use or reading of, specifically, Chapter 2 of Paulo Freire's (2009) *Pedagogy of the Oppressed*—that's the chapter where he talks about and famously introduces the idea of the banking method, or the notion that in oppressive and colonial schooling situations, teachers control knowledge, and "bank" it into students in a one-way transaction, thereby replicating the dominant narratives of colonial society. It is an important and revolutionary idea that speaks to the importance of disrupting the patterns of knowledge presented to students. But this chapter is, more than likely, also the only Freire text/chapter that most teachers see. As a result, we end up with a less than complete understanding of the banking method, and really of Freire as a whole.

Specifically, we worry that in a landscape in which efforts towards diversity, equity, and inclusion (DEI) are increasingly institutionalized as administrative imperatives and messaged as simply questions of representation (e.g., #diversetexts), or multicultural (and even sometimes decolonial) *content*, the core message that flows through the rest of Freire's work is missed. You see, Freire's banking method is not just about the content of the curriculum, but about our cultural practices and relationality. Disrupting the normalcy of the banking method is not just about switching to a new body of content knowledge from a new diverse, critical, representative, or even decolonized perspective. It is about shaking up our core assumptions about how we do things in the classroom, and, particularly, how we might relate to one another in ways that move past an adversarial, dehumanizing, and colonial conception of other people (either oppressed or oppressor) as Others. Humanization and critical engagement with all content is central for Freire.

We, of course, are not suggesting that we DON'T need to diversify our texts or work to shake up the terrifying Eurocentrism of the curriculum. Instead, we want to ensure that we point out that challenging what is considered 'normal' *practice* for how we organize learning and relating to one another in the classroom is just as important— maybe even a little bit more so—because schools have operated in much the same way as they do today for literally generations. That sense of normalcy, of expecting—both as a teacher and student—a school and a classroom to work logistically and relationally in much the same way as it has since the 1930s and 1940s is a reflection of all three dimensions of coloniality: knowledge, being, and power. It is why our classrooms are designed the way they are. It is why most textbooks are written and structured the way they are.

It is why our schedules and school years are broken down the way they are. And it is why our go-to practices and the interactions they invite (for instance, Cornell notes or a structured presentation that consistently repeats every unit) likely look very similar, if not identical, to the tasks that we did ourselves in school. Normal is historically embedded, reinforced, and comfortable. It is easy to fall back into normal because it feels safe and familiar both to teacher and student, even as it might make us miserable. But we do not know anything else, and the unknown of alternatives can be terrifying.

But normal is not going to move us towards decolonization. If coloniality is the norm, disrupting it necessarily means doing something different, and simply swapping in a more diverse set of content readings is not enough. We need to imagine how we can conceptualize and organize our classrooms in ways that rethink Eurocentric knowledge, but also colonial relationships, ways of being, and interpersonal power dynamics. Here, we offer a few examples of different approaches to literacy skills, so that whether you are in a position to make big changes or to just navigate in tight spaces and make small ones, you can envision how to challenge the colonial normal.

Reading and Speaking Instruction to Build Radical Consensus

One of the time-honored, normal, tasks we take up in literacy classrooms is the debate. This can vary from a somewhat informal challenge of taking and defending a position to actually encouraging students to engage in formal, rhetorical debate as it is practiced in debate clubs and by debate teams. In our experience, we see teachers using this as a way to invite students to more authentically, or at least excitedly, engage with informational and non-fiction texts and materials or to develop media literacy skills.

Here is the trick, though: there is something deeply colonial about a debate and the central premise of this practice, which is to defeat the ideas, values, and commitments held by another position. Debate as an exercise in taking and defending a position ultimately becomes less about understanding a complex dilemma in the world and its many sides and more about the competitive aspect. In cases where students are simply taking random positions on topics (like the old, painful classic, Pro/Con: School uniforms are a good idea), we diminish the importance of holistic and reflective learning and incentivize doing and saying whatever is necessary to win. Worse yet, in cases where we are asking students to debate or defend issues on which they have a personal stance (for instance, debating perspectives on immigration), we are encouraging them to deepen their existing position and intolerance of counter-ideas as a literal exercise in public defense. In an absolutely worst-case scenario, we force students for whom these issues are existential and personal into positions where they are either forced for a grade to argue against their sincerely held moral beliefs or put in a space where they and other students are arguing over their right to exist. We implore you: please, never place students in these positions, and never create a scenario where identities that may or may not be present in your classroom are 'up for debate.' No one should ever have to feel as if their right to exist is in question, especially not in their school classroom.

Essentially, debate does not solve problems or teach how to engage with them. It encourages us to remain in the normalized, colonial relational pattern of seeing the world in zero-sum, adversarial, Us/Them terms. This division is a core element of the coloniality of knowledge, because an Us/Them world is one that rewards and reinforces the colonial notion that someone must always win at the expense and loss of others. It normalizes oppression and marginalization as a by-product of how society *must* work. Yet this is not the only way to be. Indigenous and Global South thinking does not follow this zero-sum approach to solving problems and coexisting in a diverse society. Rather, in other thought traditions outside Western coloniality, the emphasis is on building consensus, not winning the argument. So how can we do that as we read informational, non-fiction texts, and do away with the Us/Them logic normalized in debates? We think that a great way is to, essentially, get a little weird with it, and shake up—with great intentionality—how we think about reading about and discussing social challenges and dilemmas. We call this consensus building.

Step 1: Identify Tensions and Contradictions, Not Areas of 'Debate'

Right from the start, move away from the normal ways we often understand and read about social issues and problems. Imagine you have selected a core text, informational or otherwise, that raises a compelling social dilemma for consideration. For the remainder of this unit, you want students to build towards an exploration of this social dilemma, drawing on other informational texts you have found related to the topic/issue and, perhaps, conducting some outside research to develop their media literacy skills. Rather than approaching even the initial examination of the topic/issue as one of identifying the 'positions' (i.e., 'sides') of the debate around it, have them work to identify the tensions and contradictions that relate to the topic: What reasons make this such a challenging problem to solve? What different concerns are in tension with one another? What contradictions in our social world does this point or connect to?

This may not be easy, but by identifying the different tensions and contradictions in the topic, not as fixed locations, but as issues that need to be resolved, we shake up the normal way youth approach and frame social issues and problems that they observe in their lives. We find Alan Luke's (2017) Four Resources model approach to reading to be an excellent way to help structure such resource collection—helping students ask the right types of questions about texts and media to prime them for honest, solution-oriented conversations later.

Step 2: Explore Shared and Divergent Values and Beliefs

Now that you and your students have explored the points of tension and contradiction around a social dilemma, you can start to do some of the deeper analysis around these dilemmas and ideas in order to position them as part of a community challenge and collective endeavor. We like to start by asking students to create a list of shared values around a particular contentious issue. What are beliefs and values around this thing that anyone with a respect for community and humanity would agree to? That might appear challenging in our polarized world and climate, and it might seem that it would yield a very short list (and in some cases it might), but we think you will be surprised to find that in many cases we can derive quite a few shared, core values. Indeed, we have dilemmas because we have shared values that possess a variety of solutions, tensions, and positions. This process is crucial because it reinforces our shared humanity and the collective aspect of the task any time we come face to face with a dilemma. On a literacy level, it also encourages analysis and deductive reasoning as we tease apart the core values that exist and produce competing perspectives on social tensions.

Once you've got your list of shared values, you can turn your attention to those that are not shared. What are values, beliefs, or concerns that are pressing for only one constituency involved? Build out these lists as well, ensuring that as you do so, you are engaged in analysis and reflection on the roots and rationale for those differing values. Read texts and engage in analysis that tries to fully understand the logic, needs, and desires behind a value that exists for only one constituency (one 'side') involved in a dilemma. We want to frame this task not as a task of figuring out which side has the longest or best list, but rather as an exploration, a process of fully understanding why different people and perspectives feel the ways they do.

Step 3: Set Up the Challenge and Seek Out Resources

With the social dilemma and landscape of values set out before you, you are ready to dig into the research and media literacy work that often accompanies the examination of social dilemmas in informational texts. Ensuring we get away from the normal starts with how we lay out the challenge for students as they begin their inquiries. The challenge you want to set for students is not for them to determine which position is best (a debate), but rather, to explore perspectives on the issue and determine a solution that meets the needs and respects the interests of as many of the values you have identified on all sides of the dilemma as possible. Essentially, rather than competing to see who can dismiss other arguments most effectively in favor of their own, the goal is to envision ideas that best address as many of the values—shared and divergent—as possible.

With this challenge in place, directing students to seek out resources through various research strategies can take on a very different look. We are setting out to build consensus and critically assess ideas and texts, rather than just seeking out things that will serve our limited purpose. Ultimately, this encourages students to see and practice the reading of informational text not just as a process of dismissing media sources or resources that do not align with their perspectives but as an opportunity to critically examine them to understand their logic, the veracity of their sources, the ways their arguments play on rhetorical strategies (things like ethos, pathos, and logos), and how they advance positions that may or may not be compatible with the shared, core values and broad array of the divergent values. Again, Alan Luke's Four Resources model can be hugely effective in supporting this type of re-framed engagement with reading.

Step 4: Create Dialogues for Solution Building

The ultimate task that we are building towards (i.e., what we are doing with the reading) is to still provide students an authentic opportunity to talk about competing ideas and solutions to compelling real-world problems. This is often why teachers assign debates in the first place. Debates offer an approximation of an authentic ending to the task of reading informational writing. That impulse is sound. We want tasks to be authentic; we want to encourage translating reading analysis skills into oral literacy skills; and we want to encourage agency to engage with social issues. But as we have suggested, we need to shake up this colonial normal.

So, after taking the steps suggested above, organize the task as a roundtable of ideas in which each student or group could present solutions, as well as their rationale for how these solutions meet the most needs with the fewest and least impactful compromises to divergent values and positions. Logistically, assign each student a set amount of time for presenting their ideas and then provide discussion time for the group to ask questions and consider the proposals. This allows space for dialogue and disagreement, but constructive disagreement, about whether those solutions would authentically meet the needs of the most people or whether a value that a solution failed to cover was critically important or not. Moreover, this should not be framed as selecting a winner, but rather acknowledging that solutions were not necessarily mutually exclusive or a zero-sum proposition. Multiple ideas with different approaches can, in fact, co-exist, perhaps building or bridging consensus across positions or proposals that were mutually exclusive.

All of this allows us to be honest about our ideas (naming what we did not solve) and to be solution oriented in our discourse and discussion (asking hard questions, not to tear down another argument but to propose substantive solutions). Assessment, as with any oral presentation, can still assess and evaluate robust analyses and accurate readings of texts, as well as emphasize consideration of complex positions.

We cannot eliminate moral debate or disagreement. It is the nature of our vast and diverse society that there are many different culturally informed ways of being that must find, often tenuous, ways to co-exist. There will always be many perspectives on how to address the social problems and issues of scarcity and shared governance we face. We cannot, and will not, solve any of these great questions in our middle-grades literacy classroom, but what we can do is help students engage with a process of resolving, reconciling, and discussing issues in which compromise is valued and in which solutions are built around an appreciation of consensus, and around respect, care, and understanding for those positions that may ultimately be left out of that consensus.

The cultivation of this sort of approach to reading informational texts and engaging in analyses that balances singular solutions and cultural relativism, that remains aware of and attentive to ways that address unmet needs, and that understands why and how unmet needs often produce frustration, is abnormal to schooling and to society. We are encouraged to take partisan positions and hunker down into them. How humanizing for our students might it be to invite them to not reduce the world to such Us/Them propositions?

Disrupting the Activity System of Normalized Schooling

In the spirit of disrupting the normal, instead of a writing strategy for students, we're going to offer something a little bit different—a bit of a writing task for you. We want you to get weird with things in your classroom, so we will do the same in this chapter and break from our own normal, to have you think about writing activities you might engage in, not just those for your students.

The instructional strategies we have suggested throughout this book are, of course, crucial to great teaching and working towards decolonization in our praxis. But we are also often wary (as we have expressed throughout this book) of trying to boil anything down to discrete tasks, skills, practices, or lesson plans. Yes, we need curricular changes, strategies, and plans that put ideas into practice, but we also need to reflect more broadly in order to really shake things up and get away from the colonial 'normal' that has dominated our schools, curriculum, and pedagogy for so long. With that in mind, we want to encourage you to think holistically, and even *geographically*, about your classroom, your school, and the way it operates as a cultural system so that you can begin to imagine and map out your way to escape the logic of 'the way it has always been done.'

What we mean by this is that, as we have noted, *normal* is imbued in our schools, classrooms, and pedagogies on many, many levels. Our classrooms are obviously spatial in the sense of the layout of the desks or tables, the position of the board, the arrangement of different resources, and the location of power outlets. The things that are available to you such as the kind of furniture you can use or even the simple size of your space all constrain the choices available to you and necessarily push you towards expected outcomes. For example, you deliver instruction from a lecture-type position because that's where the board and computer were installed. Essentially, some architect's and engineer's vision of how you should normally arrange learning in your classroom—based on their own, historically rooted conception of schooling—makes choices for you. But beyond this very material example, it is important to recognize that our classrooms and the normal that dominates them are also emotional or affective geographies, where routines, norms, values, and social power shape how we navigate through those spaces. The way we think of students, the agency we give them, the value we place on the resources they arrive to us with, and the attitudes and beliefs that we show through our pedagogical choices all create a landscape that is easier or more difficult, comforting or treacherous, through which students must navigate. Our choices to either adhere to the colonial norms of schooling or find ways to disrupt them shape this terrain.

To visualize all of this, we find Engeström's (1987) idea of the Activity System incredibly useful as a way to imagine what the cultural geography and terrain features of our classrooms look like. While Engeström gets quite a bit more complicated in his analysis, explanation, and the full scope and conception of how an activity system operates and captures what goes on in a cultural setting than we do here, we can use this framing to understand how the various elements of classroom culture and social interaction combine to produce or reproduce learning outcomes, often in ways that we do not fully expect or intend.

In Engeström's (2001) diagram of an activity system, there are six key elements—Subject, Object, Tools, Rules, Community, and Division of Labor—to pay attention to, each of which interacts with the others, together producing the social, academic, intellectual, and cultural outcomes of learning in any given activity or setting, like, say, our classroom.

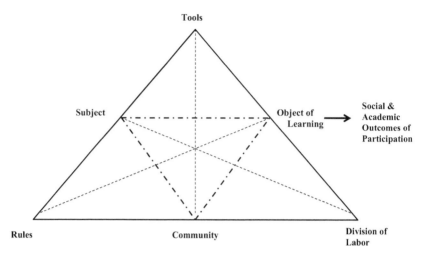

Figure 7.1 Engeström's (1987) visualization of a cultural activity system (Bury, 2012).

What Engeström's theory assists us in paying attention to is how interrelated and interdependent all of these elements are. No matter how ambitious or thoughtful the object of learning we aim to accomplish is, if the other dynamics of the classroom—who the student-subject is allowed to be, the tools available, the rules and community defining participation, and the way the labor around thinking and engaging with information is divided—remain obedient to the 'norms' of coloniality, the outcomes will continue to be limited.

Think back to our opening vignette. Here was a case where the teacher had set a thoughtful vision, ambitiously wanting her students to critically reflect on and explore cultural marginalization in history. Yet the actual object of learning she had on offer was essentially regurgitating information. This object, as well as the tools that were available (Cornell notes, a textbook), who the students were allowed to be (quietly sitting at tables and completing prescribed tasks in order), how the community operated (individual assignments on one-to-one computers), and how the labor was divided (passive note taking before a lecture, then passive synthesis around pre-selected topics) was never going to really get us towards a vision of critically engaging with historical marginalization. It was, as we discussed earlier, the banking method with new content. The cultural activity was not meant to be restrictive, but it was deeply, profoundly, *normal*. And by obeying the logic and expectations for how we organize classrooms—obeying the *normal*—it had inadvertently replicated colonial ways of being. The tools available were always going to limit who the student-subject could be in the classroom. The division of labor would always leave the community disconnected and less than vibrant. The rules may have been flexible and respectful, but the organization of the community made them a moot point. We could go on, but the point is that this educator needed to change more than just having an exciting vision and switching up some of the tools (curriculum, texts). So before we move on from considering the disruption of the normal, we want to offer you a reflective task: mapping the activity system of your classroom. Here's how it works.

106

First, write down a few thoughts about your vision for your classroom. What is it you really want for the outcomes your students will leave your space with? What is the learning that is important to you? Additionally, think seriously about who you want your students to be as learners. What is your vision for them, and how will they be able to learn and grow? Once you have done that, go ahead and draw a triangle diagram like the one above, and mark or label the six key elements that drive cultural activity: Subject, Object, Tools, Rules, Community, and Division of Labor (you can also do this as a series of lists, though we like the spatial relationship the diagram captures).

Next, take some time to reflect, honestly, on how each of these elements shows up in your classroom *as it is*. That means doing some real reflection on how things actually shake out, and the constraints that make that happen, not your intentions or aspirations (that will come later).

- **Subject**: The subject represents the individual(s) taking part in the activity and who they are invited to be. How do they understand and see themselves? How are they understood and seen by others? What sort of agency do they have, and who are they allowed to be in your classroom? And where do those expectations come from? You? The school?

- **Tools**: The tools represent just that—the tools available to accomplish a task within an activity. What actual tools are present, like computers, texts, writing utensils, etc.? What non-material tools, like peers, elders, languages, etc. are available and allowed? Are there things that could be tools, but which are made impermissible?

- **Rules**: Rules are a fairly straightforward part of the activity—what is and is not allowed—but requires some reflection, because not all rules are consciously stated. What are the posted, written rules and guidelines of the cultural activity? What norms and expectations exist that act as rules, even if they are not written down?

- **Community**: Community refers to how we organize and relate to one another in a cultural activity. How have we organized and arranged and grouped learners in the space? How accessible are different members of this community, ourselves included, to one another? How much agency does the community have?

- **Division of labor**: The division of labor involves understanding who is doing what work, both real and intellectual, in an activity. How is work distributed across tasks? What products is everyone responsible for? Are the students or the educator doing the intellectual heavy lifting?

- **Object**: Different than the outcomes (what is *actually* produced by a cultural activity), or your vision (what you aspirationally *hope* your classroom community will be like), the object represents the functional goals for learning in an activity, or the actual things students are having to produce/tasks to do. What have we set out to accomplish? What are the stated, and implied, ideas and skills we are reinforcing?

Now that you've got the reality of your situation mapped out—what the *normal* affordances and constraints in the activity system of your classroom are and look like—go ahead and look back at that vision you wrote down. Go through each category—we suggest starting with the object—and assess how well the way these things manifest actually reflects and aligns with your vision. If (hopefully) our vision is to shake things up in a decolonial way, is our object, subject, tools, etc. actually offering something different than the normal?

With that done, we can start to think aspirationally, with a bit of pragmatic vision, and we can begin—and we say this with total sincerity—to get a little weird with it. Go ahead and examine each category. What are things that, in your context, are parts of the normal which you truly cannot alter? We are thinking here of things like if your classroom community is necessarily impacted by the material space of having desks in a limited floor plan, rules that are school policies, or expectations of using certain texts and tools. These might be a bummer to accept, but decolonization is not just about the big show, but about navigating in tight spaces.

Now, start getting creative. Where is there room to change things up a little? Can we shift some rules? Can we change the community layout or relationships? Can we rethink the pattern of our lessons so that we as educators are doing less of the intellectual labor, and more is shifted towards students? Can we introduce, or permit, some tools that flip things around? Or maybe take away some that led to limited ways of being and social interaction? What can we do to shake up the way student-subjects are positioned or the way we set up the object of learning? As you go, think about the impacts and interconnections among all these elements. Remember that any change you make in one category will necessarily have ripple effects and exist in conversation with the constraints we cannot change. Be creative, and once you're done, you'll have a map of ways to organize the learning activity of your classroom so that, regardless of constraints, you are getting as close to your vision as possible.

Moving forward, keep this visualization, map, diagram, or set of lists handy, and revisit it as you tweak and fine-tune the organization of your learning space for different modules, tasks, groups, and content. Keep analyzing those six elements, how they are showing up, and how they are changing. Try to think of strange, unsettling, disruptive ways to modify ways the subject, tools, community, etc. are being framed in your classroom. Keep students, and yourself, guessing as you pursue that vision of something different than the normal.

Decolonization is not normal. It is, necessarily, abnormal in the best way possible because decolonial liberation isn't normal. Across the globe, and certainly in the U.S., coloniality dominates our lives and experiences. It is, as Maldonado-Torres says, the "air we breathe" (2007). If we want to move towards decolonial classrooms, we need to lean into abnormalcy, open that long-shut window, and get a lungful of new air. We have to find weird, new, and different ways to do things, even if those changes might be a little scary, or uncomfortable, or messy, or unclear, or unsupported by those around us, or at times unwelcome by students who are locked into their own expectations and comfort with the colonial norm. Our example here of shaking up 'the way it's always been done' with classroom debate was just an example—we need to extend the same spirit of disruption and reimagination to other tried and true elements of literacy teaching and pedagogy in general. And if our context and conditions only allow for small changes in our activity system, well, make those small changes. Even a subtle change to one aspect of the activity system will necessarily alter the others, and change the outcome. We suppose "get a little weird with it" may be strange advice to hear, but if there is any group and any setting where the challenges of fitting in to normal are understood, it's middle school. So lean into that most middle school of experiences, and embrace being a little weird.

Challenge in Practice

Mr Ngyuen has just been hired mid-year to teach 8th-grade ELA at a large, suburban school in a very affluent area of his community to replace a teacher who was a fixture of the school but has decided to retire early. He is thrilled to get started with his classes in the new semester and puts together an exciting plan of interesting and engaging pedagogical activities and assignments, including newly published middle-grades texts that include author chats, multimedia writing projects, escape-room styled activities, QR code-driven gallery walks, and Socratic Seminars to center student voices.

But as the semester begins, his innovative lessons run into some serious student apathy and resistance, with students being incredibly reticent to speak, skeptical of the new assignment products, and dismissive of the in-class activities. After a few weeks of lessons going far differently than he hoped, Mr Ngyuen takes some time to have a conversation with his students about how they feel things are going and what they think would help their learning. He is taken aback by their response: they don't really want to do any of these things. They would rather just keep doing what their old teacher did—read the stories from the textbook that the 8th graders in previous years read, answer the questions at the end of each chapter, and write essays or take multiple choice tests at the end of units. That was how school was supposed to work, and they just wanted to keep their routine.

How can Mr Ngyuen respond? What strategies, compromises, or approaches might he use to get his students to engage with and embrace a less reductive view of schooling, and their own learning?

Questions to Consider While Planning to Disrupt Normal

1   What is the normal at my school and among my teaching peers? What are the 'ways it has always been done' that are just not working for students?

2   What sort of alternative methods, materials, products, or outcomes can I use to shake up the way I invite students to participate in literacy tasks, lessons, and units?

3   How have I brought the 'arts' into language arts? How have I structured my lessons to be transdisciplinary and not just siloed as 'ELA'?

4   Within the confines of my classroom space, what can I do to change the physical layout and geography? How would that change the intellectual and emotional geography (where knowledge and social experiences flow)?

Resources to Explore

Looking Beyond the ELA Staples

To shake up the normal of our classrooms, we need to look beyond those resources and staples of ELA instruction that have persisted for generations. With that in mind, a few suggestions include looking to the following:

- *The Secret Language of Maps: How to Tell Visual Stories with Data* by Carissa Carter is a text that gets at the questions of story-ing we are interested in language arts, but does so from a different and unique angle. Further, it is worth exploring anything else coming out of the Stanford Design school series, like this text did.
- *Braiding Sweetgrass: Indigenous Wisdom, Scientific Knowledge and the Teachings of Plants* by Robin Wall Kimmerer is a spectacular text that weaves story and biology together in transdisciplinary fashion to highlight indigenous ways of knowing and being. There's now a young adult version of the book as well!
- On these same notes, we just encourage you to shake up the things you read, and that you bring into the classroom as resources. Explore materials meant for athletic coaches, rather than just teacher texts. Read some things that are peripheral to science, not just literature, like Lauret Savoy's *Trace: Memory, history, race, and the American landscape*. Read things about artists and art history to inspire you, and bring some of these—often visually exciting—texts into your class for students to explore. Basically, get weird with your reading.

Assessment Alternatives

When we start to think of assessment alternatives to break away from the normal, there are some obvious suggestions: get away from having everything end with a five-paragraph essay, and explore options like podcasting, art, re-mixing, and other non-traditional suggestions we have included in other chapters. But these are just pieces of disrupting the normal of assessment.

As we are thinking about this section, we are reminded of a scene from the television show *Arrested Development*, where a character attends a new-age, progressive school with a wild system of assessing learning (she earns a 'Crocodile' in spelling) but, ultimately, still flunks out. Where we are going with this is that often, even when we change the mode of the assessment, it is still all about the grade. So while we can't make grades disappear from our current educational landscape, we can still get weird with assessment by disaggregating it from grading. What we mean by this is to create spaces where students can give and receive honest, critical, substantial feedback—both from you and from their peers—without that feedback or task being linked to any sort of scaled grade. Have them do roundtable discussions to share their projects. Let them workshop things. Essentially, to really get weird with assessment, allow assessment to be one thing—a space where we receive the feedback needed to grow and develop—and grading in relation to whatever standards the district gives us to master something separate.

Technology Spotlight

While there are a number of digital tools available that offer educators and students the possibility to showcase, explore, and engage in their literacy practices in ways that shake up the normal, we would be remiss if we did not point out the potential of 'flipped lessons' as a tool of disrupting the normal. Flipped lessons, of course, involve an arrangement wherein instruction is essentially sent as homework, usually via digital lessons, preserving time in class for direct practice and engagement among the students, educators, and authentic learning tasks.

As we have talked elsewhere about transdisciplinary work, flipping elements like that through take-home video lessons that establish background knowledge can be incredibly useful and position you to cover information and context that is enriching, but would have been laborious to your instruction and time-consuming for students' class time. While some existing resources, like Khan Academy or John Green's Crash Course videos, are accessible on Youtube as flipped lessons, we would encourage you to use screencasting software—things like Camtasia, Voila, Quickcast, Screencast Maker, or Quicktime—to make flipped lessons of your own, recording your screen, voice, and even video as you cover material (Khan 2022). Though obviously a bit more labor-intensive, students will appreciate hearing from you.

There certainly remain constraints on this method in terms of accessibility (who has access to devices and high-speed internet), comprehension (flipped lessons tend to only offer one means of explanation, which may not resonate with all students), and pedagogy (sometimes, flipping a classroom can lead an instructor to neglect the need to ensure the material was understood), but if you ensure you do not pass too much of the labor and instructional responsibility on to the digital space, imagining how you can leverage existing flipped materials, and perhaps create your own, is an excellent way to shake up the normal, colonial way instruction is delivered and accessed in schools.

References

Bury, M. (2012). Illustrative diagram of Scandinavian activity network. [Image] https://commons.wikimedia.org/wiki/File:Activity_system.png

Carter, C. (2022). *The secret language of maps: How to tell visual stories with data*. Penguin.

Engeström, Y. (2015) 1987. *Learning by expanding*. Cambridge University Press.

Engeström, Y. (2001). Expansive learning at work: Toward an activity theoretical reconceptualization. *Journal of Education and Work*, *14*(1), 133–156.

Freire, P. (2009). *Pedagogy of the oppressed: 30th anniversary Edition*. Continuum.

Green, J. & Green, H. (2022). *Crash Course*. Youtube. https://www.youtube.com/channel/UCX6b17PVsYBQ0ip5gyeme-Q

Khan, S. (2022). *Khan Academy*. https://www.khanacademy.org/

Kimmerer, R. (2013). *Braiding sweetgrass: Indigenous wisdom, scientific knowledge and the teachings of plants*. Milkweed editions.

Kimmerer, R. (2022). *Braiding sweetgrass for young adults: Indigenous wisdom, scientific knowledge and the teachings of plants*. Milkweed editions.

Luke, A. (2017). Critical literacy, school improvement, and the four resources model. In P. Albers (Ed.) *Global conversations in literacy research* (pp. 1–13). Routledge.

Maldonado-Torres, N. (2007). On the coloniality of being: Contributions to the development of a concept. *Cultural Studies, 21*(2–3), 240–270.

Savoy, L. (2015). *Trace: Memory, history, race, and the American landscape*. Catapult.

8

DECOLONIZED CLASSROOMS... LEVERAGE A MULTILINGUAL WORLD

Introduction

Though we use it almost constantly, it is easy to forget how fundamentally significant and important language is to our humanity. But folks concerned with decolonization, especially indigenous folks, have always been acutely aware of this importance. Frantz Fanon noted that, "*To speak a language is to take on a world, a culture.*" Language builds worlds and possibilities. And the opposite also holds true, as Dottie LeBeau reminds us:

> Losing the language means losing the culture. We need to know who we are because it makes a difference in who our children are.

Too often, schools mandate policies that reject languages other than English or develop approaches that are out of touch with how languages are used in practice or with what languages are actually being practiced outside school.

Michael once worked with a middle school in the rural southeast U.S. that was part of what researchers refer to as the 'New Latinx Diaspora,' or regions of the country where unexpected and unprecedented demographic shifts have made Latinx youth and families unexpected new members of what were once homogenous communities. This particular school had seen a jarring shift in Latinx enrollment, going from a student population with about 3% Latinx students to having well over 30% of their student population identifying as Latinx in just under a decade. This demographic shift pre-sented staff with a staggering challenge. In this context, as the school was scrambling to figure out how to deal with these new students, they began addressing what seemed like the most obvious challenge facing Latinos: language. Without many bilingual educators, they began making a concerted effort to translate signs, posters, and classroom docu-ments into Spanish, often using Google Translate, or purchasing items from commercial sources. The trick was, these efforts had failed to connect with what the Latinx students' actual linguistic practices were. Translated signs, except those few reviewed by the ESL teacher in her very limited time, tended to either contain errors or formalized phrasing that made little sense to many of the Spanish-speaking students. Some signs were even in Castilian (the linguistic variant of Spanish used in Spain), which is markedly different from the Latin American Spanish that was spoken by most of the youth. But perhaps most striking was that a significant number of the Latinx, Mexican-origin students

DOI: 10.4324/9781003290681-10   113 weren't even Spanish speakers: they spoke Otomí, an indigenous language. When we look at a case like this, what we see is a situation in which good intentions can easily miss the mark and how crucial it is to ensure that our interventions and attempts to support students, especially linguistically and culturally, reflect who they actually are, not who we presume, or expect them to be.

Linguistic Hegemony and Coloniality

Let us be clear right from the outset here: this is not a chapter on English as a second language or bilingual teaching methods. So often when language comes up, we immediately start thinking about those students in our classes who are perceived as lacking English and are in the depths of second- (or third-)language acquisition. While those dynamics are a piece of what we will get into, we are here to invite you to think of language a bit more expansively and in the context of language hegemony, one of the ways the colonialities of knowledge and power most frequently manifest (Mignolo, 2003). With that said, understanding the complexities and technicalities of teaching emergent bi/multilingual youth and supporting language acquisition are critical and specific skill sets you may need in your teaching. We encourage you (with resources we suggest at the end of this chapter) to deepen your understanding of language acquisition processes, build out your pedagogical toolkits for that unique and specific challenge, and layer those discrete tools and strategies into the vision and approach to language we suggest here. So let's get into why language and a multilingual world are so important to a decolonial classroom vision.

Language has always been a battleground. It is a source of identity. It is a tool of colonization. It is a site of resistance. Throughout the entire 500-year history of colonial conflict and dominance, both *de jure* and *de facto*, intentionally or unintentionally, with malice or positive intentions, language hegemony has been one of the most obvious ways to see coloniality in action. Residential schools and colonial governments forced colonized peoples to learn their languages, criminalized indigenous tongues, and then codified—in *de jure* and *de facto* ways—the dominance and value of European languages as the discourses required for commerce, governance, education, and essentially, agency (Mignolo, 1993, 2003). This denial of language was not just a homogenization of communication but an exercise in control. Language, as we will get into a bit more later, is and has always been more than just the words we use. It is linked intimately to our identities, our histories, our stories. Losing language—and because of colonization, there are now a great many extinct indigenous languages—means losing culture, and, along with it, ways of knowing, ways of being, and the power to express oneself on one's own terms (Norton, 2013).

Yet the assault on language is not just technocratic. Languages are not some fixed, immovable things. They are dynamic practices, living archives, or *discourses*, contextual cultural and linguistic systems that carry social and cultural value in different ways in different spaces. Coloniality in and around language plays out by messaging and validating cultural narratives about both the nature of language (that it is fixed, distinct) and the value of certain discourses (that, for instance, the academic English spoken by upper-middle class white folks in the U.S. is the proper or best way to communicate).

Further, these messages work in reverse. Non-English languages are positioned as marginal, tainted, lacking, and often become assemblages of negative perception, of foreignness, of Other. Spanish—itself a colonial language—in the U.S., for instance, may be a language and one taught in schools, but because of its social, political, cultural, and historical positioning, it has been racialized. As Rosa (2019) notes, Spanish spoken colloquially in Latinx communities may look like a language, but when used and observed by others in our political, social, and cultural landscape, it sounds like a race. The same can be said for Arabic and various Asian languages at different times and in different contexts. Socialization has racialized these languages as collections of societal and cultural fears and beliefs of Otherness—we 'see' race through phenotype, but we also 'hear' race through language. And these tensions extend beyond 'foreign' languages, and even to different dialects or discourses of English. Extensive research has shown that African American vernacular English (AAVE) is complex, distinct, and rule governed, a Creole language using vocabulary and syntactical structures from English, French, Spanish, and indigenous west African language families (e.g., Bailey & Thomas, 2021; Winford, 1998; Zeigler, 2001). Yet AAVE too has become seen/heard as a racialized assemblage of Black Otherness. All of this belies the reality that in many of these cases, the actual linguistic and literary complexity of these languages and discourses exceeds those of proper middle-class English, even if those assets and strengths are completely ignored or actually punished and invalidated in schools. The measure of a marginalized, bi/multilingual student becomes their grasp of English, their capacity to 'code-switch,' or bounce back and forth between one discourse, one cultural world, and another—with white middle-class English always the 'code' necessary for access to institutional power. Those fully adept at code-switching might even earn the dubious, colonial, and racially tinged honor of being *articulate* (Alim & Smitherman, 2012).

So when we speak here about embracing a multilingual world, what we are talking about is not just embracing and welcoming emergent bi/multilingual students into your classroom, but embracing the reality that there are linguistic practices, *discourses*, tied to important and valuable identities that might not register as 'languages' but still need to be honored, welcomed in your classroom, and sustained through purposeful instruction. We are talking about disrupting our colonial assumption that, as ELA and literacy teachers, our mission is just to teach academic English (Motha, 2014). Rather, we must see ourselves as teachers of language writ large, ensuring that we are supporting all of our students to develop multiple, contextual, linguistic skills so that they may be fluent across contexts. We need to stop looking for code-switching (as a way to prove BIPOC students can emulate whiteness when needed) and begin aiming for code-meshing, or translanguaging (e.g., García, 2009; García & Wei, 2014; Lewis et al., 2012), visions of language use in which all of the discourses students bring to the classroom and those they learn there are mastered, explored, understood, and able to be leveraged strategically to convey the meanings and messages that they wish, in any context, without compromising or concealing their ontological being and identity.

No matter what context you teach in, you exist in a space where linguistic hegemony, borne of coloniality, is all around you. Yet we should not have to point out that demographic shifts and linguistic shifts with them—and the way they impact all of us, in all aspects of our lives, even if we do not see them in pronounced ways in our particular classrooms—are changing the world we are preparing students for. We no longer have the luxury of thinking about language in narrow ways or maintaining limited conceptions of who our students, ALL of whom are language learners and prospective multilingual language users, might be. Striving for the decolonial means cultivating an environment where we reject the institutional 'English learner' designation (and its implied centering of English) for all of our students, challenge them to become fluent across contexts, and individuals who can, yes, learn English, but also a more holistic, humanizing, and asset-based understanding of language and language use. This is how we set students up to do as Fanon says, and through language, take on not just one but many cultural worlds as valuable elements of the human experience.

Reading Instruction to Master Language Use

As we have noted, our purpose here is not to provide guidance around language acquisition strategies or specific practices. Rather, we want to offer a way to think about your instruction around how you are supporting language(s) and language learning to disrupt English hegemony more holistically. To that end, the reading approach we want to suggest is Alan Luke's Four Resources Model (2017). Luke's model is not specific to, or even necessarily tailored towards, emergent bi/multilingual learners. Rather, it is a framework for thinking about and organizing reading instruction as critical literacy development that we believe complements more specific language acquisition practices in important ways, laying the foundations to decolonize and disrupt the hegemony of English.

Take for instance the importance of direct instruction around grammar, syntax, and vocabulary skills to emergent bi/multilingual students. Without question, language learners need active and intentional instruction in these skill sets. We cannot just expect them to pick things up from context without explanation or without guidance and practice. But this goes for our students who may arrive in our classroom with discourse variants of English as well. As teachers of language to emergent multilingual students, we need to provide direct, clear instruction around complex vocabulary words and grammar rules (e.g., tense changes, verb conjugation) that students will need to be able to identify and apply in the future. Yet too often, this real need for intentional instruction becomes understood as reductive instruction; we only do direct teaching of disembodied skills and vocabulary and forget the way language works as a discourse, a cultural system that provides access to a world and culture.

It is our belief that by keeping the Four Resources Model as the guiding, overarching principle that shapes and organizes your reading instruction, you will position yourself to pay attention to and make room for the multiple levels needed to support reading development, including language acquisition skills, while keeping the *telos*, or vision, of your efforts firmly centered on the decolonial. Moreover, you are setting readers up with the skills to be critical language users across the languages and discourses they may use.

Step 1: Code Breaker—How Do I Crack This Code?

The first resource that Luke lays out is the code-breaker role, which pertains to the fact that no matter what, as readers we need to be able to 'break the code' of texts by understanding their architectural fundamentals. We need to be able to tease apart phonetic sounds. We must have a familiarity with the alphabet being used. We need to have practice in spelling patterns, conventions of textual organization, and the rules and structures that govern syntax in a language. No matter what our critical literacy end-goals are for our students, without breaking the code of a text and its language, we will never be able to access higher aspirations with that text. In practice, we as educators can support code breaking by verifying the technical knowledge students bring to a text about the words and structures in it and providing explicit mention and instruction to support students in their understanding of the languages and structures of the text. That might involve, but would not be limited to:

- Encouraging students to explain the use of headings, titles, or graphics as part of understanding a text
- Teasing apart the phonics and spelling of key words or new vocabulary
- Exploring linguistic taxonomies and connections for new terms
- Pre-teaching syntax strategies used by the author prior to reading

Step 2: Meaning Maker—What Does This Mean to Me?

The second resource in Luke's model, meaning making, relates to the ways in which we construct basic meanings around texts, what they are discussing, and how it relates to and reflects a cultural knowledge system, cultural discourses, types of experiences, and other webs of meaning. All texts, we know, convey basic meanings: the words, together, relate information to us. These basic messages must be unpacked and understood. But we also know that all texts are products of their context and culture. If our students (or we) exist outside of those contexts, we are likely to find texts challenging to make sense of, to reason with, and to comprehend. How can I fathom a character's diligent description of bundling up for winter if I have never seen snow? Moreover, how can I make sense of a narrator of color's tense and foreboding tone as a police encounter begins if I do not understand that culture experiences and histories with law enforcement are different from different racialized positions?

In practice, we support students to access the meaning maker resource by making sure the literal meaning of words and sentences is clear, but also by assessing the cultural and contextual knowledge students will bring to any given text. It is contingent on us to ensure that we introduce texts with an eye to context, locate them for students within their particular cultural experience, and make no assumptions about students' prior grasp of those cultural worlds. This might involve, but would not be limited to:

- Pre-teaching historical or cultural context around the setting of a text or roles/positions of characters/individuals in that text

- Providing support to unpack the meaning of archaic words or words that have contextually or culturally specific meanings
- Teasing out personal and cultural connections to the text and the topics, issues, and dilemmas a text raises
- Providing opportunities for students to re-state and re-tell the contents of a text, including intentional support and explicit instruction on the skill of summarizing known information
- Ensuring that space is available to ask clarifying questions about text meanings and context without pressure, assessment, or judgment

Step 3: Text User—What Do I Do With This Text?

Luke's third resource is the text user role, or the ability to assess, and act upon, what a text wants us to do with it. Texts of course have basic, culturally contextual meanings which we must identify. But different texts also have different purposes, which are conveyed both structurally and ideologically. Learning the way different texts operate and serve different purposes and functions through their tone, formality, structure, organization, diction, and place of publication are critical skills that language users and readers need to be astute and critical consumers of information.

In practice, we can support students by clearly discussing and clarifying the nature and categorization of different types of texts and what their purposes and uses are. This might look like, but not be limited to:

- Comparing and contrasting different types of texts and their uses and purposes
- Explicit discussion of the context in which texts are published and the nature of those publications
- Deconstructing the common features, structures, discourse, and arguments present in different texts with different purposes

Step 4: Text Analyst—What Does This Text Do to Me?

The final resource Luke offers for our consideration is textual analysis. This is, perhaps, the one we may be most excited about and interested in. It is here where critical lenses are applied to texts, and we try to decipher and infer not just literal meaning but ideological intent. Here, we take the time to ensure that students understand that texts are not neutral, but that no matter the text, authors make choices of discourse, diction, tone, structure, and of course content, so that certain points of view are being privileged and others left out for particular socio-historic and socio-cultural reasons. We seek out the symbolic meaning that is wrapped up in why an author would write a text, and how they hope it will influence us and shape our thinking. Here is where we acquire the tools to maintain our agency as readers.

In practice, we support this fourth resource by asking ourselves what contextual knowledge students have around the ideological, thematic, and symbolic elements of a reading and providing enrichment to allow them to assess different views and positions.

And we make sure to actively and explicitly discuss the ways in which words, discourses, tone, and argument structures can be linked to particular ideological positions, and symbolic meanings. In practice, this may look like, but not be limited to:

- Pre-teaching context through reflective discussion and writing around the ideological questions and positions a text poses
- Providing intentional instruction on the ideological and historical context and meaning of certain words, phrases, or arguments
- Diagramming the different arguments, assumptions, and evidence an author is drawing upon
- Conducting analyses of word, tone, and discourse choices and their intended effects
- Articulating connections to contextual bodies of knowledge, and/or intertextual connections that may exist

Step 5: Designing the Four Resources as a Holistic Approach

Essentially, these four resources are the critical skill sets that any reader needs to access texts in any of their languages and discourses. They are also roles that we often neglect and forget to make transparent to developing readers, and especially to emergent bilingual and multilingual students. By ensuring that we are accessing each of these resources and honoring each of these roles—structuring our reading instruction and activities around these four resources and continually talking about these roles—we position language learners to be more intentional, transparent, and strategic in how they approach and understand text. Rather than feeling overwhelmed, an emergent bi/multilingual student in your mainstream ELA class or just a student who arrived in your class speaking a non-hegemonic version of English will have the tools to approach language deliberately and in ways that will help their gradual and broader language acquisition goals.

In that sense, by using the Four Resources Model to intentionally show that ALL reading is a strategic, contextual, active deconstruction process, the model serves to disrupt the mystique and hegemony of English. Too often, we allow English to be positioned as some kind of inherent cultural knowledge, unattainable for second- (or third-)language learners. Showing that English, too, is just a set of cultural patterns with codes, meanings, uses, and ideas helps to shake off this notion of it being special or better in an academic context.

With all that in mind, we recommend using these four resources as transparent guiding principles for your reading instruction, especially in spaces with emergent bi/multilingual learners. Posting them in your room, and even considering using these as regular stages that you go through as a class—either full class or in small groups, and not necessarily in any fixed order—every time you approach a new text will benefit the critical literacy of all your students and ensure that you have provided the scaffolding and transparency around language skills, meanings, and cultural discourses that are vital for emergent bilingual students to not feel left behind, left out, or marginalized by your instruction.

Writing Instruction to Encourage Code-Meshing

Again, we will note that if your context involves significant (or even singular) situations where you are supporting emergent bi/multilingual learners in the early stages of their language acquisition, we encourage you to review the literature on intentional strategies of language acquisition to use in your classroom around writing. Here, we will discuss a particular strategy we find useful when setting a tone in your classroom for more ambitious future efforts at multilingual writing.

As we mentioned above, the best approaches to literacy development for emergent bi/multilingual learners are ones that support them in developing their code-meshing and translanguaging skills, abilities to carry and leverage aspects of their full linguistic toolkits strategically in any context. But as with any skill, we need to gradually build towards and scaffold our skill sets. So to become fluent in any context, a key starting point is to make transparent the way different settings have different expectations, and what those expectations are in key contexts.

Step 1: Establish the Parameters of a Set of Contexts

This lesson activity begins by transparently setting out a series of distinct contexts in which different linguistic toolkits and discourses are spoken. This might mean literally different languages, but it might also involve variations within a language. There are an array of contexts you might choose—obviously, school, family, friend groups—and variations of these contexts you might plumb—within school, a favorite teacher v. the principal; within family, a grandparent v. an older sibling—but what is critical is to identify these settings, and with your students, articulate the linguistic expectations that come with each. Are they formal? Informal? What kinds of structures and types of communiqué are expected? What tone is preferred? What are the consequences of miscommunication? Do not hesitate to lean into the potential fun here of exploring contexts that matter to your students. Are they on Instagram? TikTok? Help them make the language and writing expectations transparent, being generous with the understanding of what text can be.

Step 2: Write the Same Content for Multiple Contexts

Now comes the heart of the writing task—and the fun part. With a set of contexts established (make sure to choose a realistic number of contexts for the labor involved), create a scenario that in real life would demand wide communication and around which they can write—for instance, their significant other has split with them, and caused them to be late with an assignment—and assign them the task of writing to communicate this information to the different contexts chosen.

As they plan their writing, remind and support them to make plans for how this will look different to different audiences. What different languages will be needed? How will the narrative and tone change? What will change in their discourse, structural, and organizational choices? Again, be creative with the challenge you pose each time you do this activity. This can be an activity that ranges from the profound to the comical, and can help draw on, invite, and validate your students' full funds of knowledge.

Step 3: Critically Analyze What Linguistic Skills Were Used and Why

With this assignment, the point is to support them not just in, for instance, imagining a response to the question *Y tu novia/o?* (And your significant other?), but to understand and make transparent how the writing and linguistic demands in different contexts require different, specific, technical, ideological, and cultural skill sets. With that in mind, once the writing is done, be sure that students have the chance to share their different, contextual creations, and as you do so, have them critically analyze what different linguistic and literacy skills they used. *Why* was their message to family so different from their note to their teacher? What expectations does their Instagram caption involve, in terms of the narrative that one creates, different than the narrative created for sharing with a parent or guardian? These critical questions help to demystify the demands of different contexts but also make it clear that students must be on the lookout for the demands of particular contexts.

Step 4: Be Sure Not to Privilege the Academic English Category

While this is a rather straightforward activity, the biggest mistake we see folks make is to allow the lesson to end with the proposition that the academic English context is the one that counts. Be incredibly careful to ensure that students understand that this activity is NOT practice for how to avoid or silo all those other discourses and linguistic skills you just uncovered while in school, but an opportunity to make transparent the expectations of different contexts, the uses of different discourses, and the breadth of the assets that students might not even know they have. For sure, this can be a useful diagnostic for you to assess students' awareness of formal writing skills, and what assets they have, but be sure not to dwell on or over-emphasize your interest or attention in what they cannot do in the more formal academic context version of their writing.

Essentially, it is critical that your framing of this activity is not around learning how to write for school differently than elsewhere, but creating a record of the writing skills and linguistic tools each student has at their disposal to draw on for later use *in the classroom*. It is not a bad idea to encourage each student to make a list of the skills they showed across their multiple iterations of the same written response.

Step 5: Leverage This Knowledge in Future Assignments to Code-Mesh Elements of Their Linguistic Ranges

Where this lesson becomes incredibly valuable is as table-setting for a future of code-meshed writing. What we are of course talking about is the ability to leverage, transform, and adapt assets, languages, and skill sets from one context of our lives and worlds across the breadth of our contexts, with particular attention to bringing those skills

from our linguistic and cultural homes into the academic context as an act of decolonial resistance and disruption of English hegemony (and thus of the coloniality of
knowledge).

After this activity has been completed, archive it in a writing folder or journal. Have
it be something that you reference back to periodically, and regularly—not to admonish
students for not sticking to the correct language or discourse for academic writing, but
to encourage them to consider how they can translate skills and practices from one
context to meet the demands and expectations of another. How can they bring their
whole linguistic selves to being fluent across contexts? Practice the strategic use of
informal voice or language. Encourage them to make attempts at including a home or
first-language voice in academic writing and examining where translation is and is not
helpful. Have them think about the syntax and structures they use in different settings
and where they might add complexity or interest to the writing they do for other audiences. Encourage them to reflect on the audience they are writing for and what modifi-
cations to their writing and voice are needed to ensure a reader can draw meaning from
their text, even if they vary some of the expected linguistic elements. Cultivating these
skills of code-meshing, made transparent by the multi-context writing task, is a powerful way to encourage students in their ability to translanguage, shifting purposefully and
with strategic variation and adaptation of the range of tools within their repertoire of
linguistic practices as they encounter different challenges, questions, and contexts in the
world.

Language, Identity, and Decoloniality

Earlier in this chapter we mentioned the ways that language was not just technical or
logistical, but cultural, and linked to identity. Here, we want to expand on that, connecting back to Chapter 2, and explaining why coloniality so often tries to attack our
views of language and, thus, why decolonial educators must work so hard to protect and
value multilingualism.

We each know, personally, necessarily, that our language practices impact our lives in
incredibly intimate ways. The language(s) we use, learn, and develop become the languages with which we quite literally narrate our lives: they become the languages with
which we talk to ourselves, in our own heads (Bakhtin, 1981). This is an ontological
vision of language; one that sees and understands that different linguistic traditions, and
the ways they structurally and epistemically name and construct things, shape who we
see ourselves to be. The relationality of the subject and object in the diagrammed sentence of a language translates into the ways we construct ourselves in relation to the
world.

This is the logic that drives the Sapir–Whorf hypothesis, which, following on what
indigenous and marginalized communities have argued for years, suggests that the languages and discourses we use shape how we see and understand the world (O'Neill,
2015). Essentially, language is ontological, and the colonial assaults on language we have
seen and continue to see are exercises in the coloniality of knowledge and power, yes,
but also the coloniality of being. As Ronald Schmidt tells us, "The dispute [over the use

of non-English languages] in society and schools is essentially a disagreement over the meanings and uses of group identity in the public life of the nation state, and not language, as such" (2000, p. 47). When we create schooling conditions that rob students of their languages, or even allow them to let their multiliteracies and languages fall into neglect, without attention, value, or purposeful development, we are robbing them of core pieces of their identity. We risk irrevocably shaping their ontological relationship with themselves and the world, a trauma that lingers intergenerationally. And when we layer over the ways that language(s) are racialized, we risk further deepening the tensions and wounds of racial marginalization by neglecting yet another aspect of racial experience in institutional settings.

In addition to all the other points we have suggested, this is why considering how you will embrace multilingualism in your classroom space is so critical. Our middle-school students are in the throes of critical moments of identity development, and language(s), as ontological, racial experiences, are key pieces of this development. To encourage humanizing, decolonial outcomes, we hope you will take the time to focus on developing and encouraging all the languages and discourses present in your learning space, because doing so is honoring, fostering, and developing the racial, ethnic, and cultural identities as well.

Challenge in Practice

Ms Baker teaches at a large urban middle school. The community that her school serves is marked by a hugely diverse population and includes some longstanding communities of color, some affluent neighborhoods, and some communities where multiple organizations place refugee and asylum seekers. As a result, her 8th-grade ELA classroom is truly multicultural and diverse: it has a complex racial and ethnic make-up of 30 students; includes students whose parents and siblings grew up in the area and attended this school as well as students who arrived in the country just this school year; and at least 12 different and distinct native languages are spoken.

Even with a push-in ESL teacher, a past course in language acquisition, and her own experience learning and speaking conversational Spanish (one of the 12 languages), Ms Baker is unsure of what needs to happen to support her course. Students appear stressed from their other courses as they arrive in her room, and teachers in other disciplines have publicly expressed that developing language skills is not part of their curricular burden, that this should be on the ELA department. Ms Baker is feeling the pressure both to set her students up for language and general academic learning, but also to feel more comfortable and welcome in the school space. But with so many different languages, she is unsure of where to even begin! Unfortunately, when she sought advice from her assistant principal, the advice she was given was simply to: "Focus on the English. That's the language they are here to learn."

What should Ms Baker do to approach this challenging situation? How could she think about this as a challenge of classroom culture and organization, without getting lost in the weeds of each student's particular languages? What resources from the community might she draw on?

Questions to Consider While Planning for a Multilingual World

1 When was the last time you tried learning an additional language? What was that process like, both intellectually, and affectively (socio-emotionally)? What does that tell you about the experiences students might be facing?

2 How are you ensuring that the classroom environment and community you are creating is language rich and intentionally transparent about language use?

3 What are you doing to purposefully message that all of your students' linguistic practices and assets are valued, welcome, and worthwhile?

4 How are you ensuring that when you need them using academic English, you are not privileging it as best, better, or more important/valuable?

Resources to Explore

Expanding our Conception of Language and Praxis

As we noted early on, this has not been a directive guide for supporting the precise skills needed around second-language acquisition instruction, but a vision of how to approach and ultimately weave those into your teaching. With that said, here are some essential readings we think pair well with what we have tried to do here:

- Suhanthie Motha's *Race, empire, and English language teaching: Creating responsible and ethical anti-racist practice* (2014) is an incredibly compelling and valuable resource for building our repertoires of practice for supporting emergent bi/multilingual students.
- *Raciolinguistics: How Language Shapes Our Ideas About Race* is a powerful and important text edited by H. Samy Alim that is essential reading. We would also recommend *Articulate While Black* and *Roc the Mic Right* by Alim, as well as *Talking That Talk* and *Word from the mother* by Geneva Smitherman, to enrich your understanding of Creole and African American Vernacular English. Jonathan Rosa's *Looking like a Language, Sounding like a Race* helps to explore how language impacts and racializes Latinx students
- Carla España and Luz Herrera's *En Comunidad: Lessons for Centering the Voices and Experiences of Bilingual Latinx Students* is a great how-to text on building multilingual lessons.
- Ofelia García's work on translanguaging, including *The Translanguaging classroom. Leveraging student bilingualism for learning* and *Educating Emergent Bilinguals: Policies, programs and practices for English Learners* are essential reading if you have substantial bilingual populations at your school.
- And finally, if you really just need technical support around language development for your students, *Techniques and Principles in Language Teaching* by Dianne Larsen-Freeman is our recommendation.

Assessment Alternatives

Turning to assessment in the context of multilingualism, we want to talk specifically about formative assessment—the ongoing assessments we do to check for understanding and shift and shape our next instructional moves—and specifically question-asking strategies. Asking students questions is by far the most frequently used formative assessment practice to gage learning and understanding that we educators engage in. Yet too often, we turn this simple, formative assessment into something that feels summative by raising the stakes through cold calling, temporal pressure, and social anxiety. Being called on in class can be a terrifying prospect for students who have to process a question, translate the question in their heads, formulate an answer, translate that response, and then create an utterance in front of a classroom. And remember that this process of processing and translation is not just for students who speak 'foreign' languages; it is all our students who are language learners, and who may have different discourses tied to their identity and the voice in their heads. Our point is that formative assessment needs to stay formative, welcoming, and not a nerve-wracking mini-exam held in public.

Let us put an end to cold-calling, and stop with the rapid-fire demands on kids whose names emblazon popsicle sticks that sit on the corner of our desks, imbued with an air of doom, and the power to induce panic. If we really want to assess learning, even learning from a particular student, let us give them warning; let them know that we will be calling on them, let everyone prepare and engage in intellectual heavy lifting by doing a turn and talk (or something similar) first, and of course, let students in your room speak in their home language with others who share those languages/discourses if it is helpful to their learning. Similarly, if during a turn and talk, you hear something valuable, let them know the thought is good and that you want to hear from them as they share this already validated idea.

For language learners, the affective pressures of speaking in class are immense, easily inducing freeze reactions that can feel humiliating and paralyzing. There are ways to assess learning without being demanding and dehumanizing, and despite old-school rhetoric that plays on colonial resentment and patriarchal logic, ideas of putting students on the spot to 'toughen' them for rigorous settings in the future hold little water. If the point of question asking is to see if students are grasping the material, we can assess this even if they need prep time to do so. There are a multitude of ways we might imagine to support and encourage student contributions, and draw out their degree of comprehension, without the need to terrify or humiliate them.

Technology Spotlight

Look, as we noted in the vignette above, one should not rely on Google Translate as a definitive source of accurate translations. But it is incredibly useful, if limited. It is a good resource, and huge labor-saving tool, so do not fear using it, but be clear and sure that you always do your best to check translations with native speakers for accuracy, and be honest about your fallibility and the likelihood of erroneous translations. Consider including a conciliatory note about the nature of the translation and your apologies if things are odd or unintelligible.

Beyond that, the tech tools we most want to point you to involve personal language learning. Knowledge about how language learning works—and feels—is crucial to being able to support emergent multilingual students as it reminds us of what the challenges of operating in a second-language context involve and the ways our brains seek to access our fully linguistic tool kits. While immersive experiences are ideal, there are a number of free and paid smartphone apps—Duolingo, Babel, Rosetta Stone—available to help you learn one of the languages spoken in your classroom. While these may not be perfect, the learning design of the tech has reached impressive levels. We highly recommend working to learn a new language, and recommending this resource to your emergent multilingual students as well, which can allow this to serve as a shared, horizontal learning experience for you and your students.

References

Alim, H. S., & Smitherman, G. (2012). *Articulate while Black: Barack Obama, language, and race in the US*. Oxford University Press.

Bailey, G., & Thomas, E. (2021). Some aspects of African-American vernacular English phonology. In S. Mufwene, J. Rickford, G. Bailey, & J. Baugh (Eds.) *African-American English* (pp. 93–118). Routledge.

Bakhtin, M. (1981). *Dialogic imagination: Four essays*. University of Texas Press.

España, C., & Herrera, L. Y. (2020). *En comunidad: Lessons for centering the voices and experiences of bilingual Latinx students*. Heinemann.

Fanon, F. (1963). *The wretched of the earth* (Vol. 36). Grove press.

García, O. (2009). *Bilingual education in the 21st century: A global perspective*. Wiley/Blackwell.

García, O., Johnson, S. I., Seltzer, K., & Valdés, G. (2017). *The translanguaging classroom: Leveraging student bilingualism for learning*. Caslon.

García, O., & Wei, Li. (2014). *Translanguaging: Language, bilingualism and education*. Palgrave Macmillan.

García, O., & Kleifgen, J. A. (2010). *Educating emergent bilinguals: Policies, programs, and practices for English language learners*. Teachers College Press.

Larsen-Freeman, D. (2000). *Techniques and principles in language teaching*. Oxford University.

Lewis, G., Jones, B., & Baker, C. (2012). Translanguaging: Origins and development from school to street and beyond. *Educational Research and Evaluation*, *18*(7), 641–654.

Luke, A. (2017). Critical literacy, school improvement, and the four resources model. In P. Albers (Ed.), *Global conversations in literacy research* (pp. 1–13). Routledge.

Mignolo, W. (2003). *The darker side of the Renaissance: Literacy, territoriality, and colonization*. University of Michigan Press.

Mignolo, W. D. (1993). Colonial and postcolonial discourse: cultural critique or academic colonialism? *Latin American Research Review*, *28*(3), 120–134.

Motha, S. (2014). *Race, empire, and English language teaching: Creating responsible and ethical anti-racist practice*. Teachers College Press.

Norton, B. (2013). *Identity and language learning*. Multilingual matters.

O'Neill, S. P. (2015). Sapir–Whorf Hypothesis. *The international encyclopedia of language and social interaction*, 1–10. doi: 10.1002/9781118611463.wbielsi086

Rosa, J. (2019). *Looking like a language, sounding like a race*. Oxford University Press.

Schmidt, R. (2000). *Language policy & identity in the US*. Temple University Press.

Smitherman, G. (2021). *Word from the mother: Language and African Americans*. Routledge.

Smitherman, G. (1999). *Talkin that talk: Language, culture and education in African America*. Routledge.

Winford, D. (1998). On The origins of African American vernacular English—A Creolist perspective: Part II: Linguistic features. *Diachronica*, *15*(1), 99–154.

Zeigler, M. B. (2001). Something to shout about: AAVE as a linguistic and cultural treasure. *Sociocultural and Historical Contexts of African American English*, *27*, 169.

9

DECOLONIZED CLASSROOMS...
NURTURE CULTURAL CHANGE

Introduction

Paulo Freire (2009) recognized that education could either continue to perpetuate systems of oppression or disrupt such systems and bring about change:

> Education either functions as an instrument which is used to facilitate integration of the younger generation into the logic of the present system and bring about conformity or it becomes the practice of freedom, the means by which men and women deal critically and creatively with reality and discover how to participate in the transformation of their world.

The question then becomes: which direction will we choose?

Currently, the culture war around literature and other forms of media is in full battle mode, with conservative companies, politicians, and media pundits decrying the liberal indoctrination of American children. This is not a new battle. Literature has long been utilized to teach about morality and social values. In early schools, this was exhibited through the *New England Primer*, a book used by colonists to teach the alphabet, but that also preached about the perils of idleness and faithlessness. However, the tenor and tone of the battle in recent years has become much louder and more intentionally divisive. States have enacted new laws such as the Parental Rights in Education Act in Florida, which prohibits teaching about sexual orientation or gender identity. And as of February 2022, 36 states have introduced legislation that "restrict[s] education on racism, bias, the contributions of specific racial or ethnic groups to U.S. history, or related topics" (Stout & Wilburn, 2022). Further, lawmakers in eight states have drafted bills that would ban the teaching of what they deem "divisive" or "racist and sexist" concepts. These bills use language that is similar to language used in an executive order from former President Trump that banned diversity training for federal workers. And despite the mythology around racism being a lingering Southern problem, these states were not Southern states. In essence, the rhetoric around the 'liberal agenda' has become anything that is inclusive of people outside of the white mainstream culture.

DOI: 10.4324/9781003290681-11

Reacting to Cultural Change

Colonialism—past *and* present—is about the erasure of culture, of groups of people. It doesn't have to be physical in nature, although physical violence is certainly a reality of the United States' past and present—and unfortunately, we fear, its future. But erasure through language and exclusion is just as damaging, and the attempts to limit what teachers can discuss and what students can read is a form of erasure. This erasure also demonstrates ways in which the coloniality of knowledge is used to reinforce the coloniality of power. Further erasure of culture can also be seen in conservative textbook series that seek to completely rewrite and whitewash American history. For our students from historically marginalized communities, the erasure of texts and culture eliminates large parts of their identities. This is damaging at any age, but in early adolescence, the impact on our students is immeasurable.

As teachers of *all* students, it is imperative that we develop a classroom that nurtures cultural change, that rejects the erasure of our students' heritages, and that builds a culture that integrates all identities. We as adults and educators need to accept that the world in which we went to school is gone. There are new cultural dynamics, new demographic realities, new interests, passions, and perspectives, and new social stories that define our students' lives. Either we embrace these, or the educative value of our efforts will be lost and our teaching just another expression of coloniality. This chapter presents approaches to nurturing that cultural change by allowing students to read and write in ways that confirm their identities, while also building a classroom that is dynamic and appreciative of the change in culture, literacy, and engagement that youth themselves are driving.

Reading Instruction to Remix Futures

Aside from literature circles, the primary texts used in reading instruction in middle level classrooms are teacher selected. In recent years, teachers have become mindful of diversifying representation in their classroom libraries and novel studies, but in our work in middle level classrooms, this doesn't seem to be as prevalent when selecting other types of texts. And the truth is, selecting texts that all students will see themselves in is next to impossible. Providing students with opportunities to select their own texts is one step toward nurturing cultural change. Textbooks convey to teachers and curriculum decision makers that all students need to be reading the same texts in order to build their reading prowess. Aside from the problematic political nature of textbooks, which often skew toward exclusionary views in order to appease their markets, it is simply not true that all students have to read the same text in order for effective reading instruction to occur. In actuality, it is more powerful to teach students how to read in ways that allow them to be a part of the process, to encourage the transactional (Rosenblatt, 1994) and participant nature of reading (Freebody & Luke, 1990). One strategy for reading instruction that can nurture cultural change is remix. In remix, which has a deep history in the music industry, creators borrow from multiple texts to create a new, personalized text. While there are various ways to use remix in the literacy classroom, one powerful way to focus on creating meaning from texts is through found poetry.

Step 1: Familiarize Yourself with the Concept of Found Poetry

Found poetry is a form of poetry that is created by finding words in different places. In some forms, such as blackout poetry, words and phrases are pulled from a single text. However, other forms pull language from across texts. When composing found poems, creators use only the language that they find. They might pull a single word from one line of text and longer phrases from other lines. Once they have gathered a collection of words and phrases, creators combine them in new ways, resulting in a poem that is new and unique to their own interpretations. And while the creators are free to arrange the words in ways that make sense to them, phrases stay syntactically intact and no additional words are added—all language must be found.

Step 2: Encourage Students to Explore Inclusivity

Nurturing cultural change means we reject erasure and work toward inclusivity. Unfortunately, students from the dominant culture often don't recognize when erasure is occurring, so teaching students explicitly about what it means to be inclusive can be a first step toward change. This also creates spaces for students from marginalized communities to share their perspectives. To be clear, teaching explicitly does *not* mean direct instruction, nor does it mean that we provide students with a shared reading around the text. While it may be tempting to select texts that we use with students, we must recognize that with each text selection we bring our own biases. Thus, by presenting a singular text, we are excluding other texts that may provide different perspectives or resonate with students in other ways. Further, by tasking students with finding texts on their own, we are teaching them how to research texts for purposes other than simply writing research papers.

To start, provide students with time to research articles, blogs, song lyrics, stories—pretty much any written text—that speaks to inclusivity. Encourage them to diversify their search by demonstrating how to identify the author, author's purpose, and audience, and then selecting texts that present a variety of perspectives. Have students select at least three different texts that they feel can teach them something about inclusivity.

Step 3: Model How to Pay Attention to Language

Once students have identified the texts that will guide their work, demonstrate how to read a text for specific purposes. Rereading for different purposes is a strategy that increases comprehension, but without an authentic purpose, readers are often reluctant to read a text more than once. Show students how to highlight words or phrases that stand out for different reasons. For example, they might start with words and phrases they just find interesting. This allows them to get a sense of the text before going back and pulling out more specific ideas. Once they have read the text through that lens, they can read with an eye on practical tips. A next read might then focus on moments of 'a-ha!' or insight. Approaching reading instruction in this way helps students develop a deep understanding of text rather than viewing text as something to hurry through.

Once students have identified words and phrases across their texts, guide them to make connections across texts. How do the words and phrases from one text support the ideas in another? How do the words and phrases in a text elaborate upon the words and phrases in another? How do the words and phrases in one text contradict or challenge those in another? This teaches them how to synthesize ideas and formulate their own ideas and beliefs. Strategies such as List, Sort, Label can help them sort their lists of words and phrases into larger groups or words and phrases that share commonalities in some way. Once students have had a chance to sort their ideas into groups, they can then label each grouping with a word or phrase that ties the group together. This also helps them see the ideas they have collected in new lights, providing them with the material they need to form their own understandings of the texts.

Step 4: Remix for New Understandings

Having sorted the words and phrases they have pulled out of each text, students are then ready to begin remixing and forming their own poetry. Ask them to consider what they now understand about inclusivity. They may choose to include ideas from each of the categories or they may choose to focus on one specific category. Most importantly, students are given the ownership to frame their own understanding of inclusivity and rearrange the words and phrases in a way that represents their learning. As they are composing, demonstrate how line breaks, repetition, and stanzas can help them convey their ideas. Emphasize that the only rules they must follow are that they can only use the words and phrases they have identified and they must use words and phrases from all texts.

As a way of teaching how to read for specific ideas and synthesize across texts, remix is a valuable approach to reading instruction. Once students understand the process of remix, it can be used in other ways across the curriculum. To encourage student understanding of diverse perspectives, students can research a topic from the viewpoint of different identity markers and then create a new text that captures each of these perspectives. In addition to written texts, students can also draw from visual and video texts.

Writing Instruction to Sustain Youth Creativity

The problem with writing instruction in most middle level ELA classrooms is that it's either this or that—it's informative or it's creative; it's written or it's digital; it's the narrative assignment or the persuasive assignment. As we've discussed in earlier chapters, writing is much more than words on a page or screen. It can span across and blend genres. When we open up the possibilities of what it can be, what students can create, we make way for writing instruction that sustains and cultivates the cultural creativity and enthusiasm of youth. Just like we tend to put boxes around writing, we also put boxes around the kinds of practices that should be taught in specific classes. Studying historical events and engaging in civic action should be confined to social studies classrooms. Calculating numbers only occurs in math class. Examining phenomena is within the realm of science labs. And creating art should only be under the guidance of the art teacher—if students are lucky enough to have an art class. But middle school is about—or should be about—engaging and re-engaging in inter- and trans-disciplinary studies (as we discuss in Chapter 3). In fact, the silo-ing of subjects—and even grade levels—is a Western construct that runs counter to Indigenous traditions (Ottmann, 2017). Most indigenous languages have no word for education. Instead, they refer to the concept of *coming to know*, which is a way of learning "that involves self, community, creation and cosmos alongside the Creator" (Ottmann, 2017, p. 100). Thus decolonizing writing instruction means that we tear down those silos and provide opportunities for students to make connections across disciplines and spaces in order to help them *come to know* the world in a more authentic way—in a way that honors the traditions of all people.

Protest art is one way to break down the silos. It draws from the civic engagement often focused on in social studies classrooms, integrates art as a way of communicating, utilizes composing practices from ELA, and allows for natural connections to science and math depending upon what students identify as an issue that matters to them. It also has rich roots in marginalized communities. Protest art is used to influence the public by informing them about a social issue, declaring an objection around the issue, and persuading others to act together and address the problem (De Nichols, 2021). It can take many forms, including displays in public spaces through street art, guerilla art, public performance, and project art; political commentary through political art and culture jamming; more traditional genres like photography, poetry, and music; and even through craftivism, a co-opting of arts that are traditionally considered domestic endeavors such as needlework or yarn bombing. Protest art is a form of writing instruction in that it requires a process of creating and communicating a message, just as we would if writing a research paper or editorial. It can sustain youth creativity and nurture cultural change by honoring students' backgrounds, knowledge and interests. Because protest art comes in various forms, students can find the medium that they best communicate in, and the language arts are about effective communication. Protest art allows students to make statements about issues they care about and demonstrates to them that they have the power to influence the conversation around those issues. Further, it allows students to draw upon the artforms that have cultural meaning to them rather than forcing them to create in ways that don't match their worldviews and experiences.

Step 1: Provide Students with Mentor Texts for Analysis

Protest art will likely be an unknown art form for many students. We venture to say that some students may have negative connotations about some of the art forms, as graffiti and other forms like yarn bombing modify public spaces, which can invite censure from those who do not support or understand the messages being conveyed. This means we must draw their attention to art that they may already be aware of in their communities, as well as examples of art in other spaces. Then, through structured analyses, we can assist students in better understanding the purposes and messages that shape the art. Begin by presenting students with mentor texts that represent multiple forms and have them work together to address questions such as (1) What is the social cause being addressed? What message is it trying to convey? (2) What stands out in the piece of art? (3) How does the art piece communicate ideas about the social issue it is commenting upon? (4) What are the most effective elements in the message? (5) What areas could be refined, revised, deleted, or added to increase the impact of the message?

After students have analyzed the mentor texts individually, with a partner, or in small groups, whole-class discussions can help groups tease out and understand the nuances of protest art. This will better prepare them for understanding its purpose and how decisions are made during composition. This will then situate them to study the art forms that speak to them in greater depth. Encourage students to identify two to four forms that they could see themselves creating and find more examples to analyze.

Step 2: Identify and Research Social Issues that Matter to Students

Once students have explored protest art, prompt them to identify social issues that they have opinions about. Encourage them to think broadly before settling on one issue, drawing from problems within their communities, as well as dilemmas that are sparking more global debate. Remind students to consider not only those problems that are widely talked about, but also those quieter, and at times more pervasive, issues that complicate the world. As students settle upon potential topics, have them identify and research multiple perspectives around the issue. Emphasize the need to find and learn about the perspectives they do not agree with—even if those perspectives may make them angry. In order to create a message that reaches the desired audience, it is important to understand their thinking. Show students how to identify the arguments of each side, as well as how they frame their arguments. This can be a good time to develop a mini-lesson on logical fallacies to help students identify flaws in arguments.

Through their research, students should be able to identify an issue they want to focus upon. For students who struggle with settling on a topic, prompt them to consider what they are thankful for and then consider others who might not have the opportunity to be thankful for that item, to reflect upon conversations in their families and communities, or to remember times that they felt angry or that an injustice was done. Help them identify why these objects, conversations, or moments matter to them, and then encourage them to research what others have said about their ideas. As students research, have them identify the audience they want to target with their art and pay close attention to how their target audience communicates about the issue. This will assist them as they begin to develop their ideas.

Step 3: Play with Ideas

As students move into the ideation stage, encourage them to begin by identifying the spaces where their target audience can be found. Are physical spaces more likely to reach them or would digital spaces make more impact? Once they have identified a space, work with them to consider the different forms of art that can enter those spaces. For example, if they can best reach their audience in online spaces, yarn bombing is likely not a great approach. Conversely, if it is easy for the target audience to avoid online spaces, then creating physical art such as street or performance art might have more impact. Prompt students to recognize the limitations of some art forms, as well. We do not want to get them in trouble with the law by creating graffiti on downtown buildings! As students consider potential art forms, make sure they consider their individual talents, as well as who might complement their talents. Art—or any form of writing—does not have to be an individual endeavor. Creating together can nurture a culture of interconnectedness.

When a decision about an art form has been made, engage students in the composition process. Just as in traditional writing instruction, students need time to play with their ideas. They need to sketch ideas and receive feedback from others. It's important that they are given a safe space to try and fail in their ideas because this develops a mindset that embraces risks—and protest art (and all real learning) is about taking risks. Make sure they know that they will likely sketch out an idea only to throw it away and go in a different direction. Encourage them to seek feedback from a variety of people, including those who might not agree with their ideas. Through the process, they can strengthen their message and increase the likelihood of impacting those in their audience.

Step 4: Construct Art

After students have developed a tight prototype of their artwork, aid them in identifying the materials they will need to complete the work. Language arts teachers frequently are not given the materials to create art—after all, art is the purview of the art room. This means that students first need a clear inventory of what they will need to bring their artwork to life. As a teacher, it helps to know where you can pool materials across groups. For example, if several groups plan to paint murals, you can acquire paint and brushes that groups can share. If students need materials that you do not have in your classroom, you can ask administration to purchase material out of their budget, write grants, or work creatively with students to locate materials in the community through donations or other inexpensive options like second-hand stores or community sales. After students have acquired the necessary materials, create time and space for students to develop their work. Make sure that there are avenues for a continual feedback process so that students learn about the value of refining their ideas even in the act of creating.

Step 5: Publish the Work

Artwork complete, it is important to publish their work in public spaces. Protest art cannot exist simply within a classroom. If students are creating simply for the teacher or even just each other, then we devalue their ideas and their work. Thus, it is important to help students identify venues where their work will have the most impact. Consider contacting public libraries for space to publicly display their work. Think about coffee shops that might be open to a presentation day. It is also necessary to consider whether all students will display their work in the same spaces—it may be that doing so will also dilute their work because some students may be trying to reach an audience that will not enter a chosen library or coffee shop. Listen closely to what your students are telling you and try to determine spaces that honor their visions and leave them feeling comfortable.

In addition to securing venues, you must also secure permissions from students' parents or guardians. As minors, when we present student work in public spaces, we have to be careful that we publish their work in ways that their families feel are safe and in harmony with their beliefs. And if families are uncomfortable with the student's desired space, work with the student to find a compromise that they are comfortable with—don't just shut them down. Consider ways they can publish within the classroom or school and brainstorm how they might continue their work in other ways. But most importantly—publicize their work! Work that stays inside the classroom has little impact on cultural change, as well as on shaping students' understanding of their role in creating change.

Step 6: Reflect on the Process

Reflection is often an overlooked part of the learning process—but it can be one of the most important steps because it is through reflection that we identify what we have learned and how we can transfer that learning to other contexts. If traditional writing instruction is required by your curriculum, you can have students compose written reflections in paper or blog form. If you are less tied to expectations or do not urgently need to practice more traditional writing, you can also expand the reflective spaces by having them reflect via video or audio recordings. Whichever approach you take, have them return to the questions they considered while analyzing mentor texts. How would they answer those questions when they look at their own work? Have them also consider new questions such as: What's next for them? Where can they take this new understanding? How can they incorporate art in other aspects of their lives? How can they help shape change in the world through art? As they start to explore these questions, they begin to nurture kernels of ideas that can result in larger cultural change—and most importantly, they begin to see that they *can* shape the conversations necessary for cultural change.

Honoring Middle-School Youth as the Creators of New Worlds

Remix and protest art position students as creators who are imagining, speculating, about potential new futures. To create, students must also learn how to effectively listen. Throughout this book, we've focused on listening to community voices and those are vital to the process of world building. Yet sometimes listening means that we listen without hearing sound. Within Aboriginal communities, the concept of deep listening is a practice that requires the listener to pay attention to the "spaces within and between stories" (Brearley & Melvin, n.d.). It helps us become aware of the stories that are told, as well as silenced. Deep listening means that we recognize relationships with each other, as well as the land; that we invest time in building those relationships; that we expand our understanding of ways of knowing and being; that we are creative in the way we learn; and that we infuse care into all our actions because we are aware of the impact we have upon ourselves and others. Miriam Rose Ungunmerr Baumann, 2021 Senior Australian of the Year and renowned Aboriginal artist and educator, explains that *dadirri*, an Aboriginal word for deep listening, is also an awareness of your roots, your purpose for why you are here, your future path, and the place where you belong. It encourages quiet stillness and an openness to waiting (Ungunmerr, 1988). Embedding *dadirri* into our practice means that we make space for that quiet, deep listening. It can be literally setting aside five minutes of our class time to sit quietly with each other and notice the sounds, see the objects, feel the room, and contemplate how these sensory details shape our understanding of the world. Deep listening requires nothing more than being in the moment.

We can also translate deep listening into practices that encourage students to go out into their communities, their worlds, and discover aspects of their world that they had never noticed before. One way to do this is to task students with noticing elements of their world that connect with them in some way and capturing those elements through video and sound recordings. When students pay attention to the details of objects, sounds, and experiences that have meaning to them, they can draw inspiration for new visions of the world. Liberation and humanization require a new cultural world to come into existence, and youth will be the cultural creators who craft this new vision. But in crafting this new vision, they must first deeply listen and identify how the world speaks to them.

We can assist students in identifying ways to create a new vision by helping them collect the artifacts they discover through deep listening, documenting them, and creating an archive that shares their world experiences with others—creating new stories for others to listen to, as well. To do so, we can introduce students to the concept of archiving by reading excerpts from books like *Lost Children Archive* by Valeria Luiselli (2020), which although an adult novel, provides middle-school students with glimpses of what it means to archive outside of museum spaces. The story follows a family's journey from New York City to the Chiricahua Apache land in Arizona. Archiving and documenting, the mother explains, help us collect the present in order to make sense of our time and space: "You just have to find your own way of understanding space, so that the rest of us can feel less lost in time." In a sense, the mother is explaining deep listening to her son. And while the book as a whole would likely not be used with middle schoolers, excerpts such as this can help students make connections between the artifacts they collect through deep listening and the need for curating their collection.

After students have collected photos and recordings of elements of the world that speak to them, students can tag each artifact with its name, when and where it was collected, who collected it, what it is composed of, and descriptors that capture the artifact's importance. Once each artifact has been documented, students can work together to sort artifacts into collections, name the collections, and compose an introduction that reflects upon how the collection embodies the community. Through this process, students will find commonalities and differences and begin to explore where they have come from, why they are here, and where they belong. Once students have answered those questions, they can begin to consider the path they want to forge next. While there are various ways to capture this path, remix, once again, offers students a tool to envision a new future. Consider ways that students can look across the collection and pull out elements they want to preserve in their world. Then, invite them to add their own dreams for the future to the mix, creating something new that draws upon the past and present to envision a new future. In doing so, students recognize the power of listening as they consider new worlds.

Challenge in Practice

Ms Green is an experienced 7th-grade teacher who teaches in a highly racially, culturally, and economically diverse middle school. She recently learned more about protest art while attending a national conference. Excited to center her students' passions and to help them learn how to leverage their voices, Ms Green designed a unit around protest art. Students have been very receptive to the unit, sharing insightful observations about the protest art they have studied and thoughtfully researching the issues they are driven to learn more about. Now, they are exploring different art forms and sketching out their ideas.

On Friday, as she is circulating the room and talking with students about their ideas, she is concerned by some of the trends she is seeing. It seems that many students, while very excited about their social issue, are playing it very safe in their designs. In talking to them about their ideas, she learns that while they have some provocative ideas, they are afraid to put those ideas into action for fear of getting into trouble with adults in the school and community. While she is talking through these fears with one student, a small argument erupts at the opposite end of the room. Walking over to them, she discovers two groups of students from the same cultural background heatedly debating what they believe to be acceptable representations of their culture. One group had run with Ms Green's suggestion to pull from the artforms that have rich traditions in their communities. The other group had been inspired by remixes they had created earlier in the year and were remixing pieces of their traditional cultures with representations of modern Anglo culture. The group that was staying true to the mentor texts they had pulled from their communities was accusing the other group of being sell-outs. The remix group was defending their ideas, claiming that the other group was too stuck in the past and afraid of change. Ms Green is alarmed that this stage of the project is not going as planned and is uncertain how to navigate the various conversations.

How should Ms Green approach these conversations with her students? How can she encourage students to take risks? How should she navigate conversations around cultural practices in communities that she is not a part of? How can she help students recognize that culture is always changing? What steps could she have taken prior to this that might have prevented some of these debates?

Questions to Consider While Planning
for Nurturing Cultural Change

1   How can you help students understand the value of both tradition and change?
2   How can you create classroom experiences that promote risk taking? How can you create experiences that help students develop confidence in their own abilities and knowledge?

3   How can you learn more about students' cultures and attitudes towards their cultures in order to build responsive and proactive learning experiences?

4   How can you create an inclusive classroom that celebrates and elevates different perspectives?

5   How can you incorporate a wide variety of mentor texts for students to draw inspiration from?

Resources to Explore

Nurturing Change Through Art

Protest art has a rich history in the United States and around the globe and has often played a role in making change. We have centered protest art in this chapter, both explicitly as well as through remix, which can also be used as a form of protest art. To better understand protest art in its various forms, as well as its impact, check out the following resources:

- The article "The 25 Most Influential Works of American Protest Art Since World War II" from *The New York Times* brings together artists, a curator, and a writer to discuss protest art that has impacted change. Following each example, the group discusses the work and why and how it made a difference: https://www.nytimes.com/2020/10/15/t-magazine/most-influential-protest-art.html
- The National Gallery of Art has designed a lesson series titled, "Uncovering America," that features a lesson on Activism and Protest. It features examples, as well as suggested lesson ideas: https://www.nga.gov/learn/teachers/lessons-activities/uncovering-america/activism-and-protest.html
- The Met provides an exploration of "Art, Protest, and Public Space," which highlights prints from the 18th century to present: https://www.metmuseum.org/perspectives/articles/2021/10/art-protest-public-space
- The book *Art of Protest: Creating, Discovering, and Activating Art for Your Revolution* by De Nichols was written to introduce students in middle and high school to the history of protest art. It introduces different genres of protest art, highlights artists, and tips for creating your own designs.
- *Détournement* is a form of remix that has a rich history in protest art. In their article "Media Literacy and American Education: An Exploration with Détournement," Seth French and Jacob Campbell explore how to use *détournement* in the classroom: https://digitalcommons.uri.edu/jmle/vol11/iss1/4/
- Although most of their exhibits can be found in the museum's physical space, the Museum of Graffiti shares past and present exhibits that can inspire ways to think about and explore the art of graffiti: https://museumofgraffiti.com/

Assessment Alternatives

Throughout this book, we have explored ways to push back at traditional assessment. As we've discussed in previous chapters, including others in the feedback loop is a more authentic and impactful way to assess the effectiveness of student work. It can also be much more meaningful to students when they see how others besides the teacher respond to the work and ideas. Due to the public nature of the work described in this chapter—as well as in other chapters of this book—teachers should consider how to help students measure the impact of their work. One way is to consider how others in public spheres, including researchers, curators, or event planners, collect feedback from the public.

Surveys are a common form of assessment when attending conferences, professional development workshops, or events. Their ability to capture feedback from a large group makes them an appealing way to measure the impact of the work or event they are trying to assess. Digital tools such as Google Forms or Survey Monkey make them easy to distribute and analyze trends, too. Working with students to develop a survey that helps them measure the impact of their artwork or other public works helps them not only learn more about how audiences respond—which measures the true impact of their work—but it also helps students reflect upon what their real intent is when creating the piece. What do they want to make sure their audience takes away from their work? What specific aspects of the work do they want feedback about? Students can draw from questions provided to them while analyzing mentor texts and creating their own work, as well as formulate questions they want to explore with their audience.

Surveys can be distributed in multiple ways. As the teacher, you can send out emails to mailing lists, you can ask the public venue to distribute the survey to their email lists, or you can add QR codes to descriptors of the work at the exhibit. Once surveys have been collected, the class can work together to analyze the responses, looking at trends that help them identify the strengths of their work, as well as at trends that highlight areas for future development. This approach to feedback can help students learn how to transfer their learning to other spaces and contexts, making it more valuable than simply assigning a grade.

Technology Spotlight

Engaging students in remix and art requires students to have access to tools that allow for manipulating images. Graphic design tools such as Photoshop and other tools within the Adobe Creative Cloud, as well as online tools like Gimp, Canva, and Inkspace provide students with the tools to manipulate images and text. There are also tools for iPads and phones, such as Snapseed and Prisma Photoeditor, that allow students to take photos and edit them all on one device. Many of these tools have templates that can help students get started while also allowing for students to start from a blank canvas. Artistic skills, like many other skills such as reading and math, are often skills that students see themselves as either possessing or not. Students who do not identify as artistic can struggle when presented with the opportunity to create from scratch. Tools such as these image editing tools can assist students in reimagining themselves as creators, paving the way for them to produce artwork that can effectively convey their intended messages.

References

Brearley, L., & Melvin, T. (n.d.). *Deep listening. The Living Circle.* https://thelivingcircle21.com.au/deep-listening-in-practice/

Freebody, P. & Luke, A. (1990). Literacies programs: Debates and demands in cultural context. *Prospect, 5,* 7–16.

Freire, P. (2009). *Pedagogy of the oppressed: 30th anniversary Edition.* Continuum.

French, S. D., & Campbell, J. (2019). Media literacy and American education: An exploration with détournement. *Journal of Media Literacy Education, 11*(1), 75–96.

Luiselli, V. (2020). *Lost children archive.* Vintage.

Nichols, D. (2021). *Art of protest: Creating, discovering, and activating art for your revolution.* Big Picture.

Ottmann, J. (2017). Canada's Indigenous peoples' access to post-secondary education: The spirit of the 'new buffalo'. In Frawley, J., Larkin, S., Smith, J. (Eds.), *Indigenous pathways, transitions and participation in higher education.* Springer. https://doi.org/10.1007/978-981-10-4062-7_7

Rosenblatt, L. M. (1994). The transactional theory of reading and writing. In R. B. Ruddell, M. R. Ruddell, & H. Singer (Eds.), *Theoretical models and processes of reading* (pp. 1057–1092). International Reading Association.

Stout, C., & Wilburn, T. (2022, February 2). *CRT Map: Efforts to restrict teaching racism and bias have multiplied across the U.S. Chalkbeat.* https://www.chalkbeat.org/22525983/map-critical-race-theory-legislation-teaching-racism

Ungunmerr, R. M. (1988). *Inner deep listening and quiet still awareness. Miriam Rose Foundation.* https://www.miriamrosefoundation.org.au/dadirri/

Part III

PRAGMATIC VISION / CONOCIMIENTOS

Anzaldúa is very clear about this: we are never really done with our learning, growth, or the ways our identities shift and change. There will always be travesias and new travesias, crossing and more crossing that continually change us. But once we have unlearned our limitations and embrace the process of change, we do come to knowledge, to *conocimientos* (knowledge) about a vision of the future that might be. Concimientos guide us forward, even as they continue to change, they sustain us, even as they are tested. This forward motion assists us in maintaining a pragmatic vision that centers students in the learning, that focuses on learning as experience, and that privileges the experiences of the students. We can develop, as Freire described it, a critical consciousness.

This last part shifts us away from focusing on the characteristics of a decolonized classroom and toward an emphasis on how to continue to nurture a vision of who we want to be as decolonizing educators. In Chapter 10, we provide approaches to identifying the attributes of our educational worlds in order to find fissures that we can dig into in order to shape new worlds. Then, we turn to approaches to sustaining our work in Chapter 11. Once again, we lean on the importance of community—this time not as a vehicle for student learning, but rather as a way to find support for and motivation to continue our commitment to our newly acquired conocimientos. And we end in Chapter 12 by leaving you with thoughts to consider as you enact your own pragmatic vision, a vision that we hope can build a less colonial figured world.

DOI: 10.4324/9781003290681-12

10

DECOLONIZED EDUCATORS…NAVIGATE TIGHT SPACES IN A CHANGING EDUCATIONAL LANDSCAPE

Introduction

Decolonizing instruction means that we have to make change. And change can be scary, particularly in current times. Yet, if we don't push past that fear, we will never see a system that celebrates and supports all students. As James Baldwin said,

> Not everything that is faced can be changed, but nothing can be changed until it is faced.

And change is needed. In the last month, one teacher with whom we work has shared three efforts by parents to stifle their work—and as we write, it is only September. First, a community member who no longer has children in school called to threaten the principal because during a lesson on identity, students were given an option to discuss their sexuality, gender, or political beliefs. Next came a different parent who complained that their child was allowed to check out a book from the school library that contained mature content, resulting in a new policy that led to the labeling and restriction of books. But what constitutes mature content? Then came a parent who sent their child's ELA teacher a note stating that their child would not be allowed to read any texts that contain "woke" ideas. It is apparent that parents and community members are becoming more and more emboldened to push back at efforts to diversify the curriculum and create learning spaces that seek to disrupt the Euro-centric power structures of schools. This leaves many educators wondering how to continue their work—or if they even have the stamina to stay in the teaching field. Indeed, right now, much of the narrative is around a teacher shortage. But we have teachers—many have just chosen to leave the classroom. And some of these decisions have been influenced by the educational spaces they have been forced to function within.

Teaching in a Neocolonial Climate of Fear

It is evident that being a decolonized educator is getting scarier and scarier. Teachers need their jobs so they can feed their own families, making it difficult to step outside the accepted norms and risk losing their jobs and often their reputations. But *society* needs teachers who work toward decolonization if we ever hope to see the changes needed for a more equitable world.

DOI: 10.4324/9781003290681-13

As we've explored throughout this book, the colonization of schools is not a new phenomenon. It's infused in the foundation of the United States' educational system. At times, colonial forces have attempted to hide in the shadows. But in recent times, the educational landscape has been less inclined to hide colonized practices. One just needs to go to social media to find numerous stories of communities that are pushing back against attempts to create a more equitable society. And alarmingly, more and more educators do not need to turn to social media to see those stories. Rather, they are happening in their own schools and districts. So how do we do what we know is right? What avenues exist? Understanding the worlds we exist within is the first step. Dorothy Holland and her colleagues (1998) developed the concept of figured worlds, which can help us explore new roads forward. Figured worlds describe how social forces shape the ways people interact in socially defined worlds. Forces such as those we just described, as well as others, impact how teachers navigate schools—and they also impact how we form our identities as teachers. Thus, as new (and experienced) teachers enter different educational worlds, it can be important to understand how those worlds have been constructed so that we can find ways to deconstruct harmful practices. What kinds of artifacts do our schools use, and what kinds of artifacts can be used to change our world? What kinds of discourse or languages are used within our worlds? How is language codified and weaponized? How can language be used to make changes? What are our identities as decolonized educators and how can we use what we know about ourselves to navigate spaces? This chapter explores these questions, as well as others, to assist us in moving forward in our work despite the obstacles that will inevitably attempt to disrupt our journey. And while we may not have all the answers, we do know, as Baldwin stated, that we must look at our landscape with open eyes if we ever hope to make a change.

Cultural Artifacts in Education

Cultural artifacts, the physical objects and concepts that symbolize our world, populate the worlds we live in (Holland et al., 1998). The world of education has its own unique set of artifacts that allow us to understand our world, as well as differentiate it from others. For example, traditional classroom rows of desks immediately signal that we are stepping into a world of school, whereas stepping into a room filled with long benches often signifies we are entering the world of church. When we interact with the artifacts within our worlds, we learn about the expectations of others, form new understandings of ourselves and our roles in the world, and perpetuate the culture (Bartlett, 1932; Piaget, 1971). Recognizing the artifacts within our worlds helps us to better understand the expectations we are being held to, consider and explore their (often colonial) origins and the ways they position us in relation to one another, and identify ways we can disrupt a culture that excludes and harms others.

While the figured world of schooling contains artifacts such as textbooks, homework, and bells to signal movement that are consistent across worlds, examining the cultural artifacts within your own context can assist you in navigating your space. Ask yourself: What are the physical artifacts that are privileged in your school and/or district and what are their roots? Is your curriculum dominated by classic novels and traditional five-paragraph essays? Are decisions mandated by standards and standardized tests? Once you have identified the physical artifacts that are valued, closely examine how they are used. What are strict mandates and what are suggestions, expectations, or traditions? Differentiate between the nuances of their use. In doing so, you can find ways to disrupt their power.

For example, if classic novels are mandated texts—you have no choice but to teach them—ask yourself: do you have to teach them in their entirety? Is that an explicit requirement? Or is it an assumption that is made based upon its sheer existence in the curriculum? Can you, rather than use the books in their entirety, pull small excerpts to examine how the novel or its ideas exist within a larger context? If you must teach them in their entirety, what other texts can you present alongside them that provide a coun-ter-story or flesh out different perspectives? And how can you ensure that you give those texts equal weight? Or rather than teaching the novel as an authority, work alongside students to interrogate the ideas it presents. As we've discussed earlier in the book, ask students to look closely at the text and raise their own questions or engage in construc-tive debates around issues within the text.

Don't stop at physical artifacts. Conceptual artifacts are just as powerful. So what are the concepts that are privileged and what are their roots? Do you have homework poli-cies that expect students to complete a specific number of hours of homework outside of school? Are students allowed to make revisions or do they have one chance to com-plete the work? Is there a focus on what students don't have or can't do rather than what they bring to the learning environment? Is the teacher considered the expert?

Conceptual artifacts are often more malleable and within our control than physical artifacts because others can control the tools they provide us and expect us to use, but they cannot control our minds (unless we let them). So how can we shift conceptual arti-facts that perpetuate colonized ideas? Recognizing and *privileging* the funds of knowledge (González et al., 2006) that students possess can assist us in making the shift. Funds of knowledge refer to students' background knowledge—personal, as well as academic, life experiences, skills and knowledge used outside of the school day, and world views struc-tured by their cultural and social contexts. Drawing upon students' funds of knowledge, we can be responsive to our students' lived experiences and develop instruction that empowers and is relevant to all of our students rather than those who have been privi-leged by the structure of schooling. We must also seek to understand our students' lived realities. How is their time used outside of school hours? Are they tasked with watching younger siblings so their parents can work later shifts? Do they have internet access in their homes or do they need to travel to public spaces like libraries to do their work?

And perhaps most importantly, consider how to shift away from the teacher-as-ex-pert artifact. At the very least, consider how you can become a facilitator of learning. As an expert, we perpetuate our own worldviews and biases. As facilitators, we help our students discover their own worldviews and biases as they learn along the way. But we also encourage you to position yourself as teacher-as-collaborator, working *with* stu-dents to develop learning experiences and identifying texts, or as teacher-as-co-con-spirator, committing to standing up to push back from others in order to assist students in becoming their authentic and best selves in school.

Discourse in Education

Like cultural artifacts, discourse helps shape our worlds. James Gee, a noted linguist and literacy researcher, differentiates between discourse and Discourse. While discourse is specific to how we use language, Discourse is more of an *identity kit* that dictates how people communicate through language, actions, thinking, and values in order to be recognized as a part of a specific community. In this way, Discourse is very similar to how Holland and her colleagues (1999) define discourse as a way for participants in figured worlds to make sense of their cultural artifacts.

In schools, discourse can be a very powerful way to sort students. It can elevate and situate students for success, and it can ensure that others cannot succeed because the discourse of school is rooted in whiteness. As students move into middle school, academic discourses become more and more important to understanding concepts and to excelling in standardized assessments. Rooted in Latin and privileging written over oral language, academic discourse determines the opportunities students have as they move along the education continuum. Students who interact regularly outside of school with people who are fluent in the language of school become more fluent in academic discourse than those who don't. And because of their fluency in academic discourse, they are often considered 'smarter,' setting them up for continued successes as they progress through school. With their focus on academic discourses, schools often ignore or punish the discourses of non-white communities. For example, as Geneva Gay (2002) noted, white teachers often tend to use a passive-receptive approach to communicating content—again, positioning the teacher as the expert who distills knowledge and expects students to sit quietly and receive the information. Yet, other cultures encourage active participatory ways of communicating, which can result in a teacher construing students who communicate in this way as rude and disruptive.

Knowing what we know about the role discourse plays in a student's success, it's vital that we begin to pay close attention to how we are using language. Academic language has been given more attention since teacher exams like the edTPA have begun to assess for teacher candidates' understanding of academic language, but academic language is just one piece of the language puzzle. As teachers, we must closely examine the discourses used in our contexts—what are students expected to know in terms of the school itself? In terms of the various disciplines being studied? In terms of their larger communities? How can we elevate discourses other than academic discourse as ways to affirm students' identities, as well as position them for success?

As we discussed in Chapter 8, the first impulse by educators is often to teach students how to code switch. For example, in their book *Code-Switching Lessons: Grammar Strategies for Linguistically Diverse Writers*, Wheeler & Swords (2010) provide teachers with strategies to help students code switch according to their audience. One example includes a t-chart that encourages students to distinguish between formal and informal language around topics such as clothing. Yet, as Baker-Bell (2020) posits, this approach privileges white mainstream English over other cultural languages. In fact, labeling the language as formal and informal reinforces this bias because it suggests that white mainstream English is the formal version of the language. While this approach may be well-intended, it sends a message that students' native languages are 'less-than,' and while they may be acceptable in some places, they are not accepted by society as a whole.

Rather than forcing students to conform to academic and white mainstream language practices, decolonized educators need to recognize how language is weaponized and assist students in finding their own voices in ways that are valued. Swales' (1990) description of how language is used to create a shared community can assist us in our efforts. According to Swales, discourse communities are made up of six elements: 1) goals, 2) intercommunication, 3) participation, 4) genres, 5) lexis, and 6) expertise. Explicitly teaching these elements will help students recognize not only how to identify the way language is used in discourse communities, it can also help them (and us!) identify places we can begin to make changes to create more inclusive communities. We can start this process by creating a discourse community for our specific classrooms that is inclusive of everyone.

First, discourse communities share a set of *goals*. Within our classrooms, we can co-construct our goals with our students and work together to determine how we want to use language to accomplish these goals. Second, *intercommunication* must be determined. What are the mechanisms we will use to communicate with each other? While email may be the preferred mode of communication by the school, it may not work for those in the community. So, it is important to work together to determine the most effective ways to communicate. This may be through a shared communication app, through regular class and community meetings, or even through a designated conversation protocol. Third, how will we ensure everyone desires to *participate* and can do so? How are we going to exchange knowledge? In what ways will we share information, and even more importantly, exchange feedback around that information? Fourth, what *genres* will we use? Genres connect to the texts we use in our classroom and become a part of our cultural artifacts. Identify the genres that have cultural significance and determine ways they can be used for teaching and learning. Fifth, pay attention to *lexis*, or specialized terminologies. Within specific disciplines, different terminologies are privileged. Sometimes we have control over this privilege, but other times we do not. Explicitly identifying the lexis within the discipline, as well as the classroom community, helps us determine whether or not we are excluding or including others. Together, identify the lexis of the community and dissect how the lexis will or can be used. Determine how to navigate instances when terminologies that may exclude are used so that everyone is equipped with the tools to learn the lexis or to eliminate lexis that only exist to exclude others. Finally, consider *expertise* within the community. How do we develop expertise across the community? How do we distribute expertise? How do we create opportunities for everyone in the community to, at times, be experts and, at other times, be novices? How will we value expertise?

By co-constructing a discourse community with our students, rather than expecting them to conform to an existing discourse community, we can build a community that values each individual. We can use language to empower rather than disempower. And we can begin to signal to students the power language has within systems, equipping them with the skills and knowledge they need to continue to make change outside our classrooms.

Identity in Education

Positionality

Our identities as educators shape how we navigate tight spaces in teaching and learning. As much as we would like an easy answer for how to work toward decolonizing the classroom, the problem is too complex for a singular solution. Who you are as a person, as well as the context you teach within, will shape your journey. We can, however, offer you questions to consider and potential pathways to explore in order to help you traverse the obstacles you will find along the way.

As you consider your identity, it is important to start by considering your positionality as an educator. The educational system is one that has long been entrenched in our society. As such, society has positioned teachers in ways that are disconnected from who they may be as people. By simply existing as a teacher in a specific space, we are automatically assigned narratives, roles, and identities that are derived from historical factors, as well as from the distribution of power and prestige that exist within the community (Holland et al., 1998; Urrieta, 2007). Historically, the educational system has positioned women as teachers and men as administrators, creating an unequal power dynamic. Schools were also initially created to serve those from privileged classes, which positions students in the system differently (Wildman, 1996). And, as we noted in Chapter 5, schooling traditional places our positionalities as teachers at a distance from those of students. These gaps can be exacerbated by the likelihood that our racial, ethnic, and cultural identities and lived experiences are vastly different from those of our students. Thus, when we set out to disrupt inequitable systems, we must first identify how we (and our students) have been positioned individually, in relation to one another, and in relation to institutional power, as well as to consider how much room we initially have to make necessary changes.

When considering your positionality as a teacher, ask yourself *What are the historical roots of the community you teach in? What are the ideologies?* Schools are rooted in communities, therefore the values of the community you work within will shape how you are seen as a teacher, as well as how much room you have to navigate. Schools that exist within more culturally conservative or racially homogenous communities will look very different from those positioned in more culturally liberal or racially diverse communities. However, while you may have less restrictions on how you go about your work as a teacher in more culturally liberal communities or diverse settings, it is important to recognize that there will still be barriers because of the way the educational system has been constructed. And while teaching in more culturally conservative or racially homogenous settings may present more obvious obstacles, constraints, and limitations, there is always room and possibility in the conceptual realm for negotiation and disruption. Thus no matter where you are, it is important to also ask *Who has the power in your school or district? Does your district operate in a hierarchical structure or are decisions made in more democratic ways?* Recognizing who has the institutional power to make decisions and change—and how that power is yielded—provides you with insights about how you are positioned in the broader colonial system, what you can do about it, and where to focus your efforts. This knowledge can assist you in understanding how to move forward, as well as how to find allies to do the work—because though they may look vastly different, making the changes possible in your community, whatever they may be, are vitally important.

Space of Authoring

In a space of authoring, we must decide if we are going to accept, reject, or negotiate the positions we are offered in our worlds (Holland et al., 1998). Often, we simply accept our positionality by doing nothing to challenge it. We may not even recognize the position we hold because it is so accepted within the world that we do not pause to question it. Yet, we do not have to accept this role. As educators seeking to decolonize education, it is most likely we *won't* accept our positionality. The schooling system within the United States, as well as in other parts of the world, has been built through a lens of colonization and very few, if any, schools are successful in completely disengaging from this foundation. Thus, educators who seek to decolonize education are faced with the choice of rejecting or negotiating their positions.

Rejecting the positions we are given means that we do not subscribe to the system we operate within and we act outside of expectations of the system. Ultimately, this is likely what most educators who are dedicated to decolonization aspire toward. Yet, the system has deep historical roots that makes it almost impossible for educators to completely reject their positionality and continue to work within a school system. This means that the most likely route toward decolonization is negotiation. Through negotiation, we can begin to work within the cracks of the foundation. And if enough of us work within those cracks, we can widen them to the point that the foundation will crumble.

So how do we use the space of authoring to negotiate our positionalities? If you've already begun to examine the cultural artifacts and discourses within your space, you've begun the process. But the success of this work relies on our identities and who we see ourselves being in the space. Holland et al. describe authoring as a process of internal dialogue and reflection. Authoring is an endeavor that is guided by your own personal context. There is no one approach. Yet, there can be no dialogue and reflection without new perspectives. So where can you find these perspectives and how do you use them to guide your navigation?

One of the easiest approaches is to simply read. Educators are professionals, and professionals are continually reading new research and interacting with new people in order to grow in the profession. There are multitudes of books that can teach you about perspectives and experiences other than your own. Often, we gravitate toward research and practitioner books such as this one when we think about professional development, and those are important. But reading other non-fiction books by authors of various identity markers can help us understand the knowledge that is valued in other communities. Reading fiction can also help us learn about others' experiences. But books are not the only texts that we can learn from. Look for blogs by educators and activists that can teach you about new ways of thinking and doing. Join social networking communities that engage in similar conversations. These communities often share resources and approaches to solving similar problems, and they are often willing to engage in collaborative problem solving around members' questions. Whatever texts you choose to read, make sure you read to learn more about the communities of the students you teach, as well as of the students you *don't* teach.

As we discussed in the cultural artifacts section, internal dialogue can also result from examining our teaching materials with an eye on biases and absences. Look closely at the books on your bookshelf. As Jenny Kimura (2019) states,

> The cover is not only the first encounter a reader will have with a book, but it is also the first indicator of whether or not a book is diverse, which is vital to teens and young adults who are seeking a reflection of themselves in the books they read.
>
> (p. 5)

Students are receiving messages about what you value before you even have a chance to open your mouth. Thus, it's important to look at your shelves—as well as other parts of your classroom—and ask yourself: How are specific identity groups being represented? What messages, key ideas, and information are expressed? What feelings and thoughts come to mind when you see your space through this lens? What are the implications for inclusion in the classroom? Once you know the answers to these questions, take the steps to fill in the identified gaps.

We cannot overemphasize how substantially discourse contributes to colonization. It is the vehicle through which coloniality reproduces itself, its logic, and its normalization as 'common sense.' So listen to the words people are using in educational spaces when engaging in reflection. Are people using coded language that tries to convey inclusivity but that really hides evidence of bias or prejudice? For example, do you hear words like 'grit' that imply hard work and perseverance but that in reality often put the burden of success on students' ability to comply with school structures rather than examining how the system devalues the students and their experiences? Be on the lookout for these kinds of colonial intellectual alibis. Look for visual representations of diverse languages. Ask yourself questions inspired by Mora et al. (2018) in their work on city literacies: What route did you take to find these languages? What means and modes of expression are present among these literacy practices? What are the implications for the promotion of diverse languages in our classrooms? How do the languages and images that are represented in the school perpetuate or dismantle culture centered in whiteness? Take steps to reframe the language you use in the classroom, as well as to promote representations of diverse languages. Find allies in the building who can help you reshape the way others in the building use language, both verbally and visually, and with whom you can work to hold yourselves accountable for maintaining your commitments and vision.

Finally, spend some time examining spaces. Look at the social media posts of your school and district. Explore websites, including the larger district's and your own. Walk through the physical spaces. Look at public art and displays. Consider furniture arrangements. Watch how instruction is delivered, both online and in physical classrooms. And as you are examining all these spaces, ask yourself variants of the critical literacy questions we explored in Chapter 6: WHO are all the possible people who made choices that helped create these spaces? HOW were these spaces constructed and accessed? HOW could these spaces be understood differently by different audiences? WHAT values, points of view, and ideologies are represented or missing from these spaces? WHY was this space created and/or shared? WHOM does this space advantage and/or disadvantage? And then use your answers to these questions to develop a plan for making changes that need to be changed.

We can only control our own spaces, so it may be that initially these are the primary spaces where we can create more inclusive and equitable classroom conditions. Yet, our efforts need to extend beyond our own spaces. This means we need to turn from internal reflection to external dialogue. Our efforts need to be seen through our actions. Ask questions of your colleagues to determine where you can find allies in the work. Ask questions of administrators when they make decisions around policies and procedures. Their answers will aid you in determining whether to accept or reject those artifacts. Don't, however, ask questions of and rely on the people you are trying to learn more about. For too long, the burden has been on the oppressed to demonstrate why and how they have been oppressed. You can find those answers by engaging in the internal dialogue previously described.

Do, however, talk to your students. Learn about their interests. Ask about their lives outside of school. Listen to their hallway conversations. Investigate how their time is spent. In general, learn as much as you can and use what you learn to guide your decisions. Be genuine, not performative. Show them that you care about them as individuals rather than as a means to a paycheck. Learn from them, grow with them, and push them to ask compelling questions about their own assumptions and positions in the world and society, even as you appreciate them for who they are.

Communicate with parents in transparent ways. Often, it's the parents and other community members and not the students who impede approaches to decolonization. Therefore, it is important to be seen as someone who is open and honest in their communication. Develop public spaces that allow parents to see the work their students are doing, as well as the unit guides and essential questions that guide instruction. Establish routines where students regularly communicate their work with their parents. Emphasize the ways students are directing instructional decisions. Invite input, but do not ask for permission. Take advantage of community resources. Visit community spaces that are devoted to supporting and enriching students from different backgrounds and cultures. Learn what they are doing and how you can mirror, partner, or extend their efforts.

World Making

When we engage within spaces of authoring, we begin to entertain the possibility of *world making*. In world making, tight spaces can begin to loosen, and we can start to realize decolonized classrooms. As we participate in world making, we also create spaces for other educators to reimagine their own figured worlds. World making involves what Holland et al. (1998) call serious play. Systems of schooling often necessitate playing in the margins but through this play educators can develop the competencies to recognize and change some of the colonizing practices of schooling and literacy instruction. Through serious play, we can develop new competencies, generate new discourse, and identify or create new physical and conceptual artifacts. If enough teachers engage in such play, we can build a new figured world, one that continually questions the artifacts, discourses, and acts within the newly imagined world to make sure they stay consistent with efforts to decolonize instruction.

Challenge in Practice

After years of teaching in public school settings where she was able to be creative and innovative in pushing students to explore literacy in critical ways, Ms Esqueda recently moved to a new city, and ended up with a position at a local private school. Though the school bills itself as diverse and lists social justice as part of its commitments, Ms Esqueda has run into the reality that the ways in which school administration, her peers, students, and families understand and construe what these things mean—and how they should shake out in the school—is vastly different than her own.

Essentially, the school understands social justice as making sure their diverse students get a "rigorous, traditional" education. There are specific, incredibly strict homework policies that must be followed, a blanket, zero-tolerance policy on late work and missed assignments, and a 'no excuses' approach to discipline and classroom management. Within her department, the department chair, though kind and thoughtful, is deeply committed to a curriculum based on the classical canon and an approach to writing that has students repetitively completing a nearly scripted version of an analysis essay for each unit and the final. More generally, the students are suspicious of anything different from rote, teacher-centric lesson activities, and parents and families have increasingly expressed concerns about changes to the 'traditional' school experience and curriculum they think their students need. The PTA has had recent discussions about whether race, ethnicity, or sexuality were even things that should come up in content-area classes, given some families' concerns about their school becoming caught up in problems of 'critical race theory' or 'political ideologies.'

Given all these constraints, where should Ms Esqueda start? Who might she begin having purposeful conversations with first? In which element of instructional praxis does it seem she could find some room for agency? In what ways could she start to disarm and deconstruct some of the more questionable understandings of ideology held by students, families, and teachers in the school, without drawing their immediate ire?

Questions to Consider While Navigating Tight Spaces

1   What ARE the constraints I face, and what are their sources/origins? If I trace them backwards, who is imposing them? Are the constraints *de jure* (hard and fast policies) or *de facto* (general community expectations)?

2   Where DO I have some agency? What are things in my curriculum and pedagogy (figured world of your classroom) that I can control, and can hold on to as expressions of my commitments, even if other things are constrained?

3   With whom can I engage in productive discourse/action about the constraints on my teaching? Are there key players I can seek to engage with in my school context? Are there community efforts, campaigns, or organizations I can seek to dialogue with?

4   (Though we don't like to be fatalistic), what is my professional and legal support network in case my teaching is challenged? Who can I count on to support me? Who will I turn to if things escalate in troubling ways?

Resources to Explore

Navigating tight spaces, as we have noted, is often about finding ways to claim agency over even potentially small aspects of our work, and begin to construct new worlds. Some organizations that might help you imagine how to do this include:

- Censorship is on the rise. Fortunately, there are organizations committed to fighting it. The National Council of Teachers of English Intellectual Freedom Center (https://ncte.org/resources/ncte-intellectual-freedom-center/) offers educators resources and guidance on how to combat censorship. The American Library Association Office for Intellectual Freedom (https://www.ala.org/aboutala/offices/oif), while targeted more specifically at libraries and librarians, offers similar resources that can be helpful for teachers. It offers free consulting services and confidential support for those who are faced with book challenges.

- Organizations such as the American Civil Liberties Union (https://www.aclu.org/), Southern Poverty Law Center (https://www.splcenter.org/), and the National Association for the Advancement of Colored People (https://naacp.org/) dedicate their work to fighting injustices against people from marginalized groups. Their sites have resources to assist those who face challenges to their human rights.

- Learning for Justice is a project developed by the Southern Poverty Law Center. Its website provides educators with resources and professional development around culture and climate, curriculum and instruction, leadership, and family and community engagement.

- The National Education Association (https://www.nea.org/) is dedicated to ensuring all students succeed, assisting educators to be aware of their rights, helping teachers develop their practices, and advocating for change in educational systems that support all students. In addition to providing resources toward these efforts, their site can also direct you to local associations.

References

Baker-Bell, A. (2020). *Linguistic justice: Black language, literacy, identity, and pedagogy*. Routledge.

Bartlett, F. C. (1932). *Remembering: A study in experimental and social psychology*. Cambridge University Press.

Gay, G. (2002). Preparing for culturally responsive teaching. *Journal of Teacher Education, 53*(2), 106–116.

Gee, J. (1999). *An introduction to discourse analysis: Theory and method*. Routledge.

González, N., Moll, L. C., & Amanti, C. (Eds.). (2006). *Funds of knowledge: Theorizing practices in households, communities, and classrooms.* Routledge.

Holland D., Lachicotte W. Jr., Skinner D., & Cain C. (1998). *Identity and agency in cultural Worlds.* Harvard University Press.

Kimura, J. (2019). A cover is worth 1000 words: Visibility and racial diversity in young adult cover design. Book Publishing Final Research Paper. 36. https://pdxscholar.library.pdx.edu/eng_bookpubpaper/36

Mora, R. A., Pulgarín, C., Ramírez, N., & Mejía-Vélez, M. C. (2018). English literacies in Medellin: The city as literacy. In S. Nichols & S. Dobson (Eds.), *Learning cities: Multimodal explorations and placed pedagogies* (pp. 37–60). Springer.

Piaget, J. (1971). The theory of stages in cognitive development. In D. R. Green, M. P. Ford, & G. B. Flamer (Eds.), *Measurement and Piaget.* McGraw-Hill.

Swales, J. (1990). The concept of discourse community. *Genre analysis: English in academic and research settings.* Cambridge University Press.

Urrieta, L. (2007). Figured worlds and education: An introduction to the special issue. *The Urban Review*, *39*(2), 107–116.

Wheeler, R., & Swords, R. (2010). *Code-switching lessons: Grammar strategies for linguistically diverse writers.* First Hand.

Wildman, S. M. (1996). *Privilege revealed: How invisible preference undermines America.* NYU Press.

11

DECOLONIZED EDUCATORS....
DISCOVER WAYS TO SUSTAIN
THEIR PRACTICE

Introduction

Indigenous scholar Jack Forbes once wrote,

> We are not autonomous, self-sufficient beings as European mythology teaches.
> Such ideas are based upon deductive logic derived from false assumptions. We
> are rooted, just like the trees....Nothing we do, do we do by ourselves.

Sustaining decolonizing practices should also be rooted in a network of educators who
support each other's efforts. We cannot do this work by ourselves. Both Michael and
Robyn have drawn upon others to sustain the work—and have worked with educators
who have done the same.

While in graduate school, Michael had the extreme pleasure of working with a coa-
lition of young pre-service educators from MEChA (Movimiento Estudiantil de Aztlán)
and the school of education at his institution to develop and launch a summer ethnic
studies program for high-school youth across their region. This group of educators, who
included both white and BIPOC folks, students coming through traditional teacher
preparation programs, and others moving into education through ethnic studies degrees
or community organizing work, came together with a remarkable, complementary set
of experiences and knowledge to not just create an exciting program with a radical,
decolonial vision of education and teaching, but to form a powerful community.

Even as they graduated, moved to different schools in different districts and even in
different states, these educators remained connected to one another through social
media, text chains, meet-ups, and reunions as a few continued to work on the summer
program. Together, they were able to support one another through intellectual and professional challenges, helping one member focus her combative commitments to equity in
a restrictive school, another determine where her red line was and how to reconcile her
commitments to youth with a need to protect herself as she left a school mid-year, and
another navigate the contradictions and false rhetoric of his school site. Together, they
supported one another through both professional and personal challenges and resisted
what researchers call 'wash-out'—or the way that the tedium and mundane frustrations
of schooling and teaching can dull or erase the aspirational commitments to equity and
justice we first bring to our classrooms. While individually each of these educators was

DOI: 10.4324/9781003290681-14

talented, together, collectively, they helped make one another exceptional by ensuring that those passions, commitments, and powerful visions of decolonial education developed in that summer program were not washed away. Shout out to you, Aquetza folks!

While cohorts within teacher education lend themselves to developing supportive communities around decolonizing education, similar communities can be built at any time in your teaching career. Robyn has had the opportunity to build such a community alongside a group of educators dedicated to self-examination and support as they, too, work toward decolonizing mindsets and practices. This group of teachers was dubbed Teacher Church by the wife of one of the members because Zoom meetings first occurred on Sunday mornings. Yet, as the community continued to develop, Teacher Church took on new meaning as it represents the fellowship and support the teachers provide each other. Made up of teachers who are at different stages in their careers— some have been teaching for 20+ years and others are in their first five—the teachers meet weekly to push their practices in student-centered ways.

Although the group began with a loose agenda of supporting each other during a time of intense racial strife (the George Floyd murder took place early in the group's development), it has gradually become more deliberate in its focus. The group participates in the restorative practice of listening circles once a month to give each of them the opportunity to express their feelings around a topic they have identified for the month. This provides them the space to blow off steam in a supportive space but also ensures they don't dwell in negative spaces. The rest of the month is devoted to reading a shared text, connecting practice to the ideas within the text, and problem-solving challenges that occur along the way. These teachers are a community, a family, that support and challenge each other to be better, to push their practices outside the boundaries of school. And together, they are making progress, including shifting away from traditional grading (a very colonial practice), inviting the community into their classrooms on a regular basis, and centering student inquiry throughout their practice. And the group has grown so close that they have come together for two summers for a retreat where they can break bread, laugh, and continue to push their thinking by co-developing instructional approaches that center decolonial practices.

Sustaining Our Commitments to Decolonization Through Interconnection

As the quote that begins this chapter explores, the idea of the individual as a totally self-sufficient, autonomous, independent being, disentangled and unbothered by connections and reliance upon others, is a colonial fiction. In fact, the idea of the radically independent individual emerges—both historically and philosophically—from the same vein of logic that produced the rationale for colonial violence and chattel slavery (see Chapter 3). While that does not make an inclination towards social autonomy somehow inherently malicious, it does mean that this way of thinking is in sharp contrast to a decolonizing, humanizing approach to the world. Global South epistemologies the world over, carrying with them the legacies of the ways of being that existed prior to colonization, speak to these appreciations of connection: Consider *In Lak' Ech*, *Ubuntu*, and *Isang Bagsak*. Each are cultural-regional philosophies that are strikingly similar in their call to embrace our connection and dependence upon others as a core cultural value. Ultimately, radical autonomy and decolonization are incompatible ideas. Colonization's central interpersonal mechanism—the coloniality of being—was to disconnect people from each other's humanity. Thus, decolonizing requires that we reconnect and re-entangle our lives to one another. Only when we accept this responsibility for interconnectedness, when we reject the coloniality of being that would divide us, can we fully value and appreciate everyone's humanity.

For educators, our interconnectedness to one another is, we suspect, already quite obvious. A school is a complex ecology (as we discussed in Chapter 7), with so many things in our professional lives dependent on the resources, actions, choices, support, and influence of others. To add to this complexity, our students arrive in our classrooms shaped by a whole host of myriad influences that we must consider, leverage, and compete with. And it is likely we have already grown (or soon will) even more suspicious of the logic of radical autonomy when we start looking towards the hard numbers, the data around which neo-colonial policy makers would have us assessed as educators. Efforts such as tying teacher salaries to student test scores, as if we and our students are dehumanized, autonomous mechanisms that can function or not regardless of social context, identity, and prior educational history, only further speak to the web of connection we all live in: Even the most generous value-added models for assessing teacher impact on academic learning show we teachers individually contribute *at best* 12–14% of a student's annual growth (see Amrein-Beardsley & Holloway, 2019). The rest is a constellation of home and community impacts, affective factors, past educational inputs, social media posts, and who knows what else. And this is not even delving into the fact that student development in middle school is about much more than grammar skill or reading comprehension (as noted in Chapter 2), and no statistical model can capture our contributions in those personal, ethical, and humanizing regards. While debating the merits of testing and teacher evaluation are a different conversation altogether, our point is simple: we as educators may be vitally important to student learning and development, but none of us operates in a classroom autonomous of the lives of others or the infinite influences and connections those lives link us to. Honestly, for teachers, the recognition of our interconnectedness and dependence on others is probably so obvious it is nearly laughable to have it pointed out.

With all this said, the point we really want to get at is that nothing we have described in this book can be done alone. And we mean that on multiple levels. Decolonization is a collective endeavor, not an individual task. You will need strong relationships with your students, a rich connection and understanding of the community(ies) you teach in, and a community of supportive peers to be a successful decolonial educator. In the remainder of this chapter, we offer three different suggestions that can help you cultivate interconnectedness to your students, to your school community, and to your peers, that we feel are critical for decolonial educators.

Sustaining Our Connections to Students and Community

We have talked a lot in this book about sustaining and nurturing the culture, literacies, practices, knowledge, and voices of the youth and families we teach. How can we do any of that if we don't take the time to explore, learn, and connect to their practices beyond just what emerges in school? We have talked a lot about appreciating, respecting, and valuing diverse racialized, ethnic, and cultural experiences in communities. How can we do any of that if we don't take the time to immerse ourselves in experiences that might be very different from our own? Simply put, we can't be culturally proactive, culturally sustaining, culturally revitalizing, or culturally nurturing if we don't authentically connect to and love those youth and community cultures we are teaching in. And it is also in this process of intentional connection that we believe you will find key elements you need to sustain yourself, to sustain your commitments and vision to decolonial work (whether you are able to do it up big or navigate it in the margins of tight spaces), and keep teaching towards a more humanizing future for years to come. When we are grounded and connected to communities, our work will feel less like labor (in an economic sense), and more like the calling that decolonial education needs to be. Moreover, the richer and more connected we are to students and communities, the better our praxis will be. Frustration in teaching comes from lots of different directions, and not all of these can be controlled. But one that we see regularly as a source of frustration for teachers absolutely can be: working in ways that are dissonant to student and community practices and ways of being. We teachers are, of course, going to struggle and get a bit frustrated if we keep advancing expectations and praxis that doesn't line up with who our students are.

But the great thing is that there are excellent, purposeful ways to address these disconnects, and in so doing, decrease the frustrations we can create for ourselves by asking students to be someone they are not and increase our own investment in the communities we teach in. Both these efforts create more sustainable futures for ourselves: they position us as more nimble, flexible, and responsive parts of a social ecology and able to lead decolonial change through our participation in community.

Learning About Student Practices: Community Ethnographies

The first of these strategies we find to be an excellent way to deepen our appreciation and understanding of our students' learning and cultural practices. It uses the strategy that sociologists and researchers have long employed to deeply know communities: ethnography. An ethnography is a systematic approach to observing, recording, and describing the interactions, practices, and perspectives of people by immersing ourselves in their cultural context, learning from them, on their terms. As much as your classroom, teacher education, or professional development work (including reading this book) might give you insight into the workings of schools and communities and how to approach pedagogy in a culturally sustaining way, it's important to note that most of life happens beyond the school—that means that the culture we need to sustain is happening beyond your classroom's walls. If we want our students to see a seamless transition between the cultural practices in their homes and lives and those that are valued in our classrooms, we need to be sure we know what those practices are. And the only way to capture this is to spend time getting to know the practices of the community on their terms. When we set about doing that strategically, we are engaged in an ethnographic exploration of our school communities.

With that in mind, we encourage you to plan to attend a community event in your school community (broadly), beyond school or after school hours. Some examples of this might be a community cultural event, a sporting event in which some of our students are playing (at the school or elsewhere), or a community play that includes some of your students. As you do this, take some serious notes, and complete a reflection on what you saw—because processing and making sense of what the cultural practices in our students' lives are and look like is the only real way to bring those into our praxis and, in so doing, sustain them. This is a task that you will need to practice, as you learn to take purposeful notes and observations and see things that might have otherwise seemed mundane or innocuous in new ways. Learning to look can take some time, so don't expect one visit to a community event will tell you all you need to know. Immerse yourself in the cultural context of your school, continually asking the questions in Box 11.1 each time. Over time, a rich picture of what your students' lives look like and involve will unfold. Done well, this is a task that will give you real insight into how your students go about learning and life when they aren't being constrained by the colonial confines of schooling. That is, we find, an illuminating and refreshing prospect that gives us new life, sustaining our decolonial commitments to praxis as we see our students in new ways and imagine how we can sustain them.

When we do this work with schools, we typically offer a tailored list of suggested community contexts. While your school community will have its own unique array of cultural events, happenings, and gatherings both formal and informal, here's an example of the types of events you might look for:

- Youth and pickup sporting events
- Farmers' markets
- Swap meets
- Seasonal festivals and street fairs
- Community aid organizations and events; charitable giving distribution events
- Community/recreation center classes and events

And always: ask your students! What do they and their families do on the weekends and evenings?

Learning About Community Dynamics: Power Analysis and Mapping

We borrow the next strategy for sustaining your practice from longstanding traditions and practices in community organizing. In community organizing, understanding who is in a community, what their roles are, how they are connected, and the ways they are linked to and influence various decisions, policies, and practices is everything.

BOX 11.1

General Ethnographic Observations:

- Who is present in this space, demographically? Who is not present? What roles are different people of different cultural, ethnic, and racial backgrounds occupying?
- Given the demographics of the school community, are all voices being heard with proportional weight? Who is more central? Who is left out? Why?
- What is the 'affect' of different individuals in this space? Does everyone seem equally comfortable? Do some seem more adept at navigating this space than others? Does anyone seem positioned at the margins?
- What is the age distribution? How would you characterize the youth–adult interactions? Whose voices are being valued? Whose interests are being served?
- How are different generations interacting? How are different segments of the community engaging with one another?
- What other patterns of interaction and behavior do you see?

Learning-Oriented Observations:

- What examples of learning and ingenuity did I observe at the site? What cultural, community, and family assets were on display?
- Who is teaching whom in this space? Who is sharing knowledge and how? What are the patterns generationally? Do different individuals communicate knowledge in different ways?
- What practices do I see happening? How are families and the community organizing themselves? How are they speaking to one another?
- How is learning and transmission of knowledge happening here in ways that converge and contrast with how learning happens in your cultural world? What does this tell you about the expectations and arrangements you create for your classroom?
- What's the division of labor? What's the level of independence and agency? How comfortable or resistant are different people to those arrangements?
- How is the context of the site unfolding? Who has agency? Who has cultural capital and power? How are youth relating to peers, to adults, to their communities, to other individuals in the space?
- How do decolonial perspectives, and other critical lenses from my teacher training, help me understand these dynamics in more nuanced, more robust ways?
- What do the participants themselves have to say about things? Is there contrast between your analysis and theirs? Are any of your students there? Who? What grades? Who are they with? What do they make of this event?

Understanding these complex ecologies is what allows great community organizers to mobilize people, to tailor their messaging, to develop meaningful programming, and to remain responsive to authentic community needs, while also advocating for new ideas and change. While we educators may not necessarily be community organizers in the sense that we aren't focused on particular policy change initiatives, we certainly share a great deal in common: Our work, too, depends on understanding our role in complex community ecologies, what those communities need, and how different elements of a community influence one another.

To do our best work and to put ourselves in a position where we can feel connected, valued, and supported requires that we understand how our communities work. When we do that, we can be strategic in our efforts, and in so doing, allow ourselves to sustain our work. Simply, if we are doing work that feels beneficial, rather than, say, just guessing at how to solve a problem we are facing, our ability to keep going, to push through difficulties, and move forward improves because we can be assured that our work will have an impact and that we won't be alone in the struggle. Power analysis and mapping allows us to create the strategic plan to make this happen.

Just like ethnography, this isn't a task you do once and then move on from. Power maps and analyses change for different dilemmas and evolve over time. The same community might be mapped differently if we are trying to address issues with students missing school, than if we were trying to imagine which new extracurriculars to offer. Additionally, an essential element of this task, mentioned in the instructions, is the need to research and explore beyond what you already know once you've done your map. You will find that there are blind spots and segments of your community that you do not know much about. We often find that folks know a lot about what institutions value and care about—something we call cultural capital—and where that exists in communities, but less about what the communities themselves value and care about. These strengths and assets that don't always register with formal institutions, but are vital to the internal practices and lives of communities are "community cultural wealth" (Yosso, 2016), and recognizing what these are is critical if we are going to leverage all of our students' strengths to support their learning. So when we do find ourselves less than familiar with a part of our community or our students' lives, think of it as an exciting opportunity to research and explore, and learn something new about this community you teach in.

In any event, the process can be incredibly rewarding and incredibly insightful. Next, we've laid out the steps and background information we use to guide folks through a *power mapping and analysis* process. We challenge you to think of a dilemma you've been facing, something that has made you feel a little frustrated and unsustainable, and either by yourself, or with colleagues, take it through this process—we suspect what you'll find is a bit of new inspiration and energy for tackling that challenge once you have explored the way that particular issue, practice, or dilemma fits into your school community, as well as where to begin targeting your efforts and conversations.

What is a Power Analysis?

Power analysis involves a systematic approach to gather political and cultural intelligence about a community which can be used to develop a plan of action informed by community needs and realities.

Why do it as educators? We cannot effectively serve our students, or know what it is about their culture that we want to sustain (let alone be responsive to), if we do not have a deep understanding and appreciation for their cultural practices and lived experiences, as well as recognizing what we don't fully know about these practices and experiences. In order to serve our students, we must constantly be learning about their worlds, and allow this to inform our curricular and pedagogical choices.

What is Power Mapping?

Power mapping involves participating in a collaborative visualization of the networks of relationships, knowledge, influence, systems, structures, resources, belonging, etc. that exist in a community, so that we can better understand how and where to intervene in the *ecology* of the community.

How Do We Approach Doing This?

The first thing to do is to recognize the dilemma, the reason why you are engaging in the task. This dilemma doesn't need to be a negative (we shouldn't only do this as a reactionary measure!), and doesn't necessarily need to be entirely specific. Basically, we engage in power analysis/mapping to solve problems or improve systems in our community ecology. For example, your dilemma might be as simple as improving your understanding of how homework is getting done, as central as wanting to better understand whose voices to include as you build your curriculum, or as big and complex as addressing a racial divide amongst your students.

Next, you want to choose a relevant focal point for your analysis. This might be a specific individual, an institution, a class/grade level, etc. based on the dilemma you are concerned with. From there, you may want to consider if there are particular, relevant lenses, concepts, or elements you want to attend to. Perhaps you really need to examine language. Or you are interested in ethnicity. Or food access is on your agenda. The possibilities are endless. As a place to start in your educational power mapping work, consider beginning with this dilemma/set of questions:

- *How can we best understand and serve the full diversity of our school community in equitable ways that advance empathy and understanding?*
- *What communities, actors, sources of capital, and perspectives do I need to engage to craft a meaningful, locally rooted approach to culturally proactive curriculum and pedagogy?*

We'll focus on your school as an institution and use the idea of "cultural community wealth" to help frame things conceptually.

So What Are the Steps of the Activity?

You are going to be creating an actual map, not just a map in name alone. This can be as artistic or simple as you would like. We do recommend trying to think geographically a bit, as it can be helpful. Ready to go? On a piece of paper, board, or some kind of shared digital document if completing this digitally with colleagues, engage in the following steps:

1   Map/diagram all the key elements of your community or the community surrounding your object of focus.

    a   What are the

        i   Different neighborhoods? Different cliques? Different constituencies?

        ii   Organizations? PTA? Boosters?

        iii   Businesses in the area? Prominent community individuals?

        iv   Sub-communities within the community?

        v   Groups, offices, organizations, etc.?

    b   Be as comprehensive as possible.

2   Identify defining elements of these parts of your community ecology.

    a   Be sure to include

        i   As many prominent contacts or individuals as you can for each item in the ecology

        ii   The demographics, stats, and characteristics of each group as you understand them

        iii   What things they care about, believe, prioritize, as you understand them

3   Map the relationships in the community ecology around and to the focal object.

    a   Mark out the relational power lines: the flows of influence, knowledge, or resources.

    b   Be sure to come up with ways to diagram and represent

        i   Connections and networks to the focal object, and to other facets within the ecology

        ii   Varying strengths and intensities of influence that different parts of the ecology evince

        iii   Where BORDERS and BOUNDARIES exist in and among the ecology

4   Analyze, identify, and *name* larger patterns.

    a   From what you've got down so far, what do you notice? Annotate your map as you go

        i   Who has the most lines drawn to them?

        ii   Where are gaps in your own knowing beginning to appear? Where are there patterns or trends across the ecology you've drawn?

    b   Note points of disagreement or different knowing.

        i   Do some of us know more about certain parts of the ecology than others?

        ii Do we have different perceptions on certain parts of the ecology than others?

    c   In sociological terms, how would you describe that pattern?

5   Identify community cultural wealth and cultural capital

    a   *Community cultural wealth*: For each constituency within the larger ecology that is OUTSIDE of the main networks/relationships of influence, what do we know about their

        i   Navigational capital—the skills they use to engage with different official and unofficial institutions?

        ii Resistant capital—the ways they define themselves in opposition to outside pressures?

        iii Linguistic capital—the language skills, multiliteracies, and discourse practices they use?

        iv Social capital—the personal networks and connections they rely upon?

        v   Familial capital—the ways they are connected to family near and far, and the ways they define family and family relationships?

        vi Aspirational capital—the goals and aspirations they have for themselves, and their children?

    b   *Cultural capital*: For the core institutions (like your school), and those groups on the 'inside' of the key networks of power and influence

        i   What are the valued elements of cultural capital? What does it take to be part of the 'in' crowd?

        ii Who are the gatekeepers? Where is knowledge of this valued cultural capital housed?

6   Pause. Reflect.

    a   What do you notice?

    b   How does this map make you feel about confronting the challenge?

7   Make a plan.

    a   Figure out

        i   How will you fill in gaps in your knowledge of key parts of the ecology? Of neglected parts of the ecology? Who will you need to talk to?

        ii What things need to happen to shift and balance power in the ecology to make things more equitable and humanizing? Who do you need to talk to? Who needs to talk to whom? Who needs to learn what?

        iii. What will you need to do to create a complete picture of the community cultural wealth of marginalized students and families over the next months?

b   Conduct one on ones: Who will you schedule one-on-one meetings with to start these discussions?

c   Develop action steps: Inclusive of things discussed, including one on ones, what are three to five action steps that need to happen next?

For an example of what a power map may look like, see Figure 11.1, which is the Power Map Michael and a team of educators created for Community High School (a pseudonym) as they explored how to move their curriculum in culturally sustaining and proactive directions.

Building Peer Networks to Sustain Decolonial Practice

In the last section of this chapter, we want to wade into what we feel is a critically important, but rarely discussed reality of our profession: Our work, and indeed our interconnectedness through that work, is not itself some wholly rational, intellectual thing that we can box up at the end of each day when we leave the classroom. We do not roll into our classrooms each morning, unburdened, connect with our students for the hours we share together, and then walk away at the end of contract hours, off to our home relationships. Teaching is emotional, *affective* work, as much as it is intellectual and physical. Anyone who has meaningfully spent time in a classroom knows the special weight that comes after a challenging day of school, the feeling of being weighed down by a complicated mix of your own emotions and thoughts, and the weight of sensations and reactions that linger on from your students' emotional, personal, and social experiences. As educators—and especially as middle level educators—our students arrive in our classroom still figuring out how they fit into a vast, sometimes scary world. As such, we are teaching our students both literacy skills and skills to deal with all the messiness, pain, tension, highs, lows, history, and complexity of life. It is for this reason that many talk of teaching not just as a job we hold, but rather as a calling—a life mission to which we commit ourselves not for personal enrichment or gain, but for the way it resonates with our deeply felt commitments and how we want to be in the world with others (Palmer, 2003, 2017). In this sense, still invoking the decolonial, we often think of teaching as spiritual work as well as practical or intellectual labor.

Now, what we mean here is not any sort of denominational, rigid, or formal understanding of spirituality, bound up with a particular faith tradition. Rather, what we want to point towards is the reality that the work we do as educators, and necessarily as decolonial educators, challenges us with questions and sensations that go beyond the intellectual and even the emotive. Every veteran educator we know has had their share of moments when they have had to shepherd students through moments, experiences, and crises well beyond anyone's maturity level and likely more intense than anything we could have expected when we signed up to share our love of reading and writing with youth. We are faced in the classroom with moral and ethical dilemmas, questions of values, and moments that demand something beyond empathy. We experience situations and hear stories that leave us turning over in our sleep months, or even years, later, wondering if we did the right thing and did our best by that student. Whatever you want to call it, however you prefer to conceptualize it, there is something about the work of

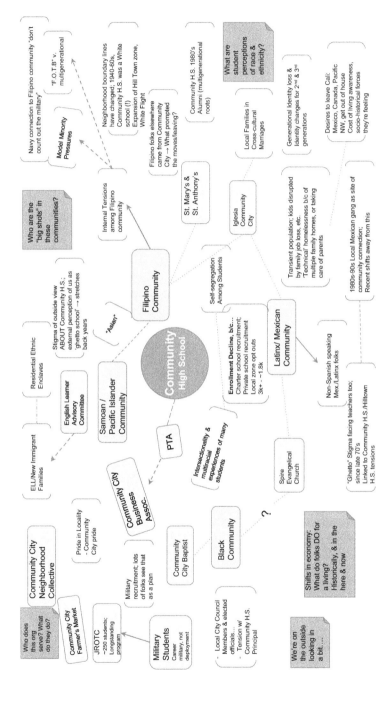

Figure 11.1 A power map created with educators to help move their curriculum toward more culturally sustaining and proactive practices.

teaching that goes deeper than the intellectual; our classrooms are not just places where we solve logistical problems and design and deliver information. They are spaces where we engage quite directly with the full scope of the human condition.

When we or others ignore this reality (or try to paper over it with Starbucks gift cards during Teacher Appreciation Week), not only do we put ourselves in a position that is ripe for burnout, but we also risk spiraling away from the humanizing, decolonial imperative we wish to strive for. Bottling up all of that affective residue from teaching— the joy, the pain, the countless sensations and feelings our students bring to us directly and indirectly in and beyond the classroom that go beyond description with simple emotional labels—puts us in an unsustainable position. Think back to Chapter 2, and our discussion of students experiencing the tension and emotion of dealing with the idea of race for the first time. As an educator, perhaps implementing one of the strategies from this text to dive into a novel about race and racism, you are likely to become the point of confluence for all of your students' complicated emotions and misconceptions about race, all at once. You need to absorb some students' problematic statements and negative, possibly aggressive, emotions and frustrations with being asked to confront the reality of race and racism, while at the same time making emotional space for other students' stories of marginalization. Both need to be meaningfully heard by yourself and others, all while balancing the messaging necessary to keep your classroom a brave space for vulnerability. That is not just a logistical challenge of ensuring different students' needs are being met, nor an intellectual challenge of imagining what to say and how to organize things; it is also a spiritual challenge of figuring out how you are going to carry all of that emotional baggage because you've got to do that same thing several times a day in different classes, come back each day of the week and do it again, and repeat it all the next unit, semester, or year as you explore new content—all while dealing with the weight that failing to do so means risking whether youth can learn, grow, and make progress in understanding others and the world. We are under no illusions that this is easy work. It isn't, and it surely speaks to a career that we must be called to. As decolonial teachers, we are stepping up to help others manage their historical burdens and move towards a more humanizing world. The labor of that leaves a mark.

We cannot meaningfully humanize others if we deny ourselves the humanizing experience of being honest about all the weight we are carrying, have carried, and will carry. Sustaining our practice requires that we find a community of reciprocal, authentic care that is not just professional or intellectual, or even emotional, but is spiritually (in the way we have described) supportive as well. We need a space that leans into the reality of our work and helps us feel humanized, so that we can continue the difficult, affective work of helping students navigate through and beyond the legacies of coloniality that surround us. With this in mind, and reflecting back on the vignettes above, we will suggest that you work to find yourself a 'Teacher Church.'

Now, the very idea of church is itself heavy with social, cultural, political, and emotional baggage, especially in a conversation relating to coloniality and colonial legacies. Weighing in on all the varied and contradictory ways that the Church (as formal institution) has been implicated in both dehumanizing and liberatory moments in colonization's 500-year history is well beyond our scope here, and there are countless texts on that.

Rather, what we are pointing towards is the holistic, purposeful spirit of community that both the educators in Michael's and Robyn's vignettes created. Here were groups of people who shared values, commitments, interests, and experiences, and wanted to be intentional in creating space to process and grow these values and ethical commitments beyond what was on offer in, for instance, their department meetings or school-organized PLC. They talked shop for sure, but they also talked about those deeper things that challenged, puzzled, scared, excited, and *called* them to their work. They didn't just come together because they were teachers—they came together because of more robust ontological connections: moral, ethical, philosophical, spiritual, however you want to describe them.

As you consider our suggestions for what to do with this idea for sustaining your practice, we encourage you to use whatever discourse suits you best, excising the word 'church' for something else, if it feels more comfortable and contextually resonant. For us, here, as we explain what we mean, we are going to use 'Teacher Church' as our phrase, following the discourse used by the group of critical and decolonial educators who coined it, for they were the ones who helped us crystallize how we thought about this vital way to sustain practice.

Step 1: Find Peers Who Share Something Bigger than a Curriculum

We've already covered this point in the preceding section, so we won't belabor it, but it is, really, the crucial piece: whether you are just starting your teaching career or you are a veteran, start seeking out a network of educators who share the same moral, ethical, and philosophical commitments as you. Look for these folks both near and far. These folks may be in your school, but maybe not in your department. They may be in your district, but not in your school. They may be in a professional network, but not in your district or state. While we may be literacy and humanities educators, there's lots of places to find quick support and guidance for lesson ideas, but intentional community comes from finding folks who share our same commitments to justice and humanity. Our core point is this: don't just network to connect with folks who can help you with lesson ideas. Network to connect with folks whom you can share aspirations, tensions, moral dilemmas, and ideological quandaries with *while* talking about praxis. In the long run, that personal sustenance will help you persevere in the profession as a critical, decolonial educator quite a bit more than just a crowd of folks who can give you the worksheet they used for that next book you have to teach.

Finding these people isn't necessarily going to be easy. It will mean taking some conversational and relational risks. It will mean finding some folks who seem promising, but maybe ghost out. But we think the rewards of building that community are worth it. Start by thinking of folks already in your networks. Can you deepen these connections with intentionality? What about the professional organizations or teachers' unions you are a part of? Look for opportunities there. Are there communities, people, or ideas that excite you on social media networks? Reach out, since communities aren't bound by location any more.

Be bold. Speak to your commitments. We believe a humanizing, decolonial vision of education is exciting, and think you're more than likely to find others who feel the same and who would be eager to share space and dive deep so they can sustain their praxis too.

Step 2: Don't Shy Away from the Hard Questions

There is a considerable amount of research that shows that Americans in general are increasingly less connected, polarized, and with fewer deep friendships. Anecdotally, we certainly find that to be the case in schools we visit, where teacher conversations in department- or grade-level meetings or PLCs stay superficial, talking about surface-level professional and social items, but not about moral values or beliefs. There seems to be a sense that this polite distance is a way to be kind, careful, and not make anyone uncomfortable in an increasingly diverse world.

But we don't decolonize by just talking about praxis. Things have to get a little personal, a little deep, a little spiritual. We need to exercise a more authentic vision of care. Because care involves difficulty too, not just empty kindness. Real care pushes you to confront and engage with the questions behind our superficial dilemmas. Real care pushes to create space to be authentic and share those things we are struggling with and work through discomfort. Real care seeks to ameliorate. And real care involves relational risks.

Our point, then, is that in the spaces we create, we need to ask one another robust, authentic, deep questions that may seem scary, but are the ones we need to talk about to sustain our commitments. Ask one another about race and ethnicity in our classrooms and lives. Ask one another about how we see our moral obligations to our students, and where the limits of our commitments need to be. Ask one another about why we do this work, about what calls us back to the classroom each day. Asking deep questions doesn't just help us sort through particular dilemmas, but it provides sustenance to remind us why we came to this work in the first place.

Step 3: Avoid Becoming an Echo Chamber

It would be understandable to think that finding a group of folks who share similar commitments to equity and justice might seem like we are advocating for silo-ing oneself with like-minded folks. Certainly, the vision of a Teacher Church we are talking about does require that we share some deep values and beliefs so that we can feel safe to be honest and connected. But sharing values does not preclude challenging one another, holding one another accountable, or pushing one another to grow and change.

Essentially, while our Teacher Churches should involve a community that shares core values, don't let them become echo-chamber spaces, where complaints and frustrations are met by empty platitudes and agreement. The community we build should encourage us as a space for personal, professional, emotional, and spiritual growth. They should be spaces for encouraging us to be our best selves and continuing to pursue our values, not to dwell in complaints, concerns, limitations, and constraints. This kind of, we will just say it, whining to one another has its place. It can be and feel therapeutic to get frustrations off our chests, to be heard, and to feel others agree with you. But while this might be an element of our space, it is not the only function you want to conceive of for this community. Now, alternatively, we are not suggesting your Teacher Church should refuse to let folks share their frustrations or silence needs to share complaints. Nor should you think that playing devil's advocate every time someone has a concern is a helpful way to encourage their growth. Rather, what we hope is that you will pursue a Teacher Church space that sets norms for how your connection time will unfold, how you will relate to one another during that time, and how you will create a space in which authentic care—care that is supportive but challenges one another to be engaged in growth—is consistently practiced.

Step 4: Set Regular Meeting Times, Stick to Them, and Stay Connected in Between

This one is pretty straightforward, but it matters. When you look at the way any faith tradition organizes itself, there are ritualized times for connection. Whether those are weekly, seasonal, or based upon other ways we mark time in nature and society, groups of interconnected peoples ensure that their communities have regular times to come together, meet, and engage in the important community building and connecting work they traffic in. This goes for educators as well. From our experience, the best, strongest, most sustaining 'teacher church' communities set up times to connect and stick to them. They reflect and adjust these as they need to be based on what is sustainable, practicable, and necessary. And because of the nature of these groups, they are honest with one another when life makes meeting these commitments difficult, because doing so allows others in the community to offer support.

This last point is important, because modern life and existence is, without a doubt, faster paced and more intense than ever. Things move at a lightning speed in the world and social media ecosystem, and that translates into our school and professional life. More than that, we are also often spread out geographically, perhaps with different time zones, at different schools, and certainly with different family commitments. It is hard to schedule around an array of different back-to-school nights or unexpected family crises. So being thoughtful about your casual, sustainable connection matters too.

As Michael's former students did, keep that text chain going. Seriously—right now, go fire off a text to some close friends. Basically, make sure you are finding small ways to remain connected and supportive of one another, so that we aren't putting too much pressure on major meet-ups that are more challenging to plan and could fall through. The cruel optimism of hanging too much hope on complicated plans that fall apart is a sure-fire killer of motivation and momentum. So the suggestion or step is simple: as you build a community of shared values, make sure you have a plan to stay connected and figure out ways you will keep in touch earnestly, and authentically, as a sustainable community in both formal and informal ways.

Step 5: Mix Up How You Learn, Grow, Challenge, and Support Together

As we discuss in step 3, we don't think a community where the extent of connection is rehashing classroom complaints is necessarily the most productive. Sure, there may be space for that, but we encourage you to think of your Teacher Church network as a bit more robust. Approach your connections in a variety of ways. Read a new book together and talk about it. Attend a conference or community event together, and then dissect what it means for your teaching and classrooms. Sit down together to take turns evaluating one another's curricular plans. Go learn a new skill or activity together and reflect on how you approached learning differently. And if you do want to do some addressing of complaints, think about doing it either as a part of your time together for therapeutic venting or connected to collectively completing problem–solution chains. In any event, as you build your community, make sure to keep things interesting and enriching, and of course, joyful. We can maintain our critical, decolonial analysis of things while still finding space for laughter, positivity, and growth. If not, what really is the point?

Challenge(s) in Practice

Mr Webster is in just his second year of teaching 6th grade. During his teacher preparation program, someone gave him the advice to, "Stay out of the teacher's lounge; it's where all the negativity happens." At the time, he didn't think too much of it, and felt every school would be different. But as he started at his school, it turned out to very much be the case—the lounge at lunch time was filled with negative, complaining teachers, some whose discourse about kids was downright frightening. Though it wasn't everyone on the staff, the negative voices dominated, and Mr Webster gradually stopped going at all. Now, though less overwhelmed with negativity, he found himself out of the loop of stories about students, and access to the social capital that came with knowing all the most recent gossip. Mr Webster was certainly happier to not be in that space, but he wasn't thrilled about feeling as isolated as he did now, and worried about continuing on in a profession in which he'd have no positive relationships with colleagues. What could he do to find and build a network to help him sustain his practice?

Ms Spencer is in her seventh year of teaching but finds herself at her fifth different school. She's been bumped by district seniority practices twice, moved districts and cities twice for family reasons, and switched schools once to work closer to home. At every school she's been at, she's built mutual respect and found meaningful relationships with colleagues, but her transiency has made it challenging for her to feel grounded and comfortable in the profession and to really cultivate a network. She loves teaching, and in her seventh year, really feels like she has found a groove with purposeful, confident instruction, but there are a lot of things she wants to keep challenging herself with. Given all her moves, she's unsure of where to turn for that kind of collegial support. What could she do to find and build a network to help her continue to challenge herself and grow her praxis?

Questions to Consider for Sustaining our Practice

1   What are my existing networks of support, affirmation, and sustenance? How can I nurture these to be more intentional and active?
2   Where are there potential allies in my educational landscape? How can I take the lead on inviting folks together to foster and encourage us to challenge and push one another forward?
3   Where can I find a good coach—someone who can give me constructive feedback and keep me honest to my commitments?

4   What networks and communities outside of my classroom, school, and education generally can I find to keep my passion sustained? Where are there communities committed to critical and decolonial ideas for me to participate in out in the 'real world'?

Resources to Explore

Reading as a Sustaining Practice

Sustaining your practice, as we have noted, requires connection with others, but also ongoing learning and growth. Often, we find folks tempted to see professional growth as just digging into methods texts for new ideas and lesson strategies. This is important, but it isn't everything we need to really grow in the vision part of our pragmatic visionary role. With that in mind, here are some suggested texts and ideas for how to explore and grow in new ways as an educator:

- Check out an ethnography about youth and schools. David Kirkland's *A Search Past Silence*, Lilia Soto's *Girlhood in the Borderlands*, Julio Cammarota's *Sueños Americanos*, Tim San Pedro's *Protecting the Promise*, or Julie Bettie's *Women Without Class* are all examples of excellent, recent texts that will let you explore and understand the lives of historically marginalized youth and communities on their own terms.
- If you are looking for more pedagogically oriented texts, check out *Culturally Sustaining Pedagogies*, edited by Django Paris and H. Samy Alim, for a collection of essays on how we can organize our classrooms in decolonial, culturally sustaining ways. There is a book series related to this idea edited by Django Paris that is also well worth exploring.
- We also encourage you to consider pushing the bounds of your fiction reading. Get away from your usual fare, and pick up recommendations from your students, and texts written by folks whose work challenges coloniality. *Exit West*, by Moshin Hamid, and *Tropic of Orange*, by Karen Tei Yamashita, are examples of contemporary texts whose authors have an eye towards exploring and disrupting colonial normality. Add these, and other texts like them, to your book club's reading list.
- Your own school community. What do we mean here? That your school community should be the greatest source of your sustenance and learning. Get out in the community. Be a part of it. Let yourself grow and be sustained by that energy as you contribute to it.

References

Amrein-Beardsley, A., & Holloway, J. (2019). Value-added models for teacher evaluation and accountability: Commonsense assumptions. *Educational Policy*, *33*(3), 516–542.

Bettie, J. (2014). *Women without class*. University of California Press.

Cammarota, J. (2016). *Sueños Americanos: Barrio youth negotiating social and cultural identities*. University of Arizona Press.

Forbes, J. D. (2011). *Columbus and other cannibals: The Wetiko disease of exploitation, imperialism, and terrorism*. Seven Stories Press.

Hamid, M. (2018). *Exit west: A novel*. Penguin.

Kirkland, D. E. (2013). *A search past silence: The literacy of young Black men*. Teachers College Press.

Palmer, P. J. (2017). *The courage to teach: Exploring the inner landscape of a teacher's life*. John Wiley & Sons.

Palmer, P. J. (2003). Teaching with heart and soul: Reflections on spirituality in teacher education. *Journal of Teacher Education*, 54(5), 376–385.

Paris, D., & Alim, H. S. (Eds.). (2017). *Culturally sustaining pedagogies: Teaching and learning for justice in a changing world*. Teachers College Press.

San Pedro, T. (2021). *Protecting the promise: Indigenous education between mothers and their children*. Teachers College Press.

Soto, L. (2018). *Girlhood in the Borderlands*. New York University Press.

Yamashita, K. T. (2017). *Tropic of orange*. Coffee House Press.

Yosso, T. J. (2016). Whose culture has capital?: A critical race theory discussion of community cultural wealth. In L. Parker & D. Gillborn (Eds.) *Critical race theory in education* (pp. 113–136). Routledge.

12

A FEW LAST THOUGHTS ON OUR DECOLONIZING EFFORTS

Introduction

As we end, we want to call upon the words of two leaders in decolonization who inspire us—and we hope you—to continue this important work. We cannot forget Gloria Anzaldúa, who has guided much of what we've laid out in these pages. She offers a simple, but powerful, observation:

> I change myself, I change the world.

The work starts with us, but our efforts can radiate out to places we never expect. We also want to keep the power of love in mind. It is easy to think about coloniality, constraints, and the harm schooling has done and dwell in that frustration and bitterness. But as Che Guevara reminds us, resentment is not a driving force for change:

> At the risk of seeming ridiculous, let me say that the true revolutionary is guided by a great feeling of love…We must strive every day so that this love of living humanity will be transformed into actual deeds, into acts that serve as examples, as a moving force.

A sense of anger over coloniality's impacts only takes us so far; a vision of the decolonial needs to come from genuine love and care for who we think we might all be, together.

So now, at the end of this book, having covered quite a substantial amount of conceptual and pedagogical ground, we are going to resist the urge to summarize and rehash too many of those details. Though tempted, we won't try to recap the colonialities of knowledge, power, and being again, or anything like that—though we hope you'll go back and review them!—but, rather, in this last chapter, we want to leave you with a few parting messages about everything we have shared, and you've now explored, as you look ahead with pragmatic vision.

Make Maps, Not Tracings

First, we have covered lots of ideas and strategies across all of our chapters. Some are big, some are small. Some are clear you-can-do-this-tomorrow-type lesson ideas; others

DOI: 10.4324/9781003290681-15

were more organizational and reflective. In so much as we could, we tried to call out links between different ideas and activities. But surely you know that just because we have organized the book in the way we have, with the chapter titles and themes we did, does not mean that they are siloed ideas and practices.

We hope that even having finished the text, you will go back and see the connections across the themes and across the strategies. None of these themes or practices exist alone, and mastering one thing—say, introspection—will only move you and your students so far forward unless you look to the other concepts and themes, as well. As noted, we tried to identify some of these thematic and logistical connections, but we surely did not point out all the ways things from one chapter could dovetail with parts of another. In a sense this text is a map to what can be accomplished, not a text meant for tracing. What we have shared are not finite lists of strategies, but examples we hope will inspire your thinking and pragmatic vision as you design and create lessons and experiences in your classroom that match your students and communities. We encourage you, as you tease out the pragmatic tools and ideas from these chapters, to layer them on top of one another, weave them together, take bits of one and use it in support of another, and generally, re-mix, re-vision, and re-invent the ideas you have read about here.

Epistemic Disobedience and Sustainability

Second, at several points throughout this text, we have mentioned that we are quite aware of the constraints you may be facing. Again, the decolonial is not about big, flashy, showy efforts. It is about bringing a different ontological vision to life: a different way for humans to be together and share lived experiences in community, society and culture. You should not feel any less optimistic or proud of your work if you operate under constraints that limit how much of this you can enact. You should still keep moving even if working through new conceptions of race and raising your own racial literacy is taking some emotional or intellectual time. Just keep making progress and finding small, but tangible, ways to bring these suggestions into life and the classroom.

But let's now connect back to a key concept we introduced in Chapter 1, epistemic disobedience, and once again reflect on our disobedient students. As educators, we all know that disobedience can look all sorts of different ways. There are kids who resist and push back on the confines of schooling by jumping on desks and throwing things, turning the whole classroom upside down. Then, there are kids who are sly and subtle, mischievously sneaking notes and finding little ways to express their defiance against the rules and schooling with hardly any notice, and a lot of plausible deniability. And there's everything in between.

Disobedience can be frustrating as a teacher, and to be sure, there are times and ways that it can be hurtful and harmful to our classroom communities. But disobedience can also be productive, even artful; a creative act that imagines and enacts new worlds. As we think about our students in humanizing ways, and try to think the world differently, decolonially, it's worth really trying to consider some of the motivations and rationales behind student disobedience, and the lessons that disobedience can teach us. Because what our students are doing—sometimes productively and sometimes less so—is pushing on systems, structures, and ways of being that don't resonate with who they are. For better or worse, disobedience is an act of purposeful, creative resistance, and though we may still want to be wary that no harm is done, we can also celebrate that creativity, embrace the resistance, and grow from the lessons our students teach us.

Where we're going with this is that what we really hope you will do after reading this book is this: *be disobedient*. Be bad. Now of course we don't mean in the sense of not doing good work, doing damage to your school community, or trying to actively get in trouble with your administration. We mean be *intellectually* bad. Resistant. Disobedient. We want you to channel that disobedience we've all seen from our most spirited students, in whatever way your context and personal comfort level allows, to *disobey coloniality*. Be bad at obeying coloniality. Be bad at dehumanizing others. Be bad at accepting the norms of schooling. Disobey. Resist. It might be subtle. It might be bold. Maybe you really can turn things upside down. Maybe the best you can do for the moment is step right up to the very edge, toeing the line of permissibility with a wink. You might have to make compromises. You might need to take a real stand. Whatever you can do, do it in sustainable ways that will allow you to keep doing the work, since we can't decolonize anything if we are no longer in our classrooms. And always, always, do it with love, and with the intention of being epistemically disobedient to the way schooling and coloniality want you to act and who they want you and your students to be.

Pragmatic Vision and the Decolonial

Finally, we just want to again remind you that the pursuit of the decolonial is a process, not a destination. The goals and ideals we are talking about when we talk about disrupting coloniality are huge and systemic. That does not mean that our actions and contributions and efforts to be disobedient to that colonial system are pointless; rather, the contrary is true. It is just that we are contributing in small ways to what will be a long, collective societal journey. We, personally as educators and collectively with our students, are not going to ever really 'arrive' at the decolonial. None of us can fully say we are truly and fully decolonized because the system still exists, and its shadow is going to linger for quite a while. That's OK. Our work, our acts of humanization, and the epistemic disobedience we enact, and lead and inspire our students to partake in, are the small steps that will gradually dismantle these oppressive systems and structures.

So as we leave you, we hope that you will make sure you are reflecting on your praxis with that pragmatic vision we mentioned right at the start. Do you have a clear vision of the humanizing, decolonial world you would like to see? The way that you would like your students to exist and their identities to be honored? Keep that vision close and dear. But also consider the pragmatic actions you can take towards it. What can I do tomorrow to demystify race, even if just a little bit? How can I reframe this text to invite more human connection and introspection? What can I tangibly do to be disobedient to the dehumanizing discipline policies my district insists on? Ask those questions and let those two things—vision and pragmatics—live together and carry you forward, an epistemically disobedient educator, doing everything you can to move towards a decolonial future for youth, schools, and the world.

INDEX

Pages in *italics* refer to figures.

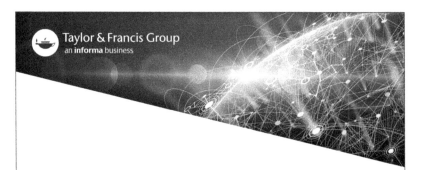

Printed in the USA
CPSIA information can be obtained
at www.ICGtesting.com
LVHW011256150324
774517LV00048B/2491